Consumer Rights and Protection in India

Consumer Rights and Protection in India

By

Mohammed Kamalun Nabi
Assistant Professor, Department of Commerce and Business Studies,
Jamia Millia Islamia Central University, New Delhi

Mohammed Irshadun Nabi
Senior Civil Judge, Cuttack, Odisha

Kishore C. Raut
Head, Post-graduate Department of Commerce,
Berhampur University, Odisha

New Century Publications
New Delhi, India

NEW CENTURY PUBLICATIONS
4800/24, Bharat Ram Road,
Ansari Road, Daryaganj,
New Delhi - 110 002 (India)

Tel.: 011-2324 7798, 4358 7398, 6539 6605
Fax: 011-4101 7798
E-mail: indiatax@vsnl.com • info@newcenturypublications.com
www.newcenturypublications.com

Editorial office:
LG–7, Aakarshan Bhawan,
4754-57/23, Ansari Road, Daryaganj,
New Delhi – 110 002

Tel.: 011-4356 0919

First Published: **2015**

ISBN: **978-81-7708-400-9**

Published by New Century Publications and printed at Salasar Imaging Systems, New Delhi.

Designs: Patch Creative Unit, New Delhi.

PRINTED IN INDIA

About the Book

The consumer protection policy creates an environment whereby the clients and customers receive satisfaction from the delivery of goods and services needed by them. One of the disquieting features of the Indian democracy, even after 67 years of Independence, is that an average Indian consumer continues to be in a pitiable condition due to poverty, illiteracy, ignorance and general apathy. Adulterated food, spurious medicines, and sub-standard domestic appliances are pushed over the counter with ease. Glossy and unethical advertisements appear in the print and electronic media. Ironically, it all happens in a country where, in ancient India, Kautilya in his epoch making *Arthasashtra* had advocated for fixing of responsibility on the State for safeguarding the interests of the consumers.

When it became imperative to protect the consumers from adulterated, sub-standard goods and deficient services and also to provide relief by way of compensation, the Consumer Protection Act was enacted in the year 1986. This Act was enacted with the objective to provide better protection to the consumers against the fraudulent practices of suppliers. The Act provides for effective safeguards for consumers against various types of exploitations and unfair dealings, relying on mainly compensatory rather than punitive or preventive approach.

The present work explains and examines the rights of the consumers and the protective measures adopted in India and other countries. It specifically deals with the statutory measures for redressal of consumer grievances provided under the Indian Consumer Protection Act, 1986.

About the Authors

Dr. Mohammed Kamalun Nabi is currently an Assistant Professor in the Department of Commerce and Business Studies, Jamia Millia Islamia Central University, New Delhi. He has to his credit 4 books and 50 research papers published in leading journals and periodicals. He specializes in consumer behaviour, advertising and services marketing.

Dr. Mohammed Irshadun Nabi is presently posted as a Senior Civil Judge in Cuttack, Odisha. He is a gold medal awardee from Berhampur University, Berhampur, Odisha for having topped the LL.M. examination. He also holds Masters Degree in Industrial Relations and Personnel Management from Berhampur University and Ph.D. in Law from Fakir Mohan University, Balasore, Odisha. His areas of interest include civil, criminal and consumer laws.

Professor Kishore C. Raut is the senior most faculty and presently head of the Post-graduate Department of Commerce, Berhampur University, Odisha. He has published 80 research articles in various journals of national and international repute. His areas of research interest include consumer behaviour, advertising, services marketing and bank management.

Contents

Preface

One of the disquieting features of the Indian democracy, even after 67 years of Independence, is that an average Indian consumer continues to be in a pitiable condition due to poverty, illiteracy, ignorance and general apathy. It is clearly discernible in the adulterated food we consume, the spurious and sub-standard products we buy, scarcity of essential commodities, black marketing, profiteering and hoarding. The hazardous drugs are pushed over the counter, and glossy and unethical advertisements appear in the print and the electronic media. Added to this is the humiliation and harassment we are subjected to by the service providers like the railways, airlines, banks, telecommunications, insurance, electricity and healthcare. Ironically, it all happens in a country where about 1,500 years ago Kautilya in his epoch making *Arthasashtra* had advocated for fixing of responsibility on the State for safeguarding the interest of the consumers.

During the pre- and post-Independence era, many legislations—Indian Penal Code, 1860; Indian Contract Act, 1872; Civil Procedure Code, 1908; Sale of Goods Act, 1930; Prevention of Food Adulteration Act, 1954; Monopolies and Restrictive Trade Practices Act, 1969; Standard of Weights and Measures Act, 1978; Motor Vehicles Act, 1988—were enacted with the object of protecting the interest of the consumers by prescribing stringent punitive measures. However, most of them, more or less, have failed in achieving anything substantial in providing respite to the hapless consumer.

When it became imperative to protect the consumers from adulterated, sub-standard goods and deficient services and also with a view to redressing consumer's grievances and providing relief by way of compensation, the Consumer Protection Act was enacted in the year 1986.

This Act was enacted with the objective to provide better protection of the interests of the consumers. The Act provides for effective safeguards to consumers against various types of exploitations and unfair dealings, relying mainly on compensatory rather than punitive or preventive approach. The Act applies to all goods and services unless specifically exempted and covers private, public and co-operative sectors and provides for speedy and inexpensive adjudication. The consumer rights under the Act are the following:

1. Right to be protected against marketing of goods and services, which are hazardous to life and property.
2. Right to be informed about quality, quantity, potency, purity, standard and price of goods and services, as the case may be, to protect consumers against unfair trade practices.
3. Right to be assured of access to a variety of goods and services at competitive prices.
4. Right to be heard and assured that consumer interest will receive due consideration at appropriate fora.
5. Right to seek redressal against unfair trade practices or restrictive trade practices or unscrupulous exploitation of consumers.
6. Right to consumer education.

Under the Act, a three-tier, simple, quasi-judicial machinery has been established at the national, state and district levels for hearing cases raised by consumers. The Act was amended in the year 1991 and again in 1993. A comprehensive amendment was made in 2002 for making the Act effective, functional and purposeful. The amended Act, *inter alia,* provides for attachment and subsequent sale of the property of a person not complying with an order.

In India, December 24 is celebrated as National Consumer Rights Day as the Consumer Protection Act, 1986 was enacted on that day.

The Act helps the consumers in two ways. In the first place, it provides cheap, expeditious, quick and swift remedy. It is a measure of swift social justice. It brings justice to the doorsteps of the common man in every district, known as the district consumer forum. Now a consumer can proceed in his own district where he suffers as a consumer.

Secondly, enough improvement has been effected in the

system of consumer remedies in vogue prior to the enactment of the Act. It is no longer necessary for the consumer to be confined for his remedies only to his immediate dealer only. He can sue in his own home town even a distant manufacturer with whom he had no direct contract relationship. The Act covers all kinds of goods and services. It also covers all kinds of consumer dealings whether cash or kind, and also protects the consumer from the vices of restrictive and unfair trade practices. It enables the consumer forums and commissions to award compensation for not only the amount lost in purchasing defective material or in hiring deficient services but also for mental agony suffered and harassment caused by defective goods or services. Properly implemented, the Act should be able to usher in a new business motto: 'Give a fair deal to the consumer'.

The level of consumer awareness and protection is an indicator of development of a country and progressiveness of civil society. The main reason for this is the rapidly increasing variety of goods and services which modern technology has made available. The increased need for consumer protection has arisen due to the following factors:

1. Growing size and complexity of production and distribution systems.
2. High level of sophistication in marketing and selling practices.
3. Aggressive advertising and other forms of sales promotion.
4. Mass marketing methods.
5. Reduction of personal interaction between buyers and sellers.

The consumer protection policy creates an environment whereby the clients, customers and consumers receive satisfaction from the delivery of goods and services needed by them. The concern of consumer protection is to ensure fair trade practices, quality of goods and efficient services with information to consumer with regard to quality, quantity, potency, composition and price for their choice of purchase. Thus, proper and effective implementation of consumer protection law promotes good governance.

Against such a backdrop, the present book is intended to examine the statutory measures for redressal of consumer grievances provided under the Consumer Protection Act, 1986 (CPA), and to evaluate the approach of the consumer grievance redressal agencies set up under the CPA, to put an end to unfair and restrictive trade practices.

October 2014

Mohammed Kamalun Nabi
Mohammed Irshadun Nabi
Kishore C. Raut

1

Consumer Rights and Protection: An Introduction

1.1 Introduction

In the present day market driven economy, consumer is the pivot around which the whole of the marketing system revolves. Marketers undertake several studies to know precisely the need and requirement of the consumers so that they manufacture goods and provide services accordingly.

However, from the practical perspective, modern day consumers are subject to innumerable forms and varieties of exploitation. In fact, consumers all around the world are victims of poor quality, unsafe goods, under measurement, adulteration and false promises. Indian consumers suffer and lose thousands of crores of rupees every year due to adulteration, quantity and quality deceptions. In the contemporary marketing environment, the consumer ultimately becomes a 'slave' though in marketing parlance he is considered a 'king'.

Modern day marketers, armed with advanced processing techniques coupled with the persuasive powers of promotion and advertising, are in a better and superior position to exploit the consumers—even the highly educated urban consumers. Deceptive advertising, misleading promotion, offering gifts, discount sales, false assurances, poor quality are some of the unfair trade practices to which consumers are often subjected. In short, modern day consumers more or less live in a sellers' market depending on the sellers' mercy. Thus, the consumer in real sense has become a silent spectator and hapless buyer in the market. Therefore, there was a need felt for consumer protection in the marketplace.

The concern for consumer protection, both in India and abroad, is not really new. It is centuries old. Consumer rights like the right to have safe unadulterated and deficiency free commodities at appropriate prices have been recognized since ancient times. History of protection of consumer rights by law has long been recognized dating back to 1824. Every year, 15th of March is observed as 'Consumer Rights Day'. On this day in 1962, President John F. Kennedy of U.S. called upon the US Congress to accord its approval to the Consumer Bill of Rights. In India, we have started celebrating 24th December every year as the National Consumer Rights Day.

Like many countries, a number of legislative enactments have been made in India from time to time to protect the interests of the consumers in the marketplace. Consumer Protection Act, 1986 was a landmark in the history of consumer protection in India which provides a system for the protection of consumer rights and the redressal of consumer disputes. The Act in fact is regarded as Magna Carta in the field of consumer protection and is intended to provide for protection of the interest of the consumers and for that purpose to make provisions for the establishment of consumer councils and other authorities for the settlement of consumer disputes and for matters connected therewith. Implementation of this legislation has raised a number of issues with wide legal and social ramifications, necessitating a systematic study to analyse their cause and effect.

1.2 Definition of the Term *Consumer* [1]

People get into different avocation and profession—as an industrialist, a farmer, a doctor, a teacher, a daily labourer, a scholar, an engineer, a scientist or a clerk either by choice or by circumstances, but everyone, in any case, is a consumer. Under the modern concept of marketing, 'consumer is the king—he is the pivot around which the whole business rotates.

The visionary in Gandhiji, way back in the year 1934, had remarked, "The customer is the most important visitor on our premises. He is not dependent on us. We are dependent on him. He is not an interruption to our work; he is the purpose of it. He is not an outsider to our business; he is a part of it. We are not doing him favour by serving him; he is doing us a favour by giving us an opportunity to do so".

For a layman, consumer is a person who makes final or ultimate use of economic goods. Therefore, it includes everyone, irrespective of the fact whether they contribute to production or not—children, aged, sick, infirm etc.

1.2.1 Recent Definitional Developments [2]: The fundamental relation between buyer and seller, to some extent remains the same till date, which was implied in the common law maxim of caveat emptor i.e. let the buyer beware. According to this, the onus is placed on the buyer to protect his own interest by insuring that what he purchases is of requisite quality to meet his needs. This doctrine, which has been progressively modified in the interests of the consumer to the extent that the law is governed more by exceptions than by the rule itself, accorded well with the principle of laissez-faire capitalism that the buyer is served best by free competition between sellers. Certain changes that have occurred over the past century—in the nature of industrial corporations and in the types of products available to the consumer—have rendered this assumption invalid.

First may be cited as the growth of large corporations, exerting monopoly influence, i.e. setting prices and standards of quality for a particular product, so that a consumer can no longer afford the opportunity to choose effectively from amongst the competing suppliers. Such corporations do not have to control a product's entire market, which may in fact be divided among several suppliers who offer the consumer, products similar in terms of price and quality, rendering an effective choice almost impossible. Sometimes, the impression of competition may be created by heavy advertising of "competing" brands or makes. Such a situation, known to economists as one of oligopoly, has often been typical of the markets for detergents and automobiles.

A second factor that has weakened the effectiveness of the

consumer in protecting his own interests by rational choice among competing alternatives is the complexity of the products that modern technology has made available. There is, for example, little basis on which the consumer can decide between the merits of two different televisions sets, vacuum cleaners, or patent drugs without a mass of technical information, which he would probably be unable to evaluate, even if it was given to him.

A third factor that is commonly alleged to have eroded the consumer's capacity to choose effectively in his own best interest is his increasing exposure to advertising and to new sales techniques. Advertising, it is argued, is predominantly persuasive rather than informative, as it serves to create demand for products that are unneeded, and often exploits the hidden fears, insecurities and prejudices of the consumer. Further, modern sales methods ranging from the so-called "introductory offers", "free gifts" and trading stamps to the "high pressure" techniques practiced by door-to-door salesmen, are found to be subjecting the consumer to an unjustified degree of influence.

Thus, due to this weak position of consumer in common law and the laws falling on the line of ejusdem generis, there arose a need for consumer protection defining clearly the perimeter of 'who is a consumer'.

1.3 Need for Consumer Protection

In the process of sale and purchase, the parties concerned i.e., the seller and the consumer are expected to achieve mutual benefits, the former getting a reasonable profit and the latter getting goods and services of desired quality and quantity at a reasonable price. Due to exploitative measures adopted by the powerful influential trading community, mutual trust that ought to be the foundation of seller-consumer relationship gradually weakens. The imbalance that results from such breaking up of trust takes the form of a social problem. In order to solve such problems, society has to evolve certain ways and means to balance the conflict of interests. The support that the society extends to the consumer to neutralize the adverse effects of various exploitative actions of the business is termed as consumer protection.

The much talked about concept of 'consumer protection' revolves around the problems of buyers in the world of sellers to protect, defend, guard and to keep them away from injury, attack, invasion, loss and injustice. There are individuals or groups in a society who by virtue of their unenviable socio-economic position are ignorant of their own interests and are thus unable to safeguard them. This results in their exploitation and suffering in various fields. This category of people needs to be protected by the society and such protection may be afforded in two distinct ways. Protection, in the first place, is tacitly transformed into 'guidance' and is applied to classes, who though not strictly 'incapable of managing their own affairs are in all likelihood, unable to protect their own interests. [3]

Secondly, protection is made to include arrangement for safeguarding, not of special classes but of all citizens against mistakes which often may be avoided by a person's own care and sagacity. The first form of protection may be afforded to the consumer by providing adequate information about various products which would guide him to make an effective purchase decision. The second one involves prescribing certain standards of duty and care to the business community or imposing ban on certain products, if necessary.

1.4 Causes of Consumer Exploitation

Various factors that contribute to a consumer falling victim to exploitation could be zeroed down broadly to issues such as social, economic or legal. Any one element out of the projected three would be dominant enough to bring to shambles the so called principle of consumer sovereignty but as commonly witnessed, all the three taken together or in twos, operate in league whereby the consumer appears completely duped in the market place. Social causes could be identifiable with certain specific characteristics of a given society which may broadly be geographical, historical, cultural, moral, ethical and the like. A particular society has its own peculiar social, moral and ethical mores that tend to develop fixed pattern of behaviour, irrespective of advantages and disadvantages inherent therein.

The second, the economic issue, is an aspect where the consumer could be undermined in economic terms which is otherwise the value, i.e. satisfaction derived in ratio to money paid either in his knowledge or beyond his knowledge and the third and the last is the legal issue, i.e. law acting as an instrument of social control in order to balance conflicting interests between individual interest and groups' interest under the value system of a given society.

1.4.1 Poverty and Ignorance: Poverty and ignorance are two major social evils which taken together, have the capacity of bringing about social exploitation. Poverty is associated with scarce economic means which cripples a person from meeting his bare necessities. Ignorance is associated with lack of proper knowledge or education which results in incapacity to judge and choose things in the right perspective, in the environment around him. These two socio-economic factors could be illustratively said to be two points of a vicious circle, the segments as if locking horns with each other. When a consumer is poor, his bargaining power in the market place becomes squeezed as he has either a small amount of money or no money at all to spend. More often than not, it is the poor who refuses to complain and resigns to fate having been exposed to the exploitative propensities of the one with whom he trades. This may be either due to low expectation of the success of his cause or complaint or hesitation to jeopardise his relations with the trader. [4]

1.4.2 Lack of Information: Knowledge is the key to the solution of major consumer problems. In a free market which promotes competition, consumer is expected to exercise his right to choose and thereby satisfy his need more efficiently.

[5] But lack of information about the product itself and sometimes similar products under varied brand names and their respective merits and availability of different varieties of products representing more than one use or capable of multiple uses, hampers his sovereignty. This lack of information may manifest either as complete ignorance of a product arising from lack of exposure to it or because of the absence of sufficient objective information to evaluate the product correctly. [6] Total ignorance about a product not only affects the poor and the underprivileged segment of the society but affects all the consumers alike. So far as access to information is concerned, the rich, educated and affluent consumers stand on a better footing than the poor, uneducated and underprivileged mass of consumers, due to their better exposure to market conditions.

The market is now flooded with a variety of goods and services having similar and marginally different characteristics under various brand names from innumerable producers or sellers. Not only the products are complex, the prices of such products are fixed in such a manner that it necessitates a lot of information for an effective purchase decision. The more the necessity of obtaining the information, the more difficult it becomes to obtain the same with the best of his knowledge and experience. The consumer is no longer able to know the quality related to price of the product—the villain being the technical complexity of the products [7] so produced.

When a consumer cannot rely on his own prudence and the information available in the market is unreliable and incomplete, he has no other go than to depend on information supplied by the seller. Seller controlled information is generally biased or insufficient which stands as an impediment to the achievement of consumer sovereignty.

1.4.3 Lack of Grievance Redressal: The non-satisfaction of the consumer to get commodity as per his expectation gives rise to consumer grievance. In the days when the market offered limited number of products which were simple in nature, the buyer had a chance to detect defects, if any, in such products. In case of any complaint regarding quality, quantity and price, the issue could easily be resolved between themselves as, in most cases, the buyer and the seller were known to each other. In modern times, consumer grievances stem from the increasing complexities of products and the complex nature of marketing. When the process of production and marketing becomes associated with unethical practices like misrepresentation, fraud, deceit etc., the grievances become all the more grave.

Grievance culminates in consumer seeking a redressal. Due to the impersonal buyer-seller relationship and an ambiguous placement of responsibility, more and more grievances occur and the probability of their satisfactory resolution becomes lesser and lesser. There is an imbalance of power when the consumer confronts the business with his grievances. [8] The consumer is no match for a seller because of his respectable position in the market place. Financial resources at the disposal of the seller are enormous compared to that of the consumer. The trader, with his organized professional fraternity, panel of expert advisers in the fields of law, commerce and public relations and his symbiotic relationship with the government and trade unions, is almost invincible with so many people to support him. [9] So far as the consumer is concerned, inconvenience, time and the cost factor stand in his way in case legal action is necessary. Such inherent drawbacks of the consumer and the money power and social credibility of the seller deprive the consumer of the redress of his grievance to which he is entitled to in case of any grievance arising from fraudulent business transaction.

1.4.4 Sales Promotion Methods: Producers actively and deliberately influence consumers to buy the commodities produced by them. [10] The consumer is not competent to decide what is best for him because his tastes are influenced by the structure of the society and the economic environment. His preferences are moulded, changed and created by circumstances. Want creation through sales promotion techniques like advertisement, prizes, product warranty, samples, coupons, free trails, free offers, cash refund etc. are some of the external agents responsible for such manipulation.

Though many of these sales promotion methods theoretically appear to be beneficial to the consumer, in real practice they are not. Dishonest manufacturers and sellers use these tools to motivate the consumer to purchase without goods of such quality and quantity and at such prices, which the consumer would not have normally purchased without such motivations. Many bargain offers are at best confusing and at worst misleading. They may induce consumers to buy things they would not have bought had they been given adequate information about the nature of the offer. [11]

1.4.5 Unfair Trade Practices: Consumers are also victims of exploitation by unfair trade practices resorted to by manufacturers, distributors or retailers with the fraudulent objective of inducing them to make a purchase through false representations about the quality, standard, composition or style of goods and services. It is an unfair trade practice to make a false representation regarding goods that these are of a particular quality, composition or model or to state that reconditioned or renovated goods are new goods or to represent that goods have sponsorship or characteristics which they do not have or to make false or misleading statement regarding need or usefulness of goods. [12]

On the price front, various traders also resort to unfair trade practices by adopting deceptive pricing to attract consumers and thereby inducing them to make a purchase. The effect of unfair trade practices is most conspicuous amongst the underprivileged classes of the society as they are susceptible to the allurement of the offer and thus fail to understand the misleading motive behind such offers. These practices are not only unfair but also unethical but also affect the individual consumer and the society at large.

1.4.6 Adulteration: Adulteration is another cause of consumer exploitation. Many unfair traders use this process for easy and fabulous gain without consideration of the hazards that may be brought about to the ultimate consumers. The menace of this practice is widely felt in the field of food and drug items. Food items are normally adulterated by mixing either sub-standard categories of the same item or by mixing certain alien foreign substances, the admixture of which is not capable of identification in ordinary process of examination. Similarly, drug preparations are adulterated by mixing certain substances which depotentialise the efficacy of such drug or nullify the operation of such drug or make it noxious. Due to poor purchasing power and ignorance of consumers, it becomes difficult on their part to maintain an effective supervision of adulterated food and drugs. It is only when adulteration results in certain health hazards that the common man becomes aware of his victimization.

The legal measures to prevent adulteration are so technical that virtually it becomes impossible to take the adulterator to task. Even though at times they are punished, the quantum of punishment hardly acts as a deterrent. Hence, the practice goes on and the consumer pays the price not only in terms of money but also in terms of his health and happiness.

1.4.7 Monopoly: The practice of monopoly limits consumer's choice and thereby affects consumer sovereignty to a large extent. In general term, the word "monopoly" refers to a market where there is a single seller of a product. Actually, the term monopoly in economics is linked with the degree of competition prevalent in the market. [13] Monopoly is said to exist when one firm is the sole producer and seller of a product with no substitute. [14] The freedom of choice that the consumer enjoys under free competition lacks in a monopolistic market. The consumer is not in a position to exert any influence on the pricing of the product and is bound to purchase goods and services at the price pre-determined by the seller.

1.4.8 Legal Doctrines and Principles: Even though the purpose of legal doctrines and principles has been to protect individual or groups in certain cases, they have been noticed to be detrimental to specific groups.

1.4.9 Privity of Contract: The doctrine of privity of contract, so beloved of the common law, is a distorting factor in the law of consumer protection. [15] The general rule of common law says that no one but the parties to a contract can be bound by it. [16] Under this principle, known as privity of contract, a third party cannot be bound by the terms of a contract to which he is not a party nor can he benefit from such a contract. [17] It was at one time thought that if the person who was to take benefit under the contract was related by blood to the party, right of action would rest with him. [18] But this benefit even to blood relation was refused in the 19th century, [19] and the principle was applied with all its stringency during the early days of the present century. [20] The notable opposition that the application of this rule received was from Lord Denning who criticized it as a 19th century innovation. [21] However, his view did not find favour with the House of Lords.

This doctrine made a distinction between buyer and consumer and prevented the ultimate consumer from seeking legal redress in case of loss or damages if he himself was not the buyer.

1.4.10 Caveat Emptor: In the era of laissez faire, any restraint on the liberty of an individual was looked upon with disfavour by the society. There was a presumption that each individual was the best judge of his own interest. In this golden age of individualism, it was assumed that a buyer would use all care and skill while entering into a transaction or making a purchase. From this assumption, developed the maxim of caveat emptor—let the buyer beware. The maxim envisaged that the seller could be relieved of the obligation to make disclosures about the quality of the product. Even an enlightened consumer of soaps, drugs, fruits, radios, cars and other commodities as it is of everyday use, is unable to judge the quality of the commodities, as it cannot be expected of him to fully examine the goods on the spot and aim at the right buying decision. [22]

It was only in the 19th century that the law of Sale of Goods underwent a sea change development. The courts also developed the theory of sale by description to restrict the application of the doctrine. [23] Even changes in the law relating to Sale of Goods and change in the judicial attitude could not protect the consumer effectively against the application of this doctrine. [24]

Standard Form of Contact: One of the most important developments in the sphere of contract during the last hundred years has been the appearance of the standard form of contracts or contracts of adhesion. The idea of an agreement freely negotiated between the parties has given way to the necessity for a uniform set of printed conditions which can be used time and again and for a large number of persons. A standard form of contract devised by the supplier has either to be accepted or not accepted by the consumer. In fact, he has no alternative but to accept it, he does not negotiate, but merely adheres. [25] This principle curtails to a large extent the right of freedom of contract because there is no room for independence of the parties to decide the terms of the agreement by mutual negotiation where a standard form is prescribed. "Today, an active consumer enters scores of contracts every week without in real sense agreeing to the terms that are imposed upon him. For the very reason that these terms are imposed rather than agreed upon, they are almost universally unfair [26] as the consumer is wrongly presumed to have assented to propositions in the written agreement. [27]

1.4.11 Inaccessibility to Law: Consumer protection is mainly a matter of civil law. So far as the individual's redress is concerned, this branch of law makes good the loss suffered by providing damages. A weakness of this law is the fortuitous nature of its enforcement. A large section of consumers fail to take the advantage of the law because of their ignorance of legal procedure and lack of financial resources to institute and conduct a legal proceeding. When the consumer makes a cost-benefit analysis, the meagre quantum of relief that is expected after a prolonged period of legal battle, deters him from exercising his right to redressal in a court of law.

1.5 Law as an Instrument of Protection

Out of the two parties i.e., the buyer and the seller usually the former, is on the weaker side. This is also true in the case of employer-employee and landlord-tenant relationship. Employees are given protection under various legislations intended to promote their welfare. Similarly, the interest of tenants is protected under the rent control law. In view of the above facts, it is all the more necessary to protect the consumer from unscrupulous practices adopted by traders and service providers, be it for unsatisfactory telephone service, dirty railway compartments, adulterated food, unsafe buildings, hazardous toys, faulty gas stove or false and deceptive advertisement. [28]

When self-help fails to protect the individual, it becomes necessary on the part of the state to interfere and accord necessary protection to those whose interest are at stake. To achieve this objective, law acts as an effective instrument in the hands of the state. In a pluristic society, where there is a perpetual conflict between the interests of various groups, law balances such conflicting interests so as to achieve social harmony. In the early times, law was primarily meant for maintenance of peace with emphasis laid on rules to keep various interests on their ordered place. In contrast, the modern state has become a welfare state with obligation to provide a wide range of social services and securities.

The welfare state is a compromise between the two extremes of consumerism on the one hand and the unbridled individualization on the other and as such, in spite of all its imperfections, it set a pattern for any progressive human society. [29] A welfare state is the institutional outcome of the assumption of responsibility by the legal society for the general well-being of its members. [30] With the change in its objective from laissez faire to welfare, the modern state as and when necessary plays a pro-active role and interferes in economic matters keeping the larger interest of the weaker sections of the society in view.

The primary purpose of consumer law is the same as that of any other law, i.e. achievement of justice. Justice is the constant and perpetual will to render to everyone that to which he is entitled. Justice is identified with a certain attitude of human mind, a willingness to be fair and readiness to give recognition to the claims and concerns of others. [31] Clearly, a society depends on the interaction of the will of the members of the society, exchanging benefits and burdens, setting rewards and punishments and seeking to influence the distribution of scarce resources. The foundation of law is not force but justice. As an instrument of justice, law constitutes a permanent resistance to the forces which lead to disintegration and depersonalization of individuals. [32]

In the process of market transaction, for justice to prevail, the parties concerned i.e., consumers and sellers are expected to give each other, their legitimate dues. A reasonable profit is the sellers due which ordinarily consumers do not hesitate to provide. On the other hand, consumers expect the supply of goods and services of reasonable standards of quality, quantity and price as their legitimate claim from the business community. Invariably, business greed prompts the business community to deprive consumers of their reasonable dues by adopting various unfair trade practices and exploit the consumers thereby. This business attitude gives rise to the necessity of law in prescribing norms to make it obligatory on the part of the business to provide the consumers what is socially, morally and of course legally due to them. Hence, consumer justice requires the sellers to liberate themselves from their exclusively aggrandising impulses and help the consumers achieve their reasonable dues.

Principle of justice aims at establishing equality among the individuals and groups in a society and in its distributive aspect, is primarily concerned with the allocation of rights, powers, duties and burdens among them. [33] This concept of justice emphasizes that every individual should be given a full chance to make good in life and lead a worthwhile existence. Equality promotes justice whereas inequality leads to injustice. It is the prime concern for every orderly society to be in quest for justice and abolish the existence of injustice. Law is invariably used as an efficient tool to achieve such a goal. Law promotes equality by allocating rights, duties and power etc. among various individuals or groups in such a manner that the existing inequality is neutralized.

The consumers and the sellers are two major groups into which the entire population of the society can be divided. The dominance of the seller over the consumers is merely the outcome of unequal power, the two groups enjoy. In order for justice to prevail, this inequality is to be removed so that the consumers can make good in life and lead a worthwhile existence. With this objective in view, various consumer laws have not only recognized different rights of the consumer but also have prescribed a series of duties and responsibilities with a view to increase the power of the buyers while curtailing the same of the sellers so as to put them on an equal footing.

Endnotes

1. Sharma, D., "Consumer Grievance Redressal under the Consumer Protection Act", New Century Publications, Delhi, 2002, p. 1.
2. Mehta, S., "Evolution of Definition of Word Consumer-Recent Developments", CPJ 2010(iv), pp. 1-2.
3. Diecey, A.V., "Law and Public Opinion in England, p. 262.
4. Cranston, R., "Consumer and the Law", Weildenfield and Nicolson, London, 1978, p. 3.
5. Maynes, E.S., "Decision-making for Consumers: An Introduction to Consumer Economics, McMillan Publishing Co. New York, 1976, p. 319.
6. Feldmen, L.P., "Consumer Protection: Problems and Prospects", West Publishing Co., U.S.A., 1980, p. 26.
7. Supra, Note 2, p. 320.
8. Supra, Note 1, p. 3.

9. Ramesh, M.K., "Consumer Interest in Legal Profession: Problems and Prospective", Cochin University Law Review, 1989, p. 405.
10. Haris, C.P., "Consumerism", *European Journal of Marketing*, Vol. 12, No. 4, 1978, p. 301.
11. Fulop, C., "Buyer Be aware Shopping Laws", *Economic Affairs*, Vol. 6, No. 3, February-March, 1986, U.K., p. 13.
12. Saraf, D.N., "Law of Consumer Protection in India", Thripathy, 1990, p. 115.
13. Seth, M.L., "Principles of Economics", 6th Edition, Laxmi Narayan Agarwall Educational Publishers, Agra, 1971, p. 348.
14. Ahuja, H.L. "Modern Micro Economics", S. Chand and Co., 1990, p. 311.
15. Anson's Law of Contract, 23rd Edition, English Language Book Society, p. 377.
16. Jolowicz, J.A., "The Problem of the Consumer and Purchaser of Goods under English Law", *The Modern Law Review*, Vol. 32, No. 1, 1969, p. 2.
17. Price vs. Easton (1833), 4B and Ad 433.
18. Dutton vs. Pool (1678), 2 Leve 210.
19. Tweddle vs. Atkinson (1861), IB and S 393.
20. Dunop Pneumatic Co. Ltd. vs. Selfridge Co. Ltd., (1915), SC 847.
21. Drive Yourself Hire Co. (London) vs. Strait (1954), 1 QB 250.
22. Nayak, R.K., "Consumer Protection Law in India: An Eco-legal Treatise on Consumer Justice", Indian Law Institute, 1991, p. 50.
23. Barr vs. Gibson (1838), 7 LJEX 124, Chanter vs. Hopkins,1838 8 LJEX 14, Varley vs. Whipp (1900), 1 QB 513.
24. Saraf, D.N., "Law of Consumer Protection in India", Thripathy, 1990, p. 3.
25. Anson's Law of Contract, p. 142.
26. Stawson, W.D., "Standard Form Contract and Democratic Control of Law Making Power", *Harvard Law Review*, Vol. 84, No. 3, January 1971, p. 529.
27. Trebilcock, M.J., "Consumer Protection in Affluent Society", *McGill Law Journal*, Vol. 16, No. 2, 1970, p. 290.
28. Sharma, D., op. cit, p. 2.
29. Hobman, D.L., "Welfare State", John Morray Publishers, London, 1953, p. 1.

30. Girrets, H.K., "Welfare State", David L. Stiss Education, International Encyclopaedia of the Social Sciences, Vol. 16, New York, 1968, p. 512.
31. Bodenheimer, E., "Jurisprudence", Harvard University Press, 1981, p. 208.
32. Philip, A., "State Responsibility and the Unmaking of International Law", *Harvard International Law Journal*, Vol. 29, No. 1, Winter, 1988, p. 24.
33. Hart, H.L., "The Concept of Law", Oxford, 1961, p. 155.

2

Review of Literature on Consumer Protection

Though concerted movement for consumer protection is comparatively of recent origin, commencing from the second half of this century, the prolific literature available on the subject, both inside and outside India is indicative of the keen interest of the discerning public in the subject whose horizon is ever expanding. For the purpose of review, the available literature could be divided into two broad categories, namely, empirical and non-empirical. While empirical studies are confined to limited authorship, non-empirical studies opened wide dimensional vistas of consumerism in its varied stages of development.

In view of brazen exploitation of consumers and the growth of business and competition, urgent necessity was felt to protect the interests of consumers by the state with its law-enforcing machinery. A vast spread of literature by experts testifies the serious concern of the government in general and that of the consumers in particular on these vital issues.

Barbar (1966) [1] agrees with Adam Smith that consumption is the sole aim of production and that the interest of the producer is linked to that of the consumer. As such, it thrusts heavy responsibility on the government to protect the consumer interest, since various socio-economic factors lead to exploitation of consumers in the hands of the producers. While analysing the various protective legal measures, it is generally felt that there is still a lot to be done on this score.

Calpovitz (1967) [2] presents a study of consumer behaviour in the United States, particularly the problems faced by consumers in the low-income group. Ignorance about their rights, in the author's opinion, is the root cause of exploitation of consumers in the hands of the trading community and hence such consumers should be provided with suitable marketing guidance to enable them to effectively exercise their bargaining power.

Jolowicz (1969) [3] analysed the scope of the term "protection" and suggests it to mean the provision of financial redress when things go wrong in any market transaction. The author compares the efficacy of both civil and criminal law in protecting consumer interest and favours civil law remedies since they make good for the loss suffered rather than merely punishing the offender.

Trebilcock (1970) [4] examines the socio-economic factors influencing consumers in an adverse manner. It is opined that the lack of proper education and awareness results in exploitation of consumers. Business malpractices should not only be controlled through legislative and executive measures but also by making ordinary consumers informed about the comparative market so that they can protect their interests.

Mathew (1971) [5] observes that the Constitution of India, the fountain-head of all laws in the country, was drafted by a group of politicians who had adequate knowledge and understanding of the socio-economic and political condition of the country, its potentialities and the genuine needs and aspiration of its people. The guiding principles on which the Constitution is based are liberty, equality and the protection of the weak against exploitation in any form. Various rights guaranteed as fundamental rights and the Directive Principles are acclaimed to be the protective umbrella provided by the Constitution against exploitation and harassment in all its dimensions.

Gordon (1972), [6] an active consumerist, highlights the consumer behaviour in the competition oriented United States' economy and while discussing the pros and cons of advertising and its importance in the marketing process, emphasises the need for suitable control measures to check misleading advertisements.

Bhatt (1976), [7] in his paper, discusses the buying pattern of the urban poor and the public distribution system (PDS) that works as a major institutional framework for protecting the weak and the underprivileged consumers of the society. The paper is an outcome of a study of the buying pattern of 150 urban poor families domiciled in Ahmedabad city. The study concentrated on areas like units of buying, frequency of buying, place of buying and terms of buying. It revealed that the urban poor buy with cash and about 90 percent of such consumers depend on fair price shops for essential commodities, never bothering about quality, purity and quantity of the commodities purchased. The paper suggests that for protecting the interest of the poor urban consumers, the PDS should be properly regulated.

Mayens (1976) [8] advises that effective decision-making is necessary for consumers to obtain better quality goods at lower price and therefore they should be guided properly on evaluating purchase information. While pointing out that the U.S.A.'s economy was fast declining by the production of needless goods, the author suggests that adequate legal measures should be enforced to protect the interest of ordinary consumers from the impact of unwanted, sub-standard and unsafe goods.

Wrath (1976) [9] is of the opinion that the Molony Report, 1962 is the chief catalyst in the process of consumer protection in U.K. due to its widespread impact on standards, labelling marks, seal, comparative testing and civil redress mechanism.

Mandana (1977) [10] emphasises on consumer education and evolves various guidelines for making informed purchase with respect to basic needs like food, clothing, housing, drugs, etc. While analysing the impact of deceptive and fraudulent advertisements on innocent consumers, it is suggested that proper education be provided to the consumers to evaluate the advertisements so as to neutralise their adverse effects on them.

Boyd and Stovall (1978) [11] while attempting to discuss various issues connected with consumer protection, laid special emphasis on creating consumer awareness on various concepts of consumerism. Consumer education is highlighted as a life long process and every consumer is expected to make himself educated about the latest development in the market.

Painter (1978) [12] deals with criminal and civil acts related to consumer protection in the United Kingdom. He examines the various types of offences and responsibilities of retailers, traders and shopkeepers and emphasises on the need for registration and licensing of equipment, adequate labelling and stamping of goods and services, particularly explosives and toxins. The author also gives information on the price control method, price check scheme, offences by private and Government traders and the precautionary steps to be taken by consumers.

Cranston (1979) [13] examines the practical application of consumer protection laws by the consumer agencies created under various statutes in U.S.A. and faults them for their failure to properly enforce such laws. As a result, they have miserably failed to deter the exploitative business community.

Reich (1979) [14] opines that the consumer movement slowed down in U.S.A. during the last part of the 1970s mainly due to too much of government intervention in business practices and inadequate implementation of the regulatory provisions. It is suggested that for the healthy growth of consumerism, consumers should be well organised to take care of their own interests, with government intervention in appropriate cases only.

Shah (1979) [15] highlights the inadequacy of textile production, factors responsible thereof and unfair trade practices followed by the textile mills and opines that consumer exploitation on the price front would not be controlled unless and until the demand and supply gap in the textile market is bridged by increased production. He appeals to the industry to practice discipline and to discontinue all marketing and stamping which are defrauding, misleading and confusing to the consumers, failing which these malpractices should be restricted by legal process.

Smith and Swann (1979) [16] while acclaiming the impressive legislative and other measures of consumer protection in the United Kingdom, advise the consumer to utilise his own experience, intelligence and initiative in settling grievances through extra-legal processes—the existing legal mechanism being tardy and expensive.

Feldman (1980) [17] points out that the seller's profit motive and the consumer's desire for need satisfaction are always in conflict, thereby giving way to consumer disputes. As most of the consumer problems affect large sections of population, concerted group action is suggested to be the most effective means of dispute redressal. This way a large number of consumers can avail benefit from a single legislation.

Harvey (1980) [18] in his monograph, discusses consumer protection laws and highlights their limitations so far as the British laws are concerned. A differentiation is made between consumer laws and laws designed to protect people, not specifically the consumers. The concept of price and price mechanism emphasises that any commodity, service and even human labour has a price. The principle of supply and demand regulates major economic activities—what, how and for whom things should be produced? In a capitalistic economy, the author hopes that most of the consumer problems can be taken care of by the operation of the concept of "perfect competition".

Hinich and Staelin (1980) [19] while dealing with adulteration of food in U.S.A., observe that the government regulation along with the growing awareness of consumer in respect of the food industry has been responsible for ensuring food safety. The regulatory agencies have achieved a fair measure of success because of the support received from the educated and conscious consumers. Even so, it is suggested that service of mass media should be liberally available to make the consumers aware of the products, their quality as also the various regulatory provisions controlling the manufacture and marketing of such products.

Lowe and Woodrofe (1980) [20] focus their attention on the types of problems faced by an individual while purchasing goods or services from a supplier and the difficulties faced by him in making good the loss resulting from any defect in such goods or services. It is hoped that law as an instrument of social control firmly deals with all types of business malpractices and crimes.

Mahindra (1980) [21] analyses the development of consumer movement in India and catalogues the various shortcomings that have retarded the growth of the movement. The author feels that in a developing country like India, where most of the people are poor and uneducated, consumer protection could be meaningful by making the consumer aware of the various factors connected with manufacture and marketing of a product and the legal requirements regarding quality, quantity and price of the product.

Micklitz and Reich (1980) [22] analyse consumer law in the economic community basing on the National Reports prepared by jurists in each of the nine EEC countries and evaluate those legislative activities and reform movements which have led to many novel and unique solutions of consumer problems. While dealing with price regulation, problems of weight, marks and labels of consumer products, corrective actions like damages and penalties for the control of deceptive advertising are suggested, along with government control of unfair terms in business contracts.

Shapiro (1980) [23] deals with the concept of technical efficiency, economic efficiency and the Pareto criterion and their application to issues related with the use of societal resources. In the light of this, the author highlights the efficacy of conflict resolution-compensation model and the behaviour modification model of civil dispute resolution mechanism. It is observed that no single model ensures inexpensive, speedy and simple redressal for consumer complaints. However, the importance of both the models is necessary for dispute settlement.

Atur (1981) [24] suggests that the mass media should take up the task of consumer education in the right earnest. Separate time slots in the electronic media and separate space in the print media should be devoted for consumer related issues and programmes.

Best (1981) [25] reports on the survey conducted by the Centre for Study of Responsive Law in 34 cities in the United States covering 2,419 respondents on satisfactory purchases. The survey established that factors like threat from the sellers, confused complaining, lack of proper guidance etc. adversely affects the airing of grievances. It was suggested that improved treatment of complaint at the buyer-seller level, the technique of negotiation and above all the existence of an effective dispute settlement forum would greatly improve the situation in favour of the consumer.

Gadgil (1981) [26] emphasises on the Indian consumers' right to information that would help him in making a rational and knowledgeable choice. It is argued that the consumer is either not provided with required information about goods or services that he intends to purchase or is given false and misleading information which ultimately deprives him of the value of the money spent. As proper information about the goods or services educates the consumer for making effective marketing decision, it is further argued that consumers should be adequately informed about the various economic policies affecting them. Right to Information, it is hoped, will go a long way in making the consumer aware of the market conditions and consequently to enable him to take a perfect purchase decision.

Jayakumar (1981) [27] feels that the effectiveness of the legal provisions aimed at consumer protection would be greatly diminished without awareness among consumers about their rights and the remedies available in law. It is suggested that a concerted campaign on consumer awareness be spearheaded by the legal community—lawyers, law teachers and law students—to build up an effective consumer movement.

Malathesh (1981) [28] conducted a survey in 1980 in respect of the opinion of the members of the public about the activities of leading consumer organisations. The survey revealed that the action of the consumer organisations in seeking remedies for various issues connected with the inefficient working of many public sector corporations was welcomed by the respondents. The respondents were unanimous in their opinion that the consumer organisations should take up issues affecting large segments of the common people and seek redressal for them through appropriate forums. The survey further revealed that consumerism is gradually gaining ground in India and that consumers are becoming more and more aware of their rights.

Mathews (1981) [29] probes into the working of the Gujarat State Electricity Board in the rural sector to assess the quality of services provided by the Board to all 25 villages surveyed. Questionnaires were used to get response from 140 respondents covering a wide range of occupations. Out of 25 selected villages, electricity supply was available in 21 for agriculture, domestic and street lighting purposes. Regular power cuts, surprise cuts and random voltage fluctuation were noticed to be the main causes of loss to the consumers. Besides, the billing system based on average consumption forced the consumer to pay more than the electricity consumed. The study suggests that even though the consumers were harassed by the Electricity Board, they could not get justice mainly due to the absence of suitable mechanism for settlement of the dispute so arising and emphasises the need for immediate establishment of dispute settlement forums at appropriate levels for the rural people.

Mc Anally and Belbridge (1981) [30] examine the course of action to be taken by individuals when problems like faulty goods and services, fake guarantees and cheating by traders crop up. It is felt that attempts should be made to inform the consumers about prices, safety and reliability of goods and the usefulness of trademarks and other marks regarding the standard of goods. Special emphasis should be laid on the education of consumers regarding the existing redressal mechanism in case of loss or injury.

Mc Laughlin (1981) [31] while presenting the summary of discussions held at a conference on "The Future of Consumerism", suggests that the mutual co-operation between business and consumer activists would strengthen the consumer movement and that the mass media should endeavour to develop an effective consumer movement by highlighting important consumer issues. Emphasis is also laid on enhanced citizen participation in the consumer movement to meet the modern challenges posed by the business community.

Mohanty (1981) [32] observes that the Indian laws have not been able to keep pace with the sophisticated trade practices and have not been able to produce the desired results. It is further observed that most of the consumers being illiterate and ignorant, have not been in a position to take advantage of the benefits of the consumer laws. The remedy suggested is that the society at large should be made aware and conscious of the consumer rights and duties, and that individual consumers could protect their own interest by themselves.

Poduval (1981) [33] suggests that government in a democratic set up as in India cannot assume the role of the protector of the interests of consumers and hence there is a need for a well organised social movement by voluntary organisations with support from the government, but free from its control. Consumer representatives, in the opinion of the author, should be given autonomy in matters relating to consumer and consumer issues should be kept above the interference of officials and politicians.

Pylee (1981) [34] observes that the various rights of the consumer are no doubt fundamental to him but are hardly available to him in practice. In the author's opinion, the enacted laws fail to produce the desired results because of the poverty and illiteracy of the consumers and the consequent failure on their part to enforce their rights. Hence, proper enforcement of the consumer laws through a suitable mechanism can provide some relief to the consumers.

Harvey (1982) [35] investigates as to how law protects the consumer from unsafe products, qualitatively deficient goods and services and fraudulent trade practices. The author discusses the historical, economic and philosophical background of consumer protection and patterns of consumer legislation in the United Kingdom. Recognition of consumer rights under various laws is opined to have provided the much-needed institutional framework for consumer protection.

Goldring and Maher (1983) [36] present the Australian consumer protection law and the means to obtain redress under these laws. The authors hold that the aim of consumer protection law is to fix liabilities on the manufacturers and suppliers for breach of duty towards the consumers and provide remedy to them in case of loss or injury arising there from.

Riswadkar (1983) [37] in his research paper "Unfair Fair Price Shop" studies the working of fair price shops in the state of Gujarat. Of the 50 villages surveyed, only 21 were found to have FPS (fair price shop) while users from 29 villages had to go outside their villages to avail PDS. The study revealed that improper working of the system negated the very purpose of FPS for the benefit of the consumers. The sub-standard goods supplied, irregularity in supply and malpractices of false dealing was attributed mainly to the improper working of the system.

Bhargav (1984) [38] carried out research in Ahmedabad, India to identify the level of consumer awareness towards their right with regard to electrical and household appliances. Some of the major findings were that majority of the consumers insisted on warranty/guarantee. On high cost items, the consumers sought details on specifications and after sale services. ISI mark was believed to guarantee high quality and therefore higher prices for goods with such mark were felt to be justified.

Cranston (1984) [39] while discussing the various

regulatory and control measures available to prevent consumer exploitation, suggests that recourse to non legal way of dispute settlement would go a long way in promoting consumer interest by involving voluntary organisations in the process. He also studies the consumer protection laws of U.K., U.S.A., Canada and Australia and throws light on restrictions imposed by government regulations and controls to prevent objectionable trading practices. While focusing on the responsibilities of the manufacturers and retailers towards the consumers as regards quality, quantity and safety of goods, the study emphasises that consumers are needed to take advantage of the legal measures available to counter the exploitation by the business community.

Essien (1984) [40] examines the nature, history and international scenario of consumer protection with special reference to consumer problems in Nigeria. The use of exploitative devices and sale of defective goods are the main causes of consumer problems all over the world and Nigeria as a developing African country is not an exception. The general public was observed to have remained passive and such an attitude was attributed to large-scale illiteracy, ignorance and lack of awareness. Reference is made to an attitude study conducted by the author in 1981 on different aspects of consumer behaviour, which revealed that nearly 80 percent of the subjects experienced problem as consumers. On the willingness of consumers to register complaints and to seek redress of defective goods, nearly half of the subjects claimed to have knowledge about the available forums, but when specifically asked to name the forum, most of them were unable to do so. Under such circumstances, consumer awareness through proper consumer education is opined to be the best mode of consumer protection.

Madhukar and Sudhakar (1985) [41] carried out a preliminary research study in Ahmedabad, India to review the "information labelling" with respect to different brands of refrigerators, tape-recorders, electric irons, textiles, drugs, food products and washing powders. It was observed that most of the Indian consumers were unable to utilise "labelling" while making a purchase because of their lack of knowledge to utilise the same. It was observed that the labelling standards for product should be very high and the ordinary consumers should be properly educated to utilise the same.

Scott (1985) [42] observes that the payment systems have undergone changes at various points of time so as to protect the consumer from exploitative repayment methods. The protection measures that are incorporated in the Uniform New Payment Code are considered to be a milestone in the English consumer protection system.

Fulop (1986) [43] examines the necessity of state interference in the United Kingdom to protect consumers from misleading price claims. Besides the legislative provisions, sufficient executive initiative is suggested to be taken to save them from manipulation in price fixation. It is further suggested that a proper study of consumer behaviour should be undertaken and all consumer legislations should be based on the actual consumer behaviour.

Khanna (1986) [44] observes that in an imperfect society with weak social and legal controls, dishonest, ruthless and cunning producers prosper and flourish at the expense of the poor, ignorant and helpless consumers. In such situations, there is urgent need not only for reviewing, revising and refining the socio-legal controls, regulations and restrictions but also for development of a social movement to counter business malpractices and help protecting various consumer rights.

Kramer (1986) [45] makes a survey of community measures with regard to consumers in the European Economic Community (EEC) in the pattern of national survey made in 1981. While discussing the position of consumer in the community law, it is opined that periodical assessment of the law with respect to prices, marketing, advertising, product safety, consumer information and dispute settlement should be made to develop an effective legal network of consumer laws.

Cardwell (1987) [46] observes that even though law is the most important means of protecting the interest of the consumer, mere passing of legislations would not be sufficient in bringing about the desired result without an effective mechanism to implement and enforce such laws. He also traces the historical development of consumer protection in United Kingdom and discusses the important features of various legislations passed from time to time and the lacunas in such enactments. The provisions of the Consumer Protection Act, 1987 are analysed and innovations made in the legal principles of this Act are highlighted. Poor draftsmanship is blamed as to be the main cause for the lacunas and defects and, hence, due care is suggested to be taken while drafting legal enactments.

Fulop (1987) [47] hopes that the provisions of the Consumer Protection Act ,1987 along with the EEC directives provide a sound legal network for consumer protection in U.K. However, the author feels that in spite of the inherent strength in the legal provisions, nothing can be achieved until the law enforcing authorities implement the existing laws in letter and spirit.

Giri (1987) [48] concentrates on legal protection of the Indian consumer. With extensive analysis and by making references to developments in western countries, he examines the current state of law relating to the problems of false and fraudulent trade practices of manufacturers or dealers in food and drugs. The author evaluates the effectiveness of the existing legal mechanism in the light of current knowledge of the causes and treatment of disorder, studies and interprets factors which contribute to the perpetuation of such offences and holds that the judiciary and the executive should change their mindset while interpreting and enforcing the consumer law so that the consumer related malpractices can be reduced considerably.

Harland (1987) [49] appreciates the efforts of the various government sponsored and private consumer organisations in developing a consumer movement in different parts of the globe. In this connection, the author points out the initiative and encouragement extended by the international organisations like IOCU and the United Nations Organisation (UNO) through special programmes and guidelines for their members to build up an effective consumer movement.

Kamath (1987) [50] drawing heavily on Gandhian philosophy, upholds the view that hardship faced by the consumers is the result of various pitfalls in the existing laws and the unsuitability of the available remedies. It is further held that the legal forces should be effectively used by formulating suitable principles, strategies and practices so as to protect the rights of the ordinary consumer.

Singh (1987) [51] welcomes the independent full-fledged adjudicatory set up provided by the Consumer Protection Act, 1986. In addition to the already existing judicial mechanism to resolve consumer dispute, it is suggested that efforts should be made to harmonise the functioning of the courts so that the working of one does not hinder the working of the other.

Grant (1988) [52] observes that in spite of the enactment of various consumer protection laws, the interest of the consumer has not been effectively protected mainly because of the absence of an organised consumer movement in the Indian subcontinent. The major bottleneck in the development of a sound consumer movement is observed to be the indifference and apathy of the consumers themselves as they are not willing to fight for their rights but expect others to do the same for them. It is hoped that the simplified provisions of the Consumer Protection Act, 1986, would go a long way in inspiring the consumers to fight back.

Saxena (1988) [53] holds that the government of India enacted the Consumer Protection Act with the objective of providing socio-economic justice to all its citizens. The setting up of an independent three-tier redressal forum parallel to the existing enforcement mechanism is observed to be a unique feature of the Act. The author emphasises the need for establishment of consumer forums at the lowest possible levels throughout the country so that the objective of the Act could be achieved to the fullest measure.

Agarwal (1989) [54] gives a descriptive analysis of the rights available to the consumers in India. He critically evaluates the Consumer Protection Act, 1986 in the context of unfair trade practices and rights of consumers. The introductory part contains an elucidation of the historical background of consumer protection legislations in India and abroad. The rest that follows gives a detailed account of the provisions of the 1986 Act along with MRTP Act, designed to protect the interest of the Indian consumers.

Balchandran (1989) [55] indicates the indifferent attitude on the part of the government both at the Centre and the States for not taking initiative needed for establishment of consumer forums at the prescribed levels and providing the minimum infrastructure for such forums to function effectively. The author appreciates the initiative taken by the Hon'ble Supreme Court of India in directing the Union and State government to establish consumer forums within definite timeframe. Further, it is suggested that consumer forum should be established in the rural areas, particularly at Panchayat levels to make such forums easily accessible to consumers.

Bharatiya (1989) [56] while elaborating the various provisions of Indian Constitution to promote the welfare of the people by securing them socio-economic and political justice, feels the necessity of consumer protection to achieve their ultimate objective. It is hoped that government would provide better protection in the years to come but even this will not work without the active involvement of the consumers themselves.

Knapp and Williamson (1989) [57] highlight the efforts made by the National Coalition for Consumers in propagating consumer education in the American Society. They felt that the leaders of consumer affairs working in different fields should join together to work for a common cause by undertaking activities that would promote consumer education and formation of voluntary organisations to further the growth of consumerism.

Prasad (1989) [58] is of the view that the poor unorganised and ignorant consumers, unaware of their rights, are continuously subjected to the exploitative techniques of businessmen and consequently fail to derive proper value for the money spent. It is hoped that a strong and effective consumer movement will save the consumers from exploitation and that the enactment of the Consumer Protection Act, 1986 will strengthen the consumer protection movement in India.

Ramesh (1989) [59] introduced the readers to the deteriorating economic system and the adverse impact of trade on the consumers. The plight of innocent consumer is brought to light and the exploitation of consumer is attributed to their lack of knowledge and confidence. Consumer awareness is highlighted as the best means of consumer protection against all forms of exploitations. He also observes that the attitude of the lawyers not being quite sympathetic to the interest of consumers, they fail to derive desired advantage from the existing courts and consumer forums. It is suggested that alternative modes of dispute redressal such as *Lok Adalat* should also be put to use for resolving consumer disputes.

Sarkar (1989) [60] agrees with the proposition that not only mere passing of legislations but also their sincere implementation will be able to safeguard the interest of the consumers.

Sharma (1989) [61] observes that in the post-Independence era in India, a large number of new laws have been enacted to bring about the necessary social change and the passing of Consumer Protection Act has been the most needed legislative activity to change the socio-economic condition of the consuming public. While strongly appreciating the role of this enactment in eradicating consumer problems, the author is of the opinion that the benevolent statutory provisions would be rendered ultimately futile without the will of the people to combat the exploitative forces.

Swamy (1989) [62] expresses satisfaction over the growth of consumer movement in India even though at a very slow pace. Lack of consumer consciousness is attributed to be the major cause of the slow growth of the consumer movement in India and happiness is expressed over the constructive role played by the voluntary organisations in developing consumerism in the country.

Verma (1989) [63] feels that in a developing country like India, government is expected to play a pivotal role in protecting the consumer interest but in reality, because of its extremely diversified activities, government fails to render effective assistance to the exploited consumers. The objectives of consumer protection can best be achieved through an organised consumer movement with participation of the consumers themselves in protecting their own interest.

Zogen and Gonen (1989) [64] studied different consumer behaviours, purchasing behaviours and factors influencing such behaviours in children by conducting a research on three hundred students with different socio-economic backgrounds in Turkey. The research revealed that the influence of TV commercials on children is ultimately reflected in the purchase behaviour of the parents. The impact of advertisement on children was found to be growing with their tendency to learn about goods and getting familiar with them before buying them. Hence, emphasis is laid on the need to guide children from an early age so as to transform them into intelligent buyers by gradually increasing their level of awareness towards products and minimizing adverse effects of TV commercials on them.

Bijlani (1990) [65] assesses the potentiality of mass media and dwells on their impact on consumer education and awareness. To him, it is the prime responsibility of the consumer groups to maintain close liaison with the media to provide factual and unbiased information to the public.

Garg (1990) [66] while analysing the provisions of the Consumer Protection Act, 1986, emphasises on educating the consumers so that they are able to handle different kinds of complaints. While highlighting the various rights of the consumers, emphasis is laid on the role of voluntary organisations, international agencies and the consumer protection councils in enlarging the horizon of awareness of the ordinary consumers.

Mathur (1990) [67] examines the needs and problems of Indian consumers in the field of various services connected with their daily life, mostly provided by the public sector. While noting the utter failure of the public sector in the management of essential services, it is recommended that there should be an inbuilt system of internal check with provision to reward the good work done and penalise failure in discharge of individual responsibilities so as to revamp the image of the public sector.

Rao (1990) [68] observes that the Hon'ble Supreme Court has justified its position as the highest consumer disputes redressal authority under the hierarchical disputes settlement mechanism created under the Consumer Protection Act, 1986 when it set an example by prohibiting the public sector from becoming arbitrary in providing essential services to the consuming public.

Saraf (1990) [79] while evaluating suitability of the Consumer Protection Act, 1986, justifies the working of the three-tier dispute settlement agency created under the Act. The author expresses satisfaction over the scope of the Act and hopes that the system would prove effective in providing justice to the consumers.

Saraf (1990) [70] traces briefly the evolution of consumer laws in U.S.A., U.K. and India and presents a profile of the Indian consumer and highlights major consumer problems connected with public utility services like railways, road and air transport, telephones, banking, insurance services etc. The author critically examines the impact of the doctrine Caveat

Emptor in business transactions and the various consumer protection measures contained in the Sale of Goods Act, 1930. Emphasis is particularly laid on modification of the existing legal provisions relating to exclusion of liability in business agreements.

Singh (1990) [71] holds the view that the success of any law depends on the active participation of its beneficiaries and hence creation of consumer awareness stands first and foremost in the consumer protection movement, which is thankfully gaining ground in India. The consumers can best be organised through consumer protection associations formed at local levels to ensure effective action against those who have always taken them for a ride.

Vyas (1990) [72] holds that inequality of bargaining power between the consumer and supplier and widespread unfair practices are the main justifications for consumer protection and, in the light of such observation, discusses the importance of standard form of contracts in commercial transactions and the difficulty faced by an ordinary consumer by the use of standard forms. For effective protection of consumer interests, it is suggested that law should be evolved to regulate the use of standard forms detrimental to the interest of the consumers.

Das (1991) [73] hails the passing of the Consumer Protection Act as a milestone in consumer protection movement in India mainly because of the provisions relating to setting up of separate consumer forums for dispute settlement. The author feels that consumer forums should be established at the lowest possible levels instead of only at the district level. Alternatively, judicial magistrates may be empowered to try consumer complaints in places where no consumer forums exist.

Prasad (1991) [74] shows that deficiency in the existing laws and the cumbersome time-consuming dispute-settlement process necessitated the passage of the Consumer Protection Act, 1986 with the objective of providing easy and speedy relief to the consumers. The author expresses satisfaction over the fulfilment of the above objectives of the 1986 Act, by providing an efficient dispute settlement mechanism through a simple procedure and within a certain time frame. Serious lacunae in the working of the Act are discernible in respect of the execution of the final orders. Hence, the author advocates simple means of execution of the orders of the consumer forum. He also expresses satisfaction over the enactment of the Consumer Protection Act, 1986, with the objective of providing cheap and speedy remedies by presenting a simple procedure devoid of technicalities and by creating a three-tier redressal forum. The author hopes that the redressal forums can act as efficient dispute settlement bodies, provided suitable persons with adequate experience are appointed members of such forums.

Agarwal (1992) [75] observes that the simple procedure for filing complaints provided under the Consumer Protection Act, 1986, and the abolition of court fees has gone a long way in providing socio-economic justice to the Indian consumers. However, the author expects a welcome change in the attitude of the members of the forum while awarding meagre amount of compensation.

Kalpana (1992) [76] holds the view that consumer movement in India has unfortunately got stuck in its infancy. Hence, it is suggested that the consumers be made knowledgeable of their legitimate rights in the interest of a potent consumer movement.

Panigrahi (1992) [77] highlights the various causes of consumer exploitation and the legal measures to protect the consumers. In extending the much-needed protection to the consumers, the author emphasises the necessity of consumer awareness and suggests that voluntary organisations be entrusted with the responsibility of strengthening consumer movement with adequate government and media support.

Saraf (1992) [78] expresses unhappiness over the conservative attitude of the National Consumer Dispute Redressal Commission towards the quantum of compensation sought for on matters of harassment, humiliation, hardship or emotional distress. While appreciating the view points of the courts in U.S.A. and U.K., the author suggests that the Indian judiciary should not only take into consideration the actual loss suffered by a consumer but also the negligence and apathy of the opposite party, more so, when it is a giant business enterprise. It is further suggested that the courts should not only adequately compensate the consumer but also award exemplary damages in appropriate cases. He also examines the various aspects of Consumer Protection Act, 1986 and its contribution to the growth of judicial institutions in India. An independent enquiry is made into the qualification and terms of appointment of the judicial and non-judicial members of different consumer forums and their suitability in handling consumer disputes. Dissatisfaction is inevitable over the territorial jurisdiction of the district forums, as in certain cases forums comprising only three members are expected to impart consumer justice to a population varying from one lakh to about a crore.

Malve (1993) [79] views education as the transmission of the value and accumulation of knowledge and the total process by which a community or a social group, whether small or large, transmits its acquired power with a view to securing its continuous existence and growth. In the light of the above viewpoint, the need for consumer education regarding the quality, quantity and price of various goods and services is stressed. The creation of consumer councils under the provisions of Consumer Protection Act, 1986 is observed to be the most appropriate and the councils are called upon to take suitable steps for educating consumers on their rights, duties and responsibilities and, above all, on the ways and means of obtaining redressal in case of loss or injury, from forums established under the Act.

The quintessence that emerges from a review of the rich reading materials available on various aspects of consumer education and awareness emphatically establishes that all attempts at consumer protection would prove an exercise in futility unless the consumer is educated about his recognised rights. Such education basically depends on adequate information on the products, their quality, safety, price and, above all, the skill and technique required for application of such information in the interest of the consumer. Consumers should also be educated about the various legal remedies available to protect themselves from exploitation and also the relevance of forums for grievance redressal. The level of general education being normally low in developing countries, consumer education should be given top priority in the agenda of government policy and planning. The thrust area of consumer education and consequent awareness is aimed at instilling confidence and ability in the consumer to fight for his own rights by remaining ever alert and vigilant. The role of mass media is of paramount importance in promoting consumer awareness and education.

Lackadaisical enforcement renders many well-intended legislations ineffective, thereby adversely affecting the genuine interest of the targeted goal. Many instances have come to notice where legislative enactments designed to eradicate and uproot social evils have been reduced to the status of paper tigers due to lopsided implementation of laws despite their inherent potentiality. The present search for literature is to verify whether the same holds good in consumer laws too.

Nabi and Raut (1993) [80] chronologically examined the history and growth of consumerism in the world and development of consumerism in the Indian society. They opine that consumerism is here to stay in India and grow into a socio-economic revolution in the near future, since an institutional structure has been built to support it.

Goyal (1994) [81] holds that even though attempts have been made for long to protect the interest of the consumers either by legislative or judicial efforts, the consumers have not reaped the desired benefit due to lack of proper enforcement mechanism. The poor and ignorant consumers could neither afford the luxury of a tortuous, expensive and time-consuming civil litigation nor the criminal law could be effectively utilised by the enforcing agencies to prevent anti-consumer activities. Under such socio-economic conditions, the passing of the Consumer Protection Act, 1986 is hailed and trust is reposed in the forums rather than the courts.

Rao (1994) [82] undertakes a systematic study of the origin and growth of consumer movement in various countries of the world and emphasises on the need for such a movement in India in keeping with the concept of welfare state—the political ideology of the country. Ignorance and illiteracy of the common people being the root cause of their exploitation, development of a strong broad-based voluntary consumer movement at the grass root level is deemed necessary for making the consumers conscious, aware and assertive. It is further suggested that law being the ideal instrument of protection, the legal community including law teachers and students should extend all possible help in giving the required push to the consumer protection programme.

Reddy (1994) [83] disagrees with the proposition that market forces can take care of consumer interest and views a perfect competitive market as a utopia. Against this backdrop, the author feels the necessity of consumer protection and observes that even though statutory protection measures play a significant role, involvement of consumers is necessary for successful implementation of its legal provisions. For making the consumer protection programme a success, voluntary consumer organisations should be given adequate representation in the consumer protection councils at the National and State levels.

Singh (1994) [84] observes that the provisions made in the Consumer Protection Act, 1986 for imposition of penalties like imprisonment and fine for non-compliance and violation of orders of consumer forums would go a long way in enforcing obedience by the defaulting parties. After an exhaustive analysis of case laws, the author opines that even though the penal provisions provide teeth and claws to the Consumer Protection Act, these provisions should be applied cautiously within the parameters of the established law.

Singh and Sangwan (1994) [85] conducted a research study on the perceptions of rural and urban consumers regarding justice through legislative measures by taking 50 respondents from each category. The study revealed that both rural and urban consumers faced problems relating to quality, quantity and price. Majority of the respondents held ignorance of the consumers squarely responsible for non-implementation of laws, while justice through legislative measures was perceived by most of the consumers as a complex process. It was therefore, suggested that consumer organisations should help promote a culture of consumerism in the society.

Srivastav (1994) [86] mainly deals with the definition of service as given in the Consumer Protection Act, 1986 and analyses the scope of the said definition to cover cases of negligence in the field of medical care. The author feels that payment of heavy compensation should be prescribed as an effective mode of punishment in curbing negligent health care practices.

Jena (1995) [87] opines that India as yet has not been able to achieve economic independence due to various socio-economic factors and suggests that for economic growth, the only solution at hand is to strengthen consumer movement to ensure public accountability by correcting malfunctioning of the entire social system. The author is of the view that the Consumer Protection Act, 1986, which is a beneficial, progressive and social legislation, can prove to be a powerful weapon in the hands of the consumers to ensure accountability and thereby, strengthen the consumer movement in the country.

Khurana (1995) [88] appreciates stringent provisions made in the Consumer Protection Act, 1986 to punish traders with imprisonment and fine for non-compliance of the order of consumer forums and hopes that such provision would force the defaulting manufacturers and traders to promptly comply with orders of the forums.

Paul (1995) [89] holds the view that while in India, common practice is to award low compensation in negligence cases, in U.S.A., the damages awarded are colossal.

Mehta (1998) [90] observes that consumer movement has no doubt done extremely well so far and has spread its message very widely. Nevertheless, it is unfortunate that of late quite a few inadequacies have crept into the functioning of its redressal agencies established at district level and state level all over the country. Happily, efforts are now being intensively made to ensure that these inadequacies are soon addressed.

Murthy (2001) [91] is of the opinion that apart from protecting environmental greenness, consumerism tends to devise a mechanism for withdrawing or preventing defective goods and services so that no consumer anywhere in the world suffers due to poor quality.

Sharma (2002) [92] examines the statutory measures for redressal of consumer grievances provided under the Consumer Protection Act, 1986 (CPA) and evaluates the approach of the consumer grievances redressal agencies set up under the CPA, in providing relief to the consumers from the supply of defective goods, deficiency in service, unfair trade practices, charging of prices in excess of the prescribed limits, and marketing of unsafe and hazardous products.

Niraj Kumar (2007) [93] opined that the law is an attempt to meet long felt need of protecting the consumer or in essence common man from disputes for which remedy under the then existing law was not sufficient. The marketing rule no longer is 'Caveat Emptor', it is 'Caveat Venditor' and the Consumer Protection Act, 1986 has emerged as a much useful and consumer friendly Act.

Compendium (2008) [94] of important Orders of State-CDR Commission and District Consumer Forums published by the State Institute of Consumer Awareness(SICA), Bhubaneswar is a compilation of landmark orders of the State Consumer Redressal Commission and of different District Consumer Fora of the State.

It was brought out on the occasion of the World Consumers Right Day, 2008 i.e. on 15th March 2008. It highlighted various types of problems faced by consumers and judicial response to the same. The endeavour is definitely a welcome step towards enlightening the consumer in general and voluntary consumer organizations (VCOs) and NGOs in particular about consumer rights and duties, grievance redressal mechanism and other related issues. It would definitely go a long way in protecting the interest of consumers as well of honest traders.

Panigrahi (2008) [95] is of the view that despite numerous laws and measures of legislative and administrative action, consumer protection has miles to go. The Central council and the State councils as well as insincere, half-hearted voluntary organisations do not stand anywhere before the well organised, well informed and well financed manufacturers.

Rajyalakshmi Rao (2009) [96] has tried to impress upon the consumer courts to provide quick and inexpensive justice in hassle free manner, to guide consumers regarding precautions to be taken while buying goods or availing services and the documents they need to preserve and has finally cited leading judgments delivered in connection with protection of consumer rights.

Proceeding on Consumer Protection and Welfare (2010) [97] No doubt advancement of technology, flooding of market with sophisticated gadgets and aggressive marketing strategies have not only thrown open a wider choice before a consumer but also exposed them to a plethora of problems. Needles to say, an enlightened consumer is an empowered consumer. He not only protects himself from exploitation but also infuses efficiency, transparency and accountability in the entire manufacturing and service sector. Therefore, it is highly important that consumer awareness is created on a mega-scale. Accordingly, top priority should be attached to consumer protection, consumer justice and the most important of all, consumer education.

The Consumer Protection Act, 1986 is a progressive and

comprehensive legislation enacted after a deep study of consumer protection laws and arrangements prevailing in different countries. While other existing laws of the land are punitive or preventive in nature, the provisions of this Act are compensatory. The Act provides for simple, speedily and inexpensive redressal to grievances of consumers.

From the review of the above studies, it is discerned that though a few researchers have made attempts in the direction of measurement of consumer awareness, perception of the working of consumer forums and complaining behaviour of the consumers, only a limited area has so far been covered in respect of the working of consumer forums for the redressal of consumer grievances.

Despite the fact that the issue of consumer protection has vital social and economic dimensions, it has not attracted much attention of research scholars. Against such a backdrop, the present study is a modest attempt to focus on the need to bridge the gap between the problems and prospects of consumerism.

Endnotes

1. Barbar, R.J., "Government and the Consumers", Michigan Law Review, Vol. 64, 1966, p. 1203.
2. Calpolvitz, D., "Poor Pay More", The Press, New York, 1967.
3. Jolowicz, J.A., "The Protection of the Consumer and Purchaser of Goods under English Law", *Modern Law Review*, Vol. 32, No. 1, 1969, p. 1.
4. Trebilcock, M.J., "Consumer Protection in the Affluent Society", *McGill Law Journal*, Vol. 16, No. 2, 1970, p. 263.
5. Mathew, K.K., "Poverty, Power and the Constitution", *The Academic Law Review*, Vol. 1, 1971, p. 1.
6. Gordon, L.J. and Lee, S.M., "Economics for Consumers", D. Van Nostrand, New York, 1972.
7. Bhatt, R., "Buying Pattern of the Urban Poor and Distribution Systems", Ahmedabad, Consumer Education and Research Centre, 1976.
8. Maynes, E.S., "Decision-making for Consumer: An introduction to Consumer Economics", McMillan Publishing Co., New York,

1976.

9. Wrath, R., "Consumer Cause: A Short Account of its Organization Development, Power and Importance," Royal Institute of Public Administration, London, 1976.
10. Mandana, J., "Indian Market Place: Guidelines to Consumer Education, Brindaban Publishing House, Bangalore, 1977.
11. Boyd, F.L. and Stovall, R., "Handbook of Consumer Education", Allyn and Bacon Inc., London, 1978.
12. Painter, A.A., "Guide to Consumer Protection Law", Barry Rose Ltd., London, 1978.
13. Cranston, R., "Regulating Business: Law and Consumer Agencies", The Macmillan Press Ltd., London, 1979.
14. Reich, R.B., "Towards a New Consumer Protection", *University of Pennsylvania Law Review*, Vol. 128, No. 1, 1979, p. 1.
15. Shah, M., "Consumer and Clothing", Consumer Education and Research Centre, Ahmedabad, 1979.
16. Smith, P. and Swann, D., "Protecting the Consumer", An Economic and Legal Analysis, Martin Robertson and Company Limited, Oxford, 1979.
17. Feldman, L.P., "Consumer Protection: Problems and Prospects", West Publishing Company, U.S.A., 1980.
18. Harvey, B.W., "Consumer Protection Laws and the Concept of the Perfect Market", Institute of Trading Standards Administration, USA, 1980.
19. Hinich, M. J. And Staelin, R., "Consumer Protection Legislation and the U.S. Food Industry", Pergamon Press, New York, 1980.
20. Lowe, R. and Woodrofe, G., "Consumer Law and Practice", Sweet and Maxwell Ltd., London, 1980.
21. Mahindra, H., "Law and Consumer", Council for Fair Business Practices, Bombay, 1980.
22. Micklitz, H.W., and Reich, N., "Consumer Legislation in the EEC Countries: A Comparative Analysis", Van Nostrand Rein Hold, New York, 1980.
23. Shapiro, A.A., "Economic Analysis of Consumer Redress Mechanism, Canada: Consumer and Corporate Affairs, 1980.
24. Alur, S.S., "Myth of Consumer Protection" in P. Leela Krishnan (ed.) Consumer Protection and legal Control, Lucknow, Eastern Book Company 1981, p. 110.
25. Best, A., "When Consumers Complain", New York, Columbia University Press, 1981

26. Gadgil, G. "Consumer' Right to Information", *The Council for Fair Business Practices Bulletin*, Vol. 15, No. 3, 1981, p. 1.
27. Jayakumar, N.K., "Consumer Justice: Strategies and Institutions", in P. Leelakrishnan (ed.), Consumer Protection and Legal Control, Eastern Book Company, Lucknow, 1981, p. 110.
28. Malathesh, S., "Consumerism: An Opinion Survey", Consumer Education and Research Centre, Ahmedabad, 1981.
29. Mathews, K., "Power that Paralysis: A Survey of Electricity Consumers in the Rural Areas of Gujarat", Consumer Education and Research Centre, Ahmedabad, 1981.
30. McAnally, M. and Belbridge, R., "Buy Rights", Pan Books Ltd., London, 1981.
31. McLaughlin, F.E. (ed.), "The Future of Consumerism", Proceeding of a Conference, Maryland Centre for Business and Public Policy, Maryland, U.S.A., 1981.
32. Mohanty, B., "Consumer Protection: A Challenging Task", P. Leelakrishnan (ed.), Consumer Protection and Legal Control, Eastern Book Company, Lucknow, 1981, p. 24.
33. Poduval, P.R., "Consumerism: Social Significance and Effectiveness", P. Leelakrishnan (ed.), Consumer Protection and Legal Control, Eastern Book Company, Lucknow, 1981, p. 41.
34. Pylee, M.V., "Consumer Protection in Developing Society", P. Leelakrishnan (ed.), Consumer Protection and Legal Control, Eastern Book Company, Lucknow, 1981, p. 10.
35. Harvey, B.W., "Law of Consumer Protection and Fair Trading", Butteworths, London, 1982.
36. Goldring, J.L. and Maher, L.W., "Consumer Protection Law in Australia", Butter Worths Pvt. Ltd., 1983.
37. Riswadkar, S., "Unfair Fair Price Shops", Consumer Education and Research Centre, Ahmedabad, 1983.
38. Bhargav, A. "Awareness and Attitudes of Consumers towards Their Rights: Case of Household Electrical Appliances", Indian Institute of Management, Ahmedabad, 1984.
39. Cranston, R., "Consumers and the Law", Weidenfeld and Nicholson, London, 1984.
40. Essien, V.L.K., "Consumer Protection in Nigeria: The Case for Reform", New York University, *Journal of International Law and Politics*, Vol. 16, No. 3, Spring, 1984, p. 515.
41. Madhukar, S. and Sudhakar, V.S., "Information Labelling

Review", Consumer Education and Research Centre, Ahmedabad, 1985.

42. Scott, H. "Consumer Protection and Payment System: Regulatory Policy for the Technological Era", *Harvard Law Review*, Vol. 98, 1985, p. 1870.
43. Fulop, C., "Buyer Be Aware: Shopping Laws, U.K.", *Economic Affair*, Vol. 6, No. 3, 1986, p. 12.
44. Khanna, R., "Law for the Welfare of Consumers in India", *Supreme Court Journal*, Vol. 1, 1986, p. 18.
45. Kramer, L., "EEC Consumer Law", Centre De Droit De La Consommution, France, 1986.
46. Cardwell, K., "The Consumer Protection Act 1987: Enforcement of Provisions Governing the Safety of Consumer Goods", *The Modern Law Review*, Vol. 50, 1987, p. 622.
47. Fulop, C., "The Costs and Benefits of a Duty to Trade Fairly, U.K., *Economic Affairs*, Vol. 8, 1987, p. 33.
48. Giri, H.N., "Consumers Crimes and the Law", Ashish Publishing House, New Delhi, 1987.
49. Harland, D.J., "Some international Dimensions of Consumer Law and Policy", *Journal of Indian Law Institute*, Vol. 29, 1987, p. 460.
50. Kamath, K.P.S., "Servants, Not Masters", Udupi, Consumers Forum, Udupi, 1987.
51. Singh, S.N., "Consumer Protection Legislation: A Critique", *Journal of Indian Law Institute*, Vol. 29, No. 3, 1987, p. 380.
52. Grant, N.B., "Consumer Movement: the Indian Experiment", *Consumer Confrontation*, Ahmedabad, Vol. 8, No. 3, 1988, p. 13.
53. Saxena, J.C., "The Consumer Protection Act, 1986: A View Point", *Journal of India Law Institute*, Vol. 30, No. 3, 1988, p. 321.
54. Agarwal, V.K., "Consumer Protection in India", New Delhi, Deep and Deep Publications, 1989.
55. Balchandran, M.K., "Consumer Protection", Comprehensive Legislation: Need of the Hour", *The Indian Journal Studies*, Vol. IX, 1989, p. 31.
56. Bharatiya, V.P., "Consumer Protection: So Much Done, Much More to be Done", *The Indian Journal of Legal Studies*, Vol. IX, 1989, p. 177.
57. Knapp, J. and Williamson, I.K., "New National Coalition for

Consumer Education", *Advancing the Consumer Interest*, Vol. 1, No. 1, 1988, p. 1.
58. Prasad, A.R., "The Consumer Protection Act, 1986: A Critical Appraisal", *All India Reporter*, 1989, Journal, p. 12.
59. Ramesh, M.K., "Consumers Interest in Legal Profession: Problems and Prospective", *Cochin University Law Review*, Vol. 13, No. 4, 1989, p. 405.
60. Sarkar, A., "Problem of Consumers in Modern India", Discovery Publishing House, New Delhi, 1989.
61. Sharma, D.D., "Some Reflections on Consumer Protection and the Role of Law", *The Indian Journal of Legal Studies*, Vol. IX, 1989, p. 49.
62. Swamy, S.N., "Consumer Protection: No Lukewarm Attitude", *Consumer Confrontation*, Vol. 9, No. 2, Ahmedabad, 1989, p. 13.
63. Verma, S.K., "Consumer Protection: Challenges and Perspective", *The Indian Journal of Legal Studies*, Vol. 9, 1989, p. 44.
64. Zogen, O. and Gonen, E., "Consumer Behaviour of Children in Primary School Age", *Journal of Consumer Studies and Home Economics*, June, 1989, p. 175.
65. Bijlani, D. "Role of Mass Media in Consumer Education", Ahmedabad, Centre for Development Communication, Gujarat University, 1990.
66. Garg, O.P., "Consumer Protection Act, 1986", Vinod Publishing House, Delhi, 1990.
67. Mathur, A.B.L., "Service Marketing by the Public sector and the Quality of Life", *The Indian Journal of Legal Studies*, Vol. X, 1990, p. 29.
68. Rao. K.S., "The Role of the Court in Protecting Consumers Vis-à-Vis Public Enterprises", *The Indian Journal of Legal Studies*, Vol. X, 1990, p. 43.
69. Saraf, D.N., "Law of Consumer Protection in India", Bombay, N.M. Tripathy, Bombay, 1990.
70. Saraf, D.N., "Some Facets of Consumer Justice through Consumer Disputes Redressal Agencies", *Journal of Indian Law Institute*, Vol. 34, No. 1, 1992, p. 28.
71. Singh, "Consumers Forum: Need of the House", *Social Welfare*, Vol. XXXVII, No. 7, October 1990, p. 6.
72. Vyas, R.C., "Consumerism and the Public Sector Industries",

The Indian Journal of Legal Studies, Vol. 10, 1990, p. 1.
73. Das, N., "Consumer Protection Act and the Common Man", *All India Reporter Journal*, 1991, p. 158.
74. Prasad, R.N., "Consumer Protection Act, 1986: Some Suggestion for Improvement", *All India Reporter*, 1991, p. 163
75. Agarwal, S.K., "Court and Accountability of Universities: Some Recent Developments", *Consumer Confrontation*, Vol. 12, No. 2, 1992, p. 35.
76. Kalpana, "Making Consumerism a Movement", *Yojana*, New Delhi, Vol. 36, No. 10, 1992, p. 10.
77. Panigrahi, B., "Consumer Protection and the Law", *All India Reporter*, 1992, p. 33.
78. Saraf, D.N., "Some facets of Consumer Justice Through Consumer Disputes Redressal Agencies", *Journal of India Law Institute*, Vol. 34, No. 1, 1992, p. 28.
79. Malve, G., "Consumer Education under Consumer Protection Act 1986", *Supreme Court Journal*, Vol. 1, 1993, p. 1.
80. Nabi, M.K., and Raut, K.C., "Whither Consumerism", *The Southern Economist*, April 1 and 15, 1999, pp.13-15.
81. Goyal, K.N., "Changing Philosophy of Consumer Protection Laws", *All India Reporter*, 1994, p. 193.
82. Rao. B.V., "Consumerism in India: A Prospect and Future", *All India Reporter*, 1994, p. 97.
83. Reddy, A.R., "Consumer Protection and Consumer Movement in India: A Perspective", *Supreme Court Journal*, Vol. 2, 1994, p. 34.
84. Singh, G., "Enforcement of Orders of the Consumer Dispute Redressal Agencies and Imposing of Penalties Under the Consumer Protection Act, 1986", *Consumer Protection Journal*, 1994, p. 17.
85. Singh, K. and Sangwan, I.V., "A Comparative Study to Assess the Problems of Rural and Urban Consumers", *Consumer Confrontation*, Vol. 14, No. 1, Ahmedabad, 1994, p. 44.
86. Srivastav, S., "Consumer Protection and Medical Profession", *Central India Law Quarterly*, Vol. VII, Part IV, 1994, p. 426.
87. Jena, K., "Role of Members of Redressal Agencies for Effective Implementation of Consumer Protection Act, 1986", *Consumer Protection Judgments*. Vol. 1, Journal Section, 1995, p. 10.
88. Khurana, L., "Consumer Protection: The Growing Concern", *Yojana*, Vol. 39, No. 5, 1995, p. 26.

89. Paul, S., "Judicial Scrutiny of Medical Negligence Cases by Consumer Forum", *All India Reporter*, 1995, p. 28.
90. Mehta, P.S., "How to Survive as a Consumer", Consumer Unity and Trust Society, Jaipur, 1998.
91. Murthy, D.B.W., "Consumer and Quality", New Age International, New Delhi, 2001.
92. Sharma, D., "Consumer Grievance Redressal Under the Consumer Protection Act", New Century Publications, New Delhi, 2002.
93. Kumar, N., "Consumer Protection in India", Himalaya Publishing House, Mumbai, 2007.
94. "Compendium of Important Orders of State CDR Commission and District Consumer Forums", Government of Orissa, Food Supplies and Consumer Welfare Department, Bubaneswar, 2008.
95. Panigrahi, B., "Popularisation of Consumer Movement", Journal of Berhampur University, Vol. XVI, March 2008.
96. Rao, R., "Consumer is King: Know Your Rights and Remedies", Universal Law Publishing Co. Pvt. Ltd., New Delhi, 2009.
97. "Seminar Proceedings on Consumer Protection and Welfare", Andhra University, Vishakhapatnam, 2010.

3

Consumerism and Consumer Protection

3.1 Introduction

Protection of consumers in any society owes largely to consumerism, consumer movement and consumer policy prevailing in that society over a period of time. Consumer protection can be better understood only when one looks at the history of consumerism and consumer movement around the world. Consumerism is the spirit of social force behind consumer movement leading to consumer awareness and consumer education with the objective of protecting the consumers at the market place.

There is a close connection between consumer protection and commerce or business which is closely related to the government and its regulations. Hence, evolution and growth of consumer protection largely depends on consumerism and consumer movement of that country over a period of time. The more the consumers are educated and organised, the better are their rights protected. In this context, consumers of developed countries are comparatively more protected because of the consumer movement and the state performing a paternal role in safeguarding consumerism through statutory enactments regulating business in comparison to developed and less developing countries.

In this chapter, an attempt has been made to examine the historical perspective of consumerism, consumer movement, consumer policies and consumer protection policy of some of the countries of the world with special emphasis on India.

3.2 What is Consumerism?

The term 'consumerism' refers to a set of policies and activities aimed at protecting the rights and promoting consumer welfare. Consumerism is on the rise, where there is consumer discontent, protests, ignorance and unfavourable economic conditions. In other words, consumerism is the manifestation of various kinds of frustration that a consumer experiences over the years. Consumerism is also defined as the organised efforts of consumers, seeking redress, restitution and remedy for dissatisfaction with their poor standard of living.

Aaker and David defined consumerism as "the widening range of activities of government, business and independent organisations that are designed to protect individuals from practices that infringe upon their rights as consumers". [1]

In an impersonal society which is the concomitant of rapid industrialization and technological advancement, individual consumer remains in the background, away from the preview sight of the leaders of manufacturing corporations. They have genuine grievances. Consumerism highlights these complaints. The purpose of doing so is to ensure equitable operation of economy in which buyers are not handicapped and their interests are adequately safeguarded. Thus, it is essentially a consumer interest campaign, advocating a social cause, championing consumer rights and pleading for a better deal for him from the seller.

As such, consumerism is understood as a social movement that has, as its objective, increase of consumer power vis-à-vis sellers of products or services. It is a movement that safeguards the consumer against market power.

Since consumerism is associated with the interwoven relationship of people, businessmen, social activists and government, an appropriate understanding of all the three parties is essential. Such an understanding may be attempted at three levels, depending on the types of relationship in question. [2]

At the first level, consumerist argues that it is the relationship between the consumer and the business enterprises which has to be modified. The following definition is typical for this level:

"Consumerism means that the consumer looks upon the

manufacturer as somebody who is interested but who really does not know what the consumers' requirements are. He regards the manufacturer as somebody who has not made any effort to find out, who does not understand the world in which the consumer lives, and who expects the consumer to be able to make distinction which the consumer is neither willing nor able to make". [3]

Operationally, at this first of the definition of consumerism, actions by consumerist forces as manufacturer—consumer relations in terms of products, services, advertising, promotion, packaging, pricing and distribution is considered.

At the second level, definition of consumerism examines interdependence between the first level of relationship described above and the societal system. The tone and tenor of the definition at this level is generally one of a perceived threat against consumers, as is evident from the following statement.

"Consumerism is generally considered to be a protection mechanism meant for consumers".

1. Physical threat to life, health and property.
2. Economic threat to consumers as a result of market imperfections, abuses, fraud and deceptions.
3. Threat from other consumers in the process of collective consumption in the modern technological mass consumption society". [4]

At the third level, consumer activism tends to become political activism. Certain organisations questioned the social fabric of the capitalistic system. They not only want to change "caveat emptor" into "caveat venditor" but also want to control the process of production. Other organisations go even further, the Marxist way, and use consumerism as a platform to take control of means of production.

3.3 Consumerism, Consumer and Business

There are various consumerist groups that are active in enhancing communication between the parties involved in the process of production and consumption. Research studies conducted among consumers and businesses have found that the issues with which consumerism should be concerned, relate mainly to information, health and safety, repairs and service, and product quality. [5] It also shows that consumer organisations operating at political level are of little practical interest to the consumer.

Marketing is seen as a link between producers and consumers; an analysis of consumer programmes shows pre-occupation with 9 rights of the consumer, viz.: (i) safety, (ii) information, (iii) truth, (iv) quality, (v) education, (vi) authenticity, (vii) health, (viii) protection, and (ix) choice.

For each of these rights, marketing strategies adopted are as under:

1. Product policy.
2. Pricing policy.
3. Advertising policy.
4. Distribution policy.

3.3.1 Product Policy: Product policy of marketing system mainly relates to product and packaging. Product policy has come under attack because of problems such as quality, proliferation of new products and too many similar products. The consumer often fails to differentiate among too many products useful for consumption. The other strategies employed by marketers are deceptive innovations, artificial differentiation, dangerous, defective, marginal products and useless gadgets.

With regard to packaging, the policy is being attacked at polluting packaging, dangerous and useless packaging, deceitful packaging which avoids possibility of comparison, labels that do not provide adequate information, lack of precise indications of use, lacks in description of ingredients and product dating. One may recall that product safety constituted Ralph Nader's entry point into the consumer movement.

3.3.2 Pricing Policy: Pricing policies have been singled out for attack for the strategy creating new products at higher prices, profit maximising, cartels, psychological pricing, fictitious prices, fake creditors, unreasonable margin, absence of unit prices, fake price/quantity relationship, fictitious promotions etc.

Consumers are at the receiving end when it comes to the pricing strategy made by the producers of goods in a strong marketing system created by them for ensuring maximum consumption of their goods.

3.3.3 Advertising Policy: Advertising strategies have been accused of turning more and more from information context to psychological positioning as a means to differentiate very similar products. Promises are often exaggerated to allure lower level instincts of market. Advertising being an effective method of communication, marketers of goods and services take its fullest advantage to manipulate consumers, create needs, contribute to inflation by raising consumption level, promote planned obsolescence and cause mental pollution. Strategic advertising methods reduce free competition, push mass-consumption society to excessive materialism, thereby giving the society false values. Advertising strategy smears image of women and does not provide adequate information to consumers. It pushes psychological non-performance character of the products in the world.

3.3.4 Distribution Policy: With regard to distribution policy, consumerists want to protect consumers from aggressive in-store merchandising technique. They seek quality of information that permits free evaluation and choice of price/quality relationship. Distribution policy in marketing system tends to high-pressure selling, deceitful promotions, aggressive merchandising techniques and pushes high-margin products in the market for most consumption. It also creates new retailing methods for pushing consumption, providing poor/sub-standard after-sales-service and high-pressure door-to-door selling.

It may be concluded that the factors contributing to the rise of consumerism are multiple and may be found at four levels: development of factors of production, changes in environment variables, changes in managerial processes, and changes in consumer-satisfaction.

3.4 Consumer Movement

An important factor for effective consumer protection is undoubtedly consumer movement. Consumer movement gives momentum to the consumerism which ultimately ends up in consumer protection. It is very difficult to define what is consumer movement?—when it started and when it will end. It is a relentless process in the society which disseminates awareness among consumers and protects consumer interests as well.

We are all consumers but most of us do not think of ourselves as such, or only at such times as circumstances force on us a change in the pattern or level of consumption. What consumers need is a fuller consciousness of their consumer function. Consumers need to develop a greater concern about quality of satisfaction derived from consumption of goods/services available to them and about values that underlie the scale of preferences which determines how they spend their money at market. Consumers need to develop greater efficiency in use of their individual resources, including how they spend money, time, and energy in the market.

This calls for an increasing awareness among consumers of their basic interest as consumers. For this, one has to know how much awareness of consumer interest already exists among consumers and how this can be stimulated and extended. Consumer organisations do protect consumer interest through consumer movement.

3.4.1 Objectives of Consumer Movement: The broad objectives for which consumers are working may be summed up in 4 keywords: (i) income, (ii) information, (iii) integrity, and (iv) independence. [6]

A. Income: Consumers want income. They are concerned with their real income, not just their money income. Consumers to get real income, are found to face many problems, such as budgeting, choice-making and the whole field of personal economics. In order to play their part effectively as citizens in economic community, consumers need to know basics of functioning of the economy as a whole. Consumer movement fills this gap by organizing consumers to assert their rights to have their money's real worth.

B. Information: The second objective of consumer movement for which consumers work together is to have information about commodities or services available to them. The quest for information about commodities or services gives them real income. Consumers cannot possibly become technical experts on all types of commodities they have to buy, but they certainly could make use of more factual information which gives them ultimately the desired return.

C. Integrity: Next, consumers are interested in integrity of those with whom they deal. The highest possible standards of honesty are to be desired not only for their own sake, but also because they enable consumers to carry on their economic activities more efficiently. What consumers feel mot concerned about in this connection is the integrity of those from whom they buy.

D. Independence: The last objective of consumer movement is independence. Consumers want independence. They want to have independence as individuals in making up their own minds about how they will spend their income; they also want independence as a class in organizing and expressing their opinions. Consumer movement promotes independence among consumers and educates them not to be influenced by manufacturers and their salesmen through powerful advertisement to purchase articles which consumers need the least.

3.5 Consumer Policy

The third and important factor for consumer protection is indeed the consumer policy. Consumer policy develops with consumerism and consumer movement. Without consumer policy, effective consumer protection cannot be contemplated.

Consumer policy promotes awareness among consumers and promotes consumer legislations. Consumer policy determines the parameters of different agencies for achieving the objective of the concept of consumer protection. Agencies responsible for carrying out consumer policy of a state may be governmental and private bodies. In private bodies, the non-governmental organizations and voluntary consumer organisations play a pivotal role.

From the above discussion, it is seen that for effective consumer protection, consumerism, consumer movement and consumer policy in harmonious cooperation are essential. Now, an attempt is being made to study the historical perspective of the above concepts in protecting consumers in India and some of the developed, developing and under-developed countries, international consumer organisations and the United Nations.

Endnotes

1. Aaker, D., and George S.D., "A Guide to Consumerism", *Journal of Marketing*, 12th July 1970, pp. 12-17.
2. Webster, F.Z., "Does Business Misunderstand Consumerism?", *Harvard Business Review*, September-October, 1973, pp. 89-97.
3. Drucker, P., "The Shame of Marketing", *Marketing Communications*, August, 1969, p. 69.
4. Sheth, J.N., and Mamera, N.J., "Recent Failures in Consumer Protection", *California Management Review*, Spring, 1947.
5. Dimond, S.L., Word, S., and Faber, R., "Consumr Problems and Consumerism: An Analysis of Calls to a Consumer Hotline", *Journal of Marketing*, June 1976, pp. 58-62.
6. Cassels, J.M., "The Clarification of Consumer Thinking" in the Proceedings of the Business-Consumer Relations Conference, New York, 1940, pp. 8-16.

4

Consumer Movements in Select Countries

Giving and taking goods and services is perhaps the oldest activity in human life. In animal life, this activity was limited to one family, until they cohabit and until kids grow up and become independent entities. Only in mankind there is a family tradition and social set up that continues for life long. We as men, women, children, as a family, as a society, and even as a nation, give and take. When there was no money currency, there was a barter system. There were some kinds of contracts, mostly yearly contracts, among residents of a village, whereby goods, services and supplies were provided by such providers to all people of the village, on yearly basis. With growth of civilization, economies, markets, knowledge of wealth and need for monetary safety and protection, use of money came into existence. This, and then Industrial Revolution, changed the world and its socio-economic order. Nations since then are coming economically so close that now the whole world is like one market. However, human beings—men, women and children live on a two-fold footing. On one side of it, we are individuals.

On the other side of it, we are family, society, state, people and nation. Giving and taking of goods and services have multiplied. Consequently, dependence on each other has enhanced. Innumerable goods and services are taken by us and given by us in our everyday life. We are all, thus, givers and takers, and therefore, we are all consumers—individually as well as collectively. This reflects two things: there always has been the factor of demand and supply. Secondly, there always has been the factor of payment in any form and satisfaction or dissatisfaction. This is what has led to the present. Since nations are made of human beings, and since this is the most common human phenomenon, consumerism has always been there in all parts, segments and forms of human society. This factor has led us to think on and study consumer movement in various parts of the world.

4.1 United States of America

Modern consumer movement in USA owes definitely to Ralf Nader, the one-man movement and then to the then President of America John F. Kennedy.

According to Henry Assael, in USA, three distinct periods have been marked by increased activities to protect consumer rights; 1890-1915, 1933-1940 and 1962-1977. Each of these periods were marked by increased prices, expenses and exposures of unethical business practices, leading to legislative protection of consumer rights.

4.1.1 First Period of Consumerism (1890-1915): During this period, huge business corporations such as Standard Oil were amassing power resulting in the passing of Sherman Antitrust Act, imposing restrictions on the big business restraining competition. In 1906, Food and Drug Administration (FDA) was set up to regulate brands by requiring disclosure of product contents. In 1914, Federal Trade Commission (FTC) was established to prevent unfair trade practices, to curb monopoly powers of big businesses and to be a watchdog over deceptive advertising and unfair trade practices.

4.1.2 Second Period of Consumerism (1933-1940): This period was sparked by the Great Depression and the 1933 book '100,000,000 Guinea Pigs', which exposed unsafe medicines, cosmetics and foods. Many books such as 'Our Master's Voice', 'The Popular Practice of Fraud', 'Eat, Drink and Be Wary', and 'American Chamber of Horrors' were published containing exposes of advertising and preparation of food-stuffs which led to formation of Consumer Union in 1936, the largest consumer organisation in the world. In 1938, Federal Trade Commission Act was amended, empowering FTC to prosecute unfair and deceptive trade practices particularly.

4.1.3 Third Period of Consumerism (1962-1977): The third period of consumerism began in 1960s when another series of exposes followed the relative quiet of World War II years. The year 1962 can be considered to be a historic year in American consumerism as it witnessed formulation of certain rights of consumers by President John F. Kennedy in a message to Congress titled, "Special Message on Protecting the Consumer Interest", where he spelled the following four rights which serve as the basis for consumer protection.

1. The right to safety—to be protected against the marketing of goods that are hazardous to health and life.
2. The right to be informed—to be protected against fraudulent or misleading information, advertising, labelling or other practices and to be given the facts needed to make an informal choice.
3. The right to choose—to be assured access to a variety of products and services at competitive prices.
4. The right to be heard—to be assured that consumer interests will receive full and sympathetic consideration in the formulation of government policy.

In addition to the above four rights, addition of a fifth right was suggested, i.e. the right to be a minority consumer without disadvantage, to ensure that the low income consumers will not be at a disadvantage in relation to any of the above rights.

In 1962, Rachel Carson's 'Silent Spring' made consumers aware of the dangers of pesticides and other chemicals in food and other products. In 1965, Ralph Nader's 'Unsafe at Any Speed' was instrumental in the enactment of laws, setting safety standards for the cars as it exposed the automobile industry's disregard for even rudimentary safety precautions. Starting with the "dissemination of relevant information, he turned to the concept of collective action. In the 1970s, he wrote, "major corporations like their consumers to remain with a capacity for group purchasing action and group participating action before regulatory agencies. The possibility that consumers banding together can muster their organized intelligence to play a major role in shaping economic policy and the future of our political economy is an unsettling one for the major corporations that plan much of the world's economy. So too would be an organised consumer initiative to assess the hazards of technology or forestall the marketing products which use consumers as test-subjects of guinea pigs".

The 1970s has been described as a period marked by an "astonishing record of legislation to protect the environment with the passage of laws to restrict our pollution, control toxic substances, promote resource conservation and protect drinking water".

4.1.4 Decline and Rebirth of Consumerism in the 1980s: Henry Assael pointed out that in the 1980s, the earlier emphasis given to consumerism declined a bit since Reagan administration believed more on self-regulations than on government regulations. The basic philosophy was stated in Reagan's 1982 economic report, 'While regulation is necessary to protect such vital areas on food, health and safety, too much unnecessary regulation simply adds costs to businesses and consumers alike without commensurate benefits'.

As a reaction to the deregulation of Reagan era, a rebirth of consumerism occurred in 1990s. The rebirth was initiated when the Bush administration came to power and the Clinton administration carried it forward. Environment, health, advertising to children and the right of privacy and non-disclosure of personal information were the key issues which engaged the attention of business, government and consumer activists.

Consumerism promotes increased awareness among the consumers for protecting the environment, resulting in what is popularly known as 'New Environmentalism'. A 1995 survey found that 63 percent of Americans placed environmental issues over issues of economic growth.

4.1.5 Waves of Western Consumerism: Yiannis Gabriel and Tim Lang identified five distinct waves of consumer activeness in the West. [1] According to them, the first wave is characterised by co-operative consumerism. The first widespread organized consumer movement—the pioneer of them all—began as working class reaction to excessive prices and poor quality goods, food in particular. This Movement, based on the principle of self-help, took off in 1844.

The second wave advocated value-for-means to the consumers. Under the cooperative manual, the second wave of consumer organisations tried to make the market place more efficient and to champion the interests of consumers. The aim is to inform and educate the consumers about the features which will enable them to act effectively as consumers. The value-for-money model places considerable stress on rights to information, labelling and the right of redress if something goes wrong. [2]

The third wave of consumer movement in the West is referred to as Nadarism. Ralph Nader, a Harvard educated lawyer, set up a Centre for Study of Responsive Law and a project for corporate responsibility in 1969. Nadarism assumed that his consumer is relatively powerless in the world dominated by corporate giants. Like the second wave of the consumer movement, Nadarism advocated that the role of information should be free and fair. [3]

The fourth wave is characterised by emergence of consumer organisations in the 1970s which gradually accelerated in the 1980s. This wave is referred to as alternative consumerism. "The movement has many elements—ethical, Third World solidarity and fair trade organizations. [4] For instance, Consumer Action is a non-profit membership based organisation that was founded in San Francisco in 1971. Since then, Consumer Action has continued to serve consumers nationwide by advancing consumer rights by publishing educational materials in various international languages and comparing prices, credit cards, bank accounts and long distance services.

The latest wave is Green Consumerism, which began in Europe and spread west to North America. "The green consumer movement forced the companies to listen to them and spawn new ranges of products, such as phosphate free detergents and cars with recyclable components which gave consumers the option of choosing green. Green consumerism has almost forced companies to conduct environmental audit with a view to gaining advantage over the competitors.

The Federal Trade Commission works for the consumer to prevent fraudulent, deceptive and unfair business practices in the market place and to provide information to help consumers spot and avoid them.

Most of the consumers in America are keen to see that the products they buy are safe to use. Usually, safety precautions are observed in respect of products manufactured and sold in USA. However, there are some instances like the following given in Consumer Report which have been disconcerting.

"Cosco and Safety First, among the largest makers of body products agreed to pay US$ 1.75 million in civil penalties for failing to report product defects to the government. (It was the second such fine for Cosco). Instead, the companies tried to quietly fix problems with their car seats, cribs, electric baby-wipe, warmness, high chairs, stockers and walkers. Two babies died and more than 300 children were injured while using these products according to the Consumer Product Safety Commission (CPSC)" (Consumer Report, July 1, 2001).

Millions of tyres were recalled by the Firestone Tyre company because of inherent defects. In USA, manufacturers are required to inform the government about the defects they find in the products manufactured by them (Consumer Report, July 1, 2001).

Consumer Union believes that in view of cases as above, there is need for stringent action against faulty products. The regional office of the Consumer Union in Texas supports legislation that would hold companies criminally liable if they make faulty products and failed to disclose problems (Consumer Report, July 1, 2001).

The West Coast regional office of Consumer Union in California, "supports state bills that would limit the sealing of out of court settlements in law suits concerning product defects, environmental hazards, unfair insurance practices and financial frauds" (Consumer Report, July 1, 2001).

"Sporadically over the past century or so, there is an ever increasing consumers' concern about the need for new protective legislation and a clearer voice in government decisions. Today's consumers after the experiences of recent years are more aware of consumer problems and more sensitive to their implications. They will not hesitate to demand action and they very well know how to go about getting it. [5]

4.2 United Kingdom

While consumer protection law is often regarded as a modern phenomenon—typical of the twentieth century—it is a fact that what is now regarded as statutes with emphasis on consumer protection had their origin in a much early age. [6] The 1932 legal articulation by the House of Lords in Donoughe vs. Stevenson [7] suit laid down the law that, "the manufacturers owed duty to the ultimate consumer in respect of the goods of the nature that is unlikely to be examined before they reach him". It perhaps was the first in time, a cognizable attempt that set the ball rolling for future consumer protection.

In the subsequent years, legislations relating to consumer protection had proliferated. Much of these legislations consisted of amendments, consolidation, simplification and modernization of existing laws as recommended by the Molony Committee Report 1962, (e.g., Trade Description Act, 1968). The other legislation enacted in response to changing social and economic conditions was the Consumer Credit Act, 1974. Basically, present day consumer protection legislation derives from the four Acts passed during the latter half of the 19th Century to protect the unwary or uninformed shopper, viz., Sale of Goods Act, 1983; Food and Drugs Act, 1860; Weights and Measures Act, 1878; and Trade and Merchandise Marks Act, 1887. [8]

Sale of Goods Act, 1893 is still regarded as the backbone of civil consumer legislation. It increased consumers' civil remedies over and above those available in Common Law. If goods prove defective under any of the provisions of the Act, a consumer can sue retailer or hire-purchase company or manufacturer to make good his loss which, however, is limited to cost compensation. Sale of Goods Act, 1983 which contained a provision that parties could agree to exclude these rights from a particular contract was made void by virtue of Supply of Goods (Implied Terms) Act, 1973 on the line of recommendations made in Molony Report.

The first Foods and Drugs Act was passed in 1860 which was replaced by the Foods and Drugs Act, 1955, prohibiting false or misleading description of food and to ensure that food offered for sale for human consumption is pure and wholesome. Subsequently, Labelling of Food Regulations, 1973 introduced stricter and wider controls over labelling and advertisement of foods and claims made for such foods; and also imposed compulsions of displaying listing of ingredients on all pre-packed foods, in order of quantity and/or percentage. The recent addition to foods law is the Foods Safety Act, 1990.

Weight and Measures Act, 1878—amended from time to time—gave a new Weights and Measures Act, 1963, which has made it a criminal offence for a shop to give short or inaccurate weight and most food-stuffs are now required to be sold by weight, and some in prescribed quantities to facilitate comparison.

The original Merchandise Marks Act, 1887 dealt with mis-description of goods and misuse of trade marks. Molony Committee Report had recommended that those provisions which had been enacted piecemeal over a long period, needed consolidation and simplification. The resulting Trade Description Act, 1968 proved much wider in scope than Molony had anticipated, covering services as well as merchandise.

The recommendations of Molony Committee, created a landmark in the history of consumer protection in UK, entailing passing of major enactments like Hire Purchase Act, 1964, Resale Price Act, 1964 and Trade Description Act, 1968. The present Consumer Protection Act, 1987 succeeding the 1961 Act, caters to the needs of contemporary society in keeping with the EEC directives and UN Guidelines of 1985. The UK government's role in the field of consumer affairs is the responsibility of several departments.

There is no single Ministry of Consumer Affairs responsible for all consumer-related problems. It has been assigned to different ministries, e.g., Home Office has the responsibility for certain aspects of prisons control and for safety of consumer goods, whereas other Departments are responsible for particular sectors, for example, food (Ministry of Agriculture, Fisheries and Food), pharmaceuticals (Department of Health and Social Security) and motor vehicles (Department of Environment). This reflects the view that particular problems affecting the consumer can most effectively be handled within the Department in which relevant technical knowledge and expertise are available. The two government departments most closely associated with the development of consumer policy are the Department of Trade and Industry and its satellite, the Office of Fair Trading.

It is to be admitted beyond any iota of doubt that the British Consumer Protection Act, 1987 has been an overall improvement over the earlier legal provisions in the field of product liability, general safety, misleading prices etc., but all the same it appears to have been received with mixed feelings when compared with its American counterpart in respect of strict liability for product defects. [9] Even though consumer protection measures by the British appear to be slow and gradual, they being a conservative society, they have not lagged much behind in protecting the consumers compared to their counterparts.

4.3 France

In France, action to protect consumer interests takes a

pluralistic form, bringing into play the public authorities, a specialised establishment (National Consumer Institute) and associations representing consumers. Two government departments have special responsibilities for consumer affairs: Director General of Internal Commerce and Prices (Ministry of Finance and Economic Affairs) and "Service de la Repression des Frands et du Controle de la Qualite" (Pure Food Department). [10] The former directorate is responsible for enforcement of the regulations concerning consumer protection. These include provisions relating to price announcement, misleading advertising, certain forms of sales (gift offers, pyramid selling, etc.) as well as competition regulations to enable customers to enjoy benefits of increased productivity and development of international competition. "Service de la Repression des Fraudes" (Pure Food Department) has the task of protecting consumers of fraud in sale of goods or for adulteration of food stuffs and agricultural products. It is also responsible for ensuring that public health measures are respected.

National Consumer Institute (I.N.C) which was set up in 1967 as a public institution acting: (A) as a testing centre, (b) as an information office, and (3) as a body for protecting consumers. It has a regular television programme in which it broadcasts information targeted for consumers. It also publishes a monthly magazine '50 Millions de Consommateurs' and a monthly bulletin titled 'Consommateur Actualites', intended especially for senior staff of consumer organisations and for teachers.

At the non-government level, a number of private associations contribute to protection of consumers' interest. Among the associations active at the national level are: Federal Consumer Union (U.F.C.), General Consumer organisation (ORGELO) and family or women's associations which devote a substantial proportion of their resources to serve the interest of consumers.

4.4 Canada

Although consumer protection was not a new idea in Canada, there were substantive developments after 1966 in this regard. The consumer movement which gained momentum in the 1960s elsewhere influenced Canada for protecting the consumers by enacting much new legislation. Developments in the year 1966 had profound impact on the Government. Two important events occurred in that year. The first was a government request to Economic Council of Canada in July, 1966 to undertake a number of special studies of particular relevance to consumers and advise regarding:

1. Interests of consumers, particularly as they relate to the functions of Department of Registrar General;
2. Acquisition, mergers, monopolies and restraint of trade; and
3. Patents, trademarks, copyrights and registered industrial designs. [11]

The second was the government's decision to designate a parliamentary committee to investigate increase in consumer prices. The Committee jointly chaired by Senators David Croll and Ron Basford, called for urgent attention to the need for consumer protection, for coordination of existing legislation and for establishment of a machinery to deal with consumer complaints. The Committee recommended creation of the Department of Consumer Protection Affairs to concentrate on three areas: (a) consumer standards, (b) consumer protection, and (c) consumer information. [12]

In Canada, the Federal Department of Consumer and Corporate Affairs, set up in 1967, has had a major influence on the development of Canadian consumer policy. Prior to the creation of this Department, Consumers' Association of Canada and other smaller private consumer groups had contributed to introducing legislations and regulations to serve consumer interests. To name a few:

1. Food and Drugs Act, 1970.
2. Precious Metals Marking Act, 1952.
3. National Trademark and True Labelling Act, 1949.

4. Bankruptcy Act, 1949.
5. Money Lender Act, 1906.
6. Small Loans Act, 1939.
7. Interest Act, 1886.

Creation of the Department of Consumer and Corporate Affairs has, however, given the consumer an official voice within the councils of the government and led to a more active policy to promote new laws and programmes for protection of consumers. [13] New legislations and programmes introduced since creation of the Department of Consumer and Corporate Affairs include the following:

1. Hazardous Products Act, 1969.
2. Consumer Packaging and Labelling Act, 1971.
3. Weights and Measures Act, 1971.
4. Textile Labelling Act, 1970.
5. Motor Vehicle Safety Act, 1970.
6. Standards Council of Canada Act, 1970.
7. Canada Cooperatives Association Act, 1970.

Bureau of Consumer Affairs of Department of Consumer and Corporate Affairs is responsible for administering consumer protection and information programmes. This Bureau is composed of the following branches:

- Consumer Research Branch which administers various Acts concerned with consumer protection and is responsible for the development of new consumer-standards, particularly safety standards drawn up for dangerous products regulated under Hazardous Products Act;
- Operation Branch which provides a detailed inspection service to ensure that the laws and regulations designed to protect consumers are being adhered to at the retail levels; and
- Consumer Services Branch which deals with consumer complaints, suggestions and inquiries and helps implement new programmes to inform and educate consumers. [14]

The Act, establishing Department of Consumer and

Corporate Affairs, also provided for establishment of Canadian Consumer Council to advise Minister of Consumer and Corporate Affairs on consumer problems. The general aim of this body is to advise ministers on ways to improve the consumer environment and to remove those imperfections which operate contrary to most efficient and productive allocation of resources.

The Consumers' Association of Canada is a major private organisation serving interests of the Canadian consumers. A non-profit, non-political organisation, it has had considerable influence in promoting the introduction of new federal and provincial legislations and programmes to benefit the consumers in Canada. To this end, it has undertaken studies and submitted briefs to the federal governments and parliamentary committees on consumer problems, and organised meetings to bring together consumer, industry and government to discuss matters of common concern. In addition, it regularly publishes a bi-monthly magazine titled "Canadian Consumer" which contains general articles on consumer problems and results of comparative tests on consumer products which are carried out in commercial testing laboratories.

4.5 European Union

Though consumer cooperatives had great success in Europe, this did not result in formation of consumer organisations. Basically, industrialisation did not lead to the same degree of affluence in Europe as in the United States. Consumer movement in Europe was fostered by the 'Consumers Union', more specifically, by the constant efforts of Colstone Worne. As early as 1939, he started to make inquiries about groups and individuals that might support his cause. In London, he was referred to as the Householders' Association, yet he was disappointed. People were not enthusiastic about testing. It took another two decades for U.K. to provide a congenial environment for consumer movement.

Consumer movement in England began in the real sense only after the Second World War. The common law did protect the consumers against aggressive selling, fraud and breach of promise. The British National Standard Institute in U.K. played a significant role in arousing the interest of the consumers. Many consumer magazines and shoppers' guides were published to educate the consumers. Consumers Association came into existence to expose undesirable as well as defective products.

It was Dorothy Goodman, an American living in London who along with Ray Goodman and Michael Young, founded the Consumers' Association (first called the 'Association for Consumer Research') in 1956. The first issue of its magazine appeared in October 1957.

Gradually, consumer organisations began to take shape in other countries. Prior to 1960, three major organisations had been founded in Europe: 'Consumen Tehand' in Netherlands, the 'Union Belge des Consummateurs (now 'Association des Consommateurs') in Belgium and 'Union Federale de la Consommation' in France. All began publishing information for and about consumers, including reports on products they had tested themselves. A consumer awakening of similar type also appeared in Netherlands in 1926. Between 1947 and 1957, there were consumer revolutions in Denmark, Federal Republic of Germany, Switzerland, Japan, Kenya, France, Hungary, Italy, Canada and Belgium.

Press campaigns in favour of the consumer in these countries played a significant role in the creation of the concept of consumerism. Women's organisations in these countries have been a mainstay of the consumer movement.

Poland was the first country in Eastern Europe to have independent consumer organisations. 'Consumer Federation' was set up in 1981 and 'Polish Home Economics Association' in 1990. Over the years, there are many consumer welfare organisations which are contributing to consumer movement, awaiting registration. One is the 'Association of Polish

Consumers' constituting 20 individuals with support of 1,000 readers of 'Test Consumer Magazine'. It has planned several campaigns on misleading advertisements, against tobacco advertising and to make banks more consumer-friendly.

The strongest organisations in the Pacific area perhaps were, in Australia and New Zealand. The Australian movement was independent and received negligible government fund as well as support. Local consumer movement existed in leading Australian cities. New South Wales and Victoria had consumer councils. New Zealand Consumer Institute, on the other hand, received support as well as patronage from the government.

The pattern of consumer protection in Europe bears a remarkable similarity to the U.S. experience. Industrialised nations in both the continents generated extensive brand name, advertising and were confronted with many consumer related problems like packaging and of ensuring the purity of food and drugs. The idea of supporting the consumer with results of product testing by brand name crossed the Atlantic after World War II. Starting with Great Britain, the Netherlands and Belgium, it spread to Scandinavian countries viz. Austria, West Germany and France and then to Australia, Japan and Israel.

Initially, European Consumer Groups feared legal consequences of publishing adverse test results by brand name, even though this had never been a problem in the U.S. Nevertheless, the movement, once started, spread so rapidly that in April 1960, the IOCU (International Organisation of Consumer Union) now known as C.I. (Consumer International) was launched at a conference in the Hague. The charter members were the 'Consumers Union of U.S.', 'Consumers' Association', London, 'Australian Consumers' Association', 'Consumerton Bond', Hague and 'The Association des Consommateurs', Brussels. The C.I. sought to become an authenticating body that would admit to membership only those organisations that accepted no income from advertising and were financially supported either by consumers or government. It stimulated interchange of techniques, test results and educational material among its affiliates. It also moved to assist consumers in less developed countries. As in 2014, it had 240 consumer groups as members in more than 120 countries.

In Britain, the privately owned Consumers' Association, assumed the exclusive role of comparative testing. Through grants, the Association established a Research Institute for Consumer Affairs which conducted investigations into governmental, professional and commercial services. It also established a National Federation of Consumer Groups to attend to matters such as complaints, store services and price comparisons and Consumer Advice Centres in London. In 1970, it had a membership of 5,32,000. A new consumer council was created by the Government in 1963 as an independent financially assisted body, designed to give advice to consumers. The British also created a Citizens' Advice Bureau.

Except for Belgium and Netherlands, European Consumer Testing organisations have followed the pattern set by Scandinavian Countries, not by Britain or the U.S. Plenty of government grants are given to consumer organisations in Norway. The main testing agency also handles complaints and publishes a monthly consumer magazine. An Institute of Informative Labelling has been established in Norway to foster growth of quality mark. In Denmark, consumer activities are divided between a government sponsored Household Advice Centre and a Consumer Testing Organisation jointly supported by members, other organisations and the government The most notable of the European efforts is Austria's 'Verein-Konsumerton-Information Centre' which issues a monthly testing publication and operates as a demonstration centre for consumer guidance. Member organisations cover 80 percent of cost, the rest being contributed by individual members and the government.

A number of co-ordinating networks exist among European groups, e.g. European Bureau of Consumer Union consisting of organisations from six E.E.C. countries, the Contact Committee of Consumers' European Economic Commission, the International Labelling Centre linked to the International organisation of standardisation and the International Electrical Technical Commission. Similarly, the Scandinavian groups established a Scandinavian Committee on Consumer Matters to co-ordinate research and information matters. The European Consumer movement, however, was weakened by the establishment of competing consumer organisations, often split on political lines.

While United States, Canada and Australia have non-governmental consumer groups and consumerism exists as a grass-root social movement, in almost all the European countries, considerable government support and patronage to consumer representation exists. The Consumer's 'Ombudsman' established in Sweden, Norway, Denmark and Finland, are perhaps the most visible examples of high level government institutionalisation of consumer representation.

An ombudsman is someone charged with investigating and resolving complaints. He is usually a government official. In the United Kingdom, National Council serves as a consumer advocate within the national government, using a combination of lobbying and research to assert its position. In Netherlands, private consumer organisations are compensated when they are consulted by the government or asked to participate in national or international committees. The Australian government helped to create the Australian Federation of Consumer Organisations (AFCO) to coordinate the activities of some fifty consumer and community groups. In addition to representing the views of its constituent organisations, AFCO also serves as a source for appointees to government and private organisations dealing with consumer matters (Committee on Consumer Policy, 1983).

The United States, on the other hand, has been the world leader in developing means of consumer redress, attempting to serve consumers better through competition rather than government regulation and finding ways to encourage but still control the advertisers. Thus, in the European countries, decisions on matters concerning consumers rests totally with the government whereas in the US, relevant policy is formulated purely on the basis of private initiative by the consumers.

4.6 Russia

Consumer protection legislation in Russia had been worked out and adopted during the times of the old Soviet Union. But it could not be implemented due to the political events of the summer 1991. [15]

When Soviet Union was dissolved and Russian Federation became independent in 1991, the newly founded Russian Republic took over the spirit of consumer protection as influenced by United Nations Guidelines of 1985. There was consensus that the difficult transition from a socialist planned economy to a market economy would not successfully be accomplished without a strong competition and consumer protection legislation and a special authority for enforcing it. [16] The Russian Government adopted the Russian Consumer Protection Act (RCPA) on 7th February, 1992 and it was put into force by an order of the Supreme Soviet of Russian Federal Republic from the same day. A State Committee of Russian Federation of anti-monopoly Practices and new Economic Structure was created in order to implement the RCPA together with Competition Act of 1991.

Preamble to RCPA states that it regulates relation between consumers and entrepreneurs. It establishes consumers' rights:

- To obtain goods (work service) of appropriate quality.
- To provide security of their life and health.
- To receive information about goods, work, services, and about producers, sellers and suppliers.
- To have their interest protected by the State and the society.
- To associate in consumer organisations.

This makes it clear that RCPA has been written in the

spirit of United Nations Declaration of 1985 on Consumer Protection and on consumer rights. These rights are protected by the State, through the agencies, authority of local administration, individual court, and conciliation procedures and via certain types of collective and group actions of consumers and other associations. An analysis of RCPA reveals that it was adopted at a time when in Russia, due to the drastic ongoing changes in the economic structure, consumer protection had the special function to make possible the transition from a planned economy which was characterised by want and scarcity, to a market economy dominated by consumer sovereignty and choice.

The Act in general has touched upon all the rights of consumers putting corresponding obligations on manufacturers, suppliers of goods or services and compensation for violation of consumer rights.

Article 4 of RCPA gives consumers indirectly a right to quality and Article 5 a direct right to safety. The quality obligation of manufacturer, seller or provider of services is defined in Article 4 by which products, works or services must correspond in quality:

- To the mandatory requirement of standard/s.
- To conditions of contract.
- To commonly held expectations.
- To information given by producers, sellers or providers of services.

Article 6 obliges manufacturers, sellers or providers of services to provide consumers with necessary and truthful information concerning their enterprise, their goods, works or services offered by such enterprise and their business hours. While Article 11 contains specific rules on how to determine amount of compensation to be paid to consumer in case of any violation of his or her rights, Article 39 spells out the enforcement provisions while rights and powers of consumer associations are provided for in Article 43 and 44.

4.7 Denmark

The consumer movement in Denmark is much older than the modern consumer movement which started in the early 1960s. "The Consumer Council" is the only association of consumers set up in 1947 solely concerned with consumer problems. The objects of the council are to pursue an active policy aiming at protecting interests of consumers, to make known consumers' views to trade and industry and to government authorities, to represent them in committees and boards dealing with questions of importance to them, to cooperate with research institutions and, finally, to work for standardisation and informative labelling of consumer goods. To disseminate consumer information, the council has since 1964 issued a monthly magazine TAENK (Think) which publishes the results of comparative tests carried out by independent laboratories, as well as other information which are of important interest to consumers.

A Consumer Council was set up in 1953 in Norway which is an independent institution. It safeguards interests of consumers at national level in cooperation with different bodies concerned with the same problem. The council, *inter alia*, submits its opinions to state authorities, protects interests of consumers in committees in which it participates, promotes research, testing of goods, informative labelling, etc., and endeavours to intensify and develop information activities. It cooperates with similar organisations abroad and organises a large number of comparative tests of goods, the results of which are finally placed in the Consumer Report published by the Council.

Although consumer interests do no normally fall within the competence of a singly public institution, there is, nevertheless, one public body, the Danish Government Home Economics Council which is responsible for household matters in the wider sense. The object of this institution, which was set up in 1935, is to improve nutritional, hygienic, economic and technical aspects of household management. The council publishes two publications 'Tek Niske Meddellser' (Technical News) and 'Rad Og Resultater' (Advice and Results) giving information to consumers.

In Denmark, no single ministry or department of the government deals with all consumer questions and no governmental institution or body is responsible for coordinating all legal provisions and other matters in this field. Ministry of Commerce is, however, responsible with regard to such laws as Monopolies and Restrictive Practices Control Act, Prices and Profits Act, Unfair Competition and Commodity Description Act. Of other ministries responsible for laws and regulations of consumer interest, mention should be made of Ministry of Justice. Questions of health, food control, social security, product safety of different kinds are dealt with by different ministries and by other public authorities generally responsible for these matters.

4.8 Norway

The Consumer policy in Norway is looked after by a special Ministry for Family and Consumer Affairs which was set up in 1956. The two-fold function of the Ministry is one, acting in an advisory capacity in certain cases relating to other ministries and directly in some other cases. As an advisory body concerning consumers, the Ministry deals, among other things, with problems of supplies, price and competition regulations, subsidies, official quality controls of consumer goods, etc. dealt with by other ministries. Inversely, it also refers frequently to other Ministries on all questions relevant to the interest of consumers. Consumer Council, State Institute for Consumer Research and Testing of Goods, Advisory Service in Home Economics and Committee for Informative Labelling come directly under it. [17] Since May 8, 1972, Ministry for Family and Consumer Affairs has been replaced by Ministry of Consumer Affairs.

4.9 Japan

After the Second World War, Japan which was devastated

by nuclear invasion, limped back with rapid industrialisation with the grit and perseverance of the Japanese within a very short period of time. Japan attained high economic growth with its technological innovation in the latter part of the 1950s, which afforded an affluent life to the people, but simultaneously as its adverse offshoot, there surfaced consumer injuries.

Interestingly, the consumer movement in Japan was first led by women's organisations. The Housewives' Association was organized in 1948 followed by the Japanese Consumers' Cooperative Union (1951), the National Liaison Council of Regional Liaison Committee of Consumers' Organisation (1956). The consumer movement during this period was conducted for the sole purpose of 'survival'. With technological innovation in the latter part of the 1950's, Japanese consumers' substantial injury was caused due to the affluent life style of the privileged people. Thus, emerged the establishment of Japan Consumer Association (1961) and the Consumption Science Federation (1964), to engage in consumer education and product testing. The movement gained momentum and extended to other areas such as product labelling and price.

The important consumer protection act was enacted in 1968 known as the Consumer Protection Fundamental Act intended to protect the right of consumers so that people could enjoy a safe and secure life. The Act defines the basic direction of the consumer protection policy and the basic framework of administration structures to carry it out. Interestingly, the Consumer Protection Fundamental Act is not empowered with legal force or penal provisions, merely a directory of laws guiding consumer administration.

The Act sets out the need for efforts by the administration, business enterprises and consumers in regard to their respective standpoints to protect and promote the interest of consumers and stipulates their roles as under:

1. The State and local governments should assume responsibility to plan and execute the measures

comprehensively in accordance with the development of the economy.

2. Business enterprises should assume the responsibility to take necessary measures to protect consumers and to cooperate with the measures planned by the administration.
3. Consumers should make efforts to acquire the required knowledge on their own and act independently as well as in a rational manner. [18]

The Consumer Protection Fundamental Act sets out basic measures for the protection of consumers with regard to the prevention of risk, proper measurement, proper standardisation, proper labelling, securing of fair and free competition, promotion of enlightenment and education, reflection of opinion, improvement of tests and inspection facilities, and improvement of systems for handling complaints. [19] Under the Act, about 70 individual laws are in operation in order to protect consumers. In addition, many local governments have established consumer protection regulations.

4.9.1 Consumer Protection Administration in Japan

A. Consumer Protection Council: Consumer Protection Council was established in 1968 in accordance with the Consumer Protection Fundamental Act, chaired by the Prime Minister and consists of 18 ministry and agency heads related to the administration of consumer protection regulations. The council meets yearly to discuss and decide/s upon the general planning and measures to be taken for consumer administration.

B. Social Policy Council: The Social Policy Council was established in 1965 in the Economic Planning Agency as an advisory organ to the Prime Minister and the ministers of related ministries. It examines and deliberates on the basic measures concerning stabilisation and improvement of national life. Consumer Policy Division of the Council examines and deliberates on basic matters concerning consumer protection and expert committees of the Division, which are established from time to time, examine and deliberate on special matters.

C. Ministry and Agency: By enforcing the relevant administrative laws under their jurisdiction, the related ministries, agencies and committees effectively protect the interest of consumers with co-ordination undertaken by the Economic Planning Agency. The major roles played by the ministries and agencies in the field of consumer protection are as under:

1. Economic Planning Agency.
2. Fair Trade Commission.
3. Ministry of Health and Welfare.
4. Ministry of Agriculture, Forestry and Fisheries.
5. Ministry of International Trade and Industry.
6. Ministry of Transport.
7. Ministry of Construction.
8. Ministry of Finance.
9. Ministry of Post and Telecommunication.
10. Ministry of Home Affairs.

Leadership of testing consumer products in Asia goes to Japan. There was competition between the Japan Consumer Association, the Japan Housewives' Association and the Japan Consumer Union.

Unlike in the U.S.A., consumer movement in Japan made its initial progress under the leadership of women. Also, while the concern of leaders of consumer movement in U.S.A. was with the safety of automobiles, in Japan it were the basic problems relating to day-to-day living.

Immediately after the end of the War in 1945, the Kansai League of Housewives was formed in Japan. This was organised further in 1948 on the occasion of a protest rally in Tokyo against inferior match sticks. The League's office tested items of daily use and exposed inferior and defective merchandise. It was on the League's discovery of false merchandising in 1960 of 'canned beef', instead of 'whale' and 'horse meat', that a law for prevention of 'false labelling' and 'false premium drawn' was enacted by the Fair Trade Commission.

However, the League lacked organisational base and hence the movement lost its potentiality. In 1956, the consumer movement was joined by men and in 1961, Japan Consumer Association came into existence. Still, Japan's consumer movement made major progress through the efforts of women only, led mainly by housewives. In 1964, the 'Livelihood-School Movement', a voluntary decentralised local body was inaugurated. In every elementary school district, groups of 50 to 100 housewives formed 'Livelihood Schools' and held meetings and discussions for problems, inviting producers, officials, scholars, etc. This created awareness about the consumer movement and moved local governments to establish consumer affair offices.

An epoch making event in the history of consumer movement in Japan was the agitation against double pricing system and boycott of colour television. This was in September 1970. The success of this agitation was seen in terms of prices being slashed. This was due to the 'Livelihood Schools' and women who were considered to be pure consumers and their movement for pure necessities of daily life. But lack of experience and awareness hindered the immediate creation of a suitable organisation that necessitated the participation of men. It was thought essential for broad basing the movement.

Today, in Japan there is still a great degree of dependence on government for support. But, there is a growing community movement in problem areas like pollution, clean environment, garbage disposal, etc. Women have thus given a new impetus to the consumer movement in Japan.

4.10 South Korea

South Korea is one of the fast developing countries in Asia along with Japan. Since the beginning of the 1960s, consumers' woes and disadvantages have aggravated and become one of the serious social problems in industrially advanced countries. Korea, being the front runner in Asian industrially advanced countries, was no exception.

However, in Korea, the government has recognised the importance and extent of consumer problems since the latter half of the 1970s and has accepted the need for action to reinforce the consumer position. As a part of this action, a bill of Consumer Protection Act was presented and passed by the 103rd National Assembly in December 1979, resulting in Consumer Protection Act becoming effective from 4th January, 1980.

In 1980, the Korean Constitution proclaimed guarantees for the consumer protection movement with an intention to encourage sound consumption activities and improvement in quality of products. This provided a constitutional basis for the consumer movement.

Besides the Consumer Protection Act, there are many laws related to consumers, directly or indirectly. The objective of Consumer Protection Act is to meet the obligations of the state and local autonomies and to focus on the fundamental rights and interests of consumers.

The Act consists of 8 Chapters and 32 Articles.

Chapter 1 contains general provisions, purpose, obligations of the State and local autonomies, obligations of business and roles of consumers.

Chapter 2 contains consumer protection measures of the State; standardisation of measuring system, standardisation of goods and services, incorporation of consumers' opinion, support to consumers' claim for damages and establishment of testing and inspection facilities.

Chapter 3 contains safety measures for consumers, standard of safety, prohibition of production and sale of violated goods and provision of safety measures.

Chapter 4 contains completeness in description of goods, standard for description and advertisement, and order of correction.

Chapter 5 contains principle of fair transaction, public announcement of unfair methods, and order to correct improper transaction.

Chapter 6 contains Consumer Protection Committee;, Chapter 7 contains supplementary provisions; and Chapter 8 penal provisions. The Consumer Protection Act of South Korea is in consonance with UN Guidelines on Consumer Protection which were unanimously adopted in the General Assembly of the UN on April 9, 1985.

Articles 22 and 23 of the Act envisages establishment of Consumer Protection Committee within the Economic Planning Board, to protect consumers and ensure quality of their life. The Committee looks into matters such as establishment or modification of the standards of safety, description and advertisement, order to correct violations against prescribed standards of advertisement and the principle of fair trade, order regarding the establishment and operation of redress and other dispute-resolving procedures, and major government policies and measures with regard to enforcement of the Consumer Protection Act.

4.11 China

In a communist country like China where socialist market economy prevails, there is a Consumer Protection Act, thanks to the consumer movement which influenced the China Government to enact a separate Consumer Protection Act in the year 1993 largely due to China's economic policy in early 1990s. The law of Peoples' Republic of China on protection of consumer rights and interests adopted by 8th National People's Congress on October 31, 1993 has 8 chapters containing 55 Articles.

Chapter I contains general provisions spelling out the objectives of the Act vide Article 1 to 6. Chapter II provides consumers' rights as under:

- Right of personal and property safety.
- Right to obtain true information.
- Rights of free choice of commodities or services.
- Rights to fair deals.

- Rights to compensation.
- Rights to set up social bodies to uphold their legal rights and interest.
- Rights to obtain knowledge concerning consumption.
- Rights of personal dignity.
- Rights to exercise supervision over commodities services.

Chapter III contains Article 16 to 25 imposing obligations on business dealers; Chapter IV incorporates administration of consumer rights: and Chapter V provides provisions for setting up consumer organisations. Chapter VI spells out settlement of disputes. According to Article 34, consumers' disputes with business dealers over consumer rights and interests can be settled through the following approaches:

1. Consultation and conciliation with business dealer;
2. Appeal to Consumers' Association for mediation;
3. Complaint to administrative department concerned;
4. Submission to arbitrating organs for arbitrating according to arbitration agreement with business dealers; and
5. Initiation of legal proceedings before People's Courts.

Chapter VII containing Article 40 to 53, imposes legal responsibilities on business dealers and Chapter VIII contains supplementary provisions.

4.12 Malaysia

Malaysia is among the most rapidly developing economies in the world. Like most ex-colonial territories, Malaysia emerged from colonial rule with laws identical in most aspects to that of the colonising country. Unfortunately, the Malaysian Parliament is yet to provide the consumer protection statutes at par with the other developing countries.

The consumer protection laws in Malaysia are scattered in a number of legislations which protect consumers. After liberation from the colonial rule in 1957, Malaysia preferred not to follow consumer protection laws of England in its entirety, as for example, Fair Trading Act, 1973; Consumer Credit Act, 1974; Consumer Protection Act, 1987.

The different statues which protect consumers in Malaysia are as follows:

Contracts Act, 1950 (revised 1974) and Sale of Goods Act, 1957 (revised 1989). Roots of both these statutes relate to the English 19th century ideal of equal bargaining power between contacting parties and the maxim of freedom of contract. The only major development in the contract related legislation to protect consumer is in the area of direct selling. In 1993, Direct Sales Act was enacted to govern door-to-door sale, telephone-sale and mail-order marketing.

For governing trade description and advertising, Malaysian Government has enacted Trade Descriptions Act, 1972 (amended 1980). It is a pure penal statute seeking to discourage false and misleading description of goods and services by imposing criminal sentence. Consumer credit is governed by Money Lenders' Act, 1951 (revised 1989); Hire Purchase Act, 1967 (revised 1978) and Pawnbrokers Act, 1972. While Money Lenders' Act and Pawnbrokers Act are enforced by Ministry of Housing and Local Government, Hire Purchase Act is enforced by Ministry of Domestic Trade and Consumer Affairs.

On product safety, laws relating to food products are Food Act, 1983 administered by Ministry of Health and for electrical goods there is Electricity Supply Act, 1990. The relevant statute for safety of vehicles and related products is Road Transport Act, 1987. The principal statute regulating import, manufacture, sale and use of pesticides is Pesticides Act, 1974. The important statutes governing pharmaceutical products and drugs in Malaysia are:

1. Prisons Act, 1952 (revised 1989).
2. Dangerous Drugs Act, 1952 (revised 1980).
3. Sale of Drugs Act, 1952 (revised 1989).
4. Medicines (Advertisement and Sales) Act, 1956 (revised 1983).

There is a Standards and Industrial Research Institute in Malaysia (SIRIM) under the Ministry of Science, Technology and environment which is the national research and standard organisation. [20] The principal functions of SIRIM are to promote public and industrial welfare, health and safety, and to promote, develop and promulgate standards for commerce and industry and for goods produced in Malaysia.

Malaysia is one of the fast developing countries to have consumer associations. Consumer Association of Penang (CAP) is probably the best known in the developing countries. Malaysia has since 1974, started the International Organisation of Consumers Union (IOCU)'s first regional office outside its headquarters in Penang. The consumer organisations of Malaysia have also played a very active role in representing the local consumer interest. CAP has adopted a strident position, publishing a feisty monthly, "The Utasan Konsumer" in four languages that enjoys a very wide circulation, raises a variety of development related issues, initiates public interest litigation and, to the chagrin of the government, even organizes protest marches.

4.13 Pakistan

In Pakistan, consumerism has got considerable recognition and a lot of work has been done in this regard. Many organisations and legislations are in place too. Consumer Rights Commission of Pakistan (CRCP), established in 1998, is an independent, non-profit, non-political and non-government organisation, also working for consumers' rights and awareness. Establishment and the active role of consumer courts have also facilitated the process of providing relief to consumers. Various consumer advocacy groups are playing an active role in the society. Many positive business responses have emerged as a result of consumerism, such as concern for total quality management, voluntary industry codes of conduct, establishment of consumers' affairs departments and encouragement of product recalls. Organisations in Pakistan are now quite conscious about the concept of consumer satisfaction and appear to be serious in formulating consumer-friendly policies.

4.14 Latin American Countries

Geographically speaking, Latin America is more than a single region, for it spans over the territories of South America, Central America and North America. As a common backbone, all Latin American countries share economic, social, political and cultural identity, including the languages (Spanish except for Brazil where Portuguese is spoken). Unfortunately, unlike in the West, comprehensive consumer protection law or policy does not exist in these developing countries. Broadly, consumer movement in Latin American countries may be discussed as follows. [21]

The earlier set of legislations in these countries involved a number of laws focusing on certain aspects of consumer protection. It was not a comprehensive or systematic regulation, rather, laws and decrees dealing with specific issues such as weights and measures, food and drug control, especially, price control. It was a feeble attempt made by the traditional legal system to provide the consumer satisfactory some degree of protection.

The second wave began in 1974 with the enactment of specific consumer protection laws in Costa Rica, Venezuela, Mexico and Columbia. Here, unlike what happened in the earlier years, the hopeless consumer was afforded ample protection.

The third wave of consumer protection in these countries started with the United Nations Guidelines for Consumer Protection adopted by General Assembly on April 9, 1985. This third wave includes comprehensive legislations adopted in countries like Guatemala, Honduras, Brazil, Peru, Ecuador, El Salvador, Paraguay, Mexico and Argentina for providing protection to the consumers.

4.15 South Africa

In the years after the Second World War, organised consumerism in South Africa was virtually unknown. The first consumer movement was founded in the 1950s by 'the grandmother of consumerism', Mrs. Dorothy Van Der Westhuizen, acting on a directive given to her at a Conference of International Council of Women in Athens. Branches were formed but organised consumerism gained momentum only when Mrs. Margaret Lessing, who saw the need of the consumer to speak with a strong united voice, encouraged the formation of an umbrella organisation to which interested bodies could affiliate. In 1961, the South African National Consumer Union was born. The Consumer Union drew in leading women's organisations and it is due to their faith in the movement that today it enjoys such a widespread support.

Endnotes

1. Yiannis, G. and Tim, L., "Unmanageable Consumer, Contemporary Consumption and its Fragmentation", Sage Publications, New Delhi, 1985, pp. 153-168.
2. Ibid.
3. Ibid.
4. Ibid.
5. Hermann, R.O., "Consumer Protection: Yesterday, Today and Tomorrow", *Current History*, May 1980, p. 227.
6. David, O., and John L., "A Text Book on Consumer Law", Blackstone Press Ltd., 1997, pp. 10-11.
7. 1932 AC 502.
8. Fulop, C., "The Consumer Movement and the Consumer", The Advertising Association, London.
9. Clark, A., "The Consumer Protection Act, 1986", *The Modern Law Review*, Vol. 50, September 1987, p. 621.
10. Consumer Policy in OECD Member Countries, 1972.
11. Federal Legislation and Programs relating to Consumer Protection, Consumer Research Report, No. 6, Department of Consumer and Corporate Affairs, Canada, March, 1973.
12. Ibid.
13. Consumer Policy in OECD Member Countries, 1972.
14. Ibid.
15. Investija, 6th June, 1991.
16. Riech, N., "Consumer Protection in Countries of Emerging Markets: The Example of Russia", Paper presented at 5th International Conference on Consumer Law, York University,

Toronto, Canada, 25-27 May, 1995.

17. Consumer Policy in OECD countries, 1972.
18. Consumer Policy in Japan, Japan Consumer Information Centre, Tokyo.
19. Ibid.
20. Established under Standards and Industrial Research Institute of Malaysia (Incorporation) Act, 1975.
21. Benjamin, A.H., "Consumer Protection in Less Developed Countries, The Latin American Experience", Paper presented at 5th International Conference on Consumer Laws, York University, Toronto, Canada, 25-27 May, 1995.

5

Consumer Protection in India

Since this treatise is meant to provide a glimpse to the consumer protection legislations in the world especially in India, it would be relevant here to examine the consumer protection measures prevalent in India since ancient times. Accordingly, the following paragraphs briefly describe the consumer protection measures available in the ancient India followed by the consumer protection legislations in its modern forms.

Consumer protection has its deep roots in the rich soil of Indian civilization, which dates back to 3200 B.C. [1] In ancient India, human values were cherished and ethical practices were considered of great importance. However, the rulers felt that the welfare of subjects was the primary area of their concern. They showed keen interest in regulating not only the social conditions but also the economic life of the people, imposing many trade restrictions to protect the interests of buyers. Here, an attempt has been made to examine the historical perspective of consumer protection in India from the Vedic age (ancient period) to the modern period. It also briefly analyses the development of consumer law in India and discusses the legal framework of the Indian Consumer Protection Act of 1986 which led to the evolution of a new legal culture in India.

5.1 Consumer Protection in Ancient India [2]

In ancient India, all sections of the society followed Dharma-Sastras (Dharma), which laid down social rules and norms and served as the guiding principles governing human relations. The principles of Dharma were derived from the Vedas. Vedas were considered to be the words of God, and law was said to have divine origin transmitted to the society through sages. Thus, Vedas were the primary sources of law in India.

Many writers and commentators of the ancient period documented the living conditions of the people through their writings, including Smriti (tradition) and Sruti (revelation), and also prescribed codes to guide the kings and rulers about the method of ruling the State and its subjects.

Among the various 'Dharma-Shastras', the most authoritative texts are: (a) the Manu Smriti (800 B.C to 600 B.C.); (b) the Yajnavalkya Smriti (300 B.C. to 100 B.C.); (c) the Narada Smirti (100 A.D to 200 A.D.); (d) the Bruhaspati Smriti (200 A.D. to 400 A.D.); and (e) the Kanyayana Smirti (300 A.D. to 600 A.D). Among these, Manu Smriti was the most authoritative.

5.1.1 Manu Smriti: Manu Smriti describes the social, political and economic conditions of the ancient society. Manu the ancient law giver, also wrote about ethical trade practices. He prescribed a code of conduct for traders and specified punishments to those who committed crimes against buyers. For example, he referred to the problem of adulteration and said "one commodity mixed with another must not be sold (as pure), nor a bad one (as good), not less (than the properly quantity or weight) nor anything that is at hand or that is concealed. Punishment "for adulterating unadulterated commodities and for breaking gems or for improperly boring (them)" was harsh. Severe punishment was prescribed for fraud in selling seed corn: "he who sells seed-corn which is not seed-corn, he who takes up seed (already sown) and he who destroys a boundary (mark) shall be punished by mutilation. Interestingly, Manu also specified rules of competency for parties to enter into a contract. He said, "a contract made by a person intoxicated or insane or grievously disordered (by disease and so forth) or wholly dependent, by an infant or a very old man, or by an unauthorized (party) is invalid".

During the ancient period, the king had the power to confiscate the entire property of a trader on two instances: (i) when the king had a monopoly over the exported goods; and (ii) when the export of the goods was forbidden. There was also a mechanism to control prices and punish wrongdoers. The king fixed the rates for the purchase and sale of all marketable goods. Manu said, "man who behaves dishonestly to honest customers or cheats in his prices shall be heavily fined". There was a process in place to inspect all weights and measures every six months, and the results of these inspections were duly noted.

All these clearly indicate that the ancient society in India was having an inbuilt and effective mechanism in the form of scripts for regulating the many wrongs of the market place. These measures also show how developed the system was in identifying the market strategies of traders. Thus, Manu Smriti effectively dealt with various consumer matters, many of which remain of great concern even in modern legal system.

5.1.2 Kautilya's Arthasastra: Written subsequent to Manu Smriti, Kautilya's Arthasastra is considered to be a treatise and a prominent source, providing various theories of statecraft and the rights and duties of subjects in ancient society. Though its primary concern is with matters of practical administration, consumer protection occupies a prominent place in Arthasastra. It describes the role of the State in regulating trade and its duty to prevent crimes against consumers.

Between 400 and 300 B.C., there was a director of trade whose primary responsibility was to monitor the market situations. Additionally, the director of trade was made responsible for fair trade practices. The director of trade was required to be conversant with the differences in the prices of commodities of high value and of low value and the popularity or unpopularity of goods of various kinds whether produced on land or in water [and] whether they...arrived along land-routes or water-routes, [and] also [should know about] suitable times for resorting to dispersal or concentration, purchase or sale. The director advised traders to 'avoid profit that would be injurious to the subjects'.

During this period, several measures were taken to maintain official standards of weight and measures. Kautilya observed, "the superintendent of standardisation should cause factories to be established for the manufacture of standard weights and measures". Further, "[the superintendent] should cause a stamping [of the weights and measures] to be made every four months. The penalty for unstamped [weights] is twenty seven panas and a quarter. [Traders] shall pay a stamping fee amounting to one Kakani every day to the Superintendent of standardisation".

According to Kautilya, "the trade guilds were prohibited from taking recourse to black marketing and unfair trade practice". Severe punishments were prescribed for different types of cheating. For example, for cheating with false cowrie-shells, dice, leather straps, ivory-cubes or by sleight of hand, [the punishment shall be] cutting-off of one hand or a fine. The rights of the traders were also well protected. Kautilya said, "On the subject of the return of an article purchased on payment of price there was a fixed rule of time, after which an article could not be returned".

During Chandragupta's period, in which Kautilya lived, good trade practices were prevalent. For example, "goods could not be sold at the place of their origin. They were to be carried to the appointed markets (panyasala) where the dealer had to declare particulars as to the quantity, quality and the prices of his goods which were examined and registered in the books". Every trader was required to take a license to sell. A trader from outside had to obtain permission. The superintendent of commerce fixed the wholesale prices of goods as they entered the customs house. He allowed a margin of profit to fix retail prices. Speculation aimed at influencing prices was prohibited. Thus, the state bore a heavy responsibility for protecting the public against unfair prices and fraudulent transaction. There were severe punishments for smuggling and adulteration of goods. For example, public health was guarded by punishing adulteration of food products of all kinds, including grains, oils, alkalies, salts, scents and medicines.

Also during Chandragupta's period, easy access to justice for all, including consumers, was considered of great importance. According to Kautilya, "The king should look to the complaints of the people [of the town and village] in the second part of the day. Mobile and circuit courts worked at night, when necessity arose. They also must work on holidays on urgent matters". The king was primarily responsible for administering justice. Everyone could approach the king's court for justice. The king only entertained cases if the aggrieved presented a valid complaint. The king was directed not to "foster litigation initiating any by action without a complainant, and moreover, [the king was told that] no complaint should be taken notice of when it proceeded from a person altogether unconnected with the person aggrieved". In addition to this, different set of courts were functional in ancient India.

The court system during Kautilya time was well organised. There were two different benches comprising judges and magistrates to try civil and criminal cases. In civil matters, the judges were empowered to take cognizance of the cases of disadvantaged persons who could not approach the court, as for example, the cases concerning ascetics, women, and minors, old sick and helpless people. Thus, rendering justice was regarded as one of the essential duties of the rulers, and care was taken to ensure that justice was accessible to all. Indeed, this emphasis on justice for all has remained a cornerstone of India's legal system till today.

5.2 Consumer Protection in Medieval and Modern India [3]

In the medieval period, consumer protection continued to be of prime concern of the rulers. During Muslim rule, a large number of units of weights were used in India. During the Sultanate period, the prices used were determined by local conditions. During the rule of Alauddin Khalji, strict controls were established in the market place. In those days, there was unending supply of grain to the city and grain-carriers sold at prices fixed by the Sultan. There was a mechanism for price-enforcement in the market. Similarly, shopkeepers were punished for under weighing their goods.

In the modern period, the British system replaced the age old traditional legal system of India. However, one of the outstanding achievements of British rule in India was the formation of a unified nationwide modern legal system. During the British period, the Indian legal system was introduced to administer justice. However, it is important to note that the traditions and customs of the Indian legal system were not ignored. The law itself underwent considerable adaptation. The British institutions and rules were combined with structural features [e.g. a system of separate personal laws] and rules [e.g. Dharma, and local custom]. The borrowed elements underwent more than a century and a half of pruning in which localisms and anomalies were discarded and rules [were] elaborated to deal with new kinds of persons, property and transactions. Despite the challenges of combining the British and Indian legal systems, the fabric of modern Indian law is unmistakably Indian in its outlook and operation and, consumer protection is not an exception.

Some of the laws which were passed during the British regime concerning consumer interests are: the Indian Contract Act of 1872, the Sale of Goods Act of 1930, the Indian Penal Code of 1860, the Drugs and Cosmetics Act of 1940, the Usurious Loans Act of 1918, and the Agricultural Procedure (Grading and Marketing Act) of 1937. These laws provided specific legal protection to consumers.

For fifty-five years, the Sale of Goods Act of 1930 [SGA] was the exclusive source of consumer protection in India. SGA, drafted with precision, is "an admirable piece of legislation as a "Consumer's Charter". The main protection for the buyer against the seller for defective goods is found in Section 16 of the Act. It provides exceptions to the principle of 'caveat emptor' ('let the buyer beware') and the interests of the buyer are sufficiently safeguarded. Phrases such as "skill and judgment of the seller", "reliance on sellers' skill", and the test of "merchantable quality" provide effective remedies to buyers. Courts interpreted these rules in consumer's favour. SGA was the exclusive consumer legislation until 1986, when Consumer Protection Act of 1986 was designed to supplement the remedies already provided under SGA.

Consumer protection was also provided under India's criminal justice system. The Indian Penal Code of 1860 has a number of provisions to deal with crimes against consumers. It deals with offences related to the use of false weights and measures, the sale of adulterated food or drinks, the sale of noxious food or drinks, and the sale of adulterated drugs.

Consumer protection legislation enacted after India's independence from Britain include: the Essential Commodities Act of 1955, the Prevention of Food Adulteration Act of 1954 and the Standard of Weights and Measures Act of 1976. A benefit of these acts is that they do not require the consumer to prove *mens rea*. Rather, "the offences are of strict liability and not dependent on any particular intention or knowledge". Criminal law in the field of consumer protection has acquired much significance, as consumers are less inclined to go to civil courts for small claims. It has been said that "the functional value of criminal law in the field of consumer protection is a high one and it has a respectable pedigree". Another view is that there has been an attempt to look at consumer protection as "a public interest issue rather than as a private issue" to be left to individuals for settlement in court.

In addition to the remedies under contract and criminal law, consumers also enjoy rights under tort law. Based on its numerous legal intricacies, tort law however is not the ideal remedy for injured consumers in India. For example, the traditional doctrine of negligence imposes heavy responsibility on the plaintiff to prove each of its grievances. These traditional legal requirements naturally encourage the injured consumers to pursue legal remedies under different laws. Not surprisingly, it is estimated that for about half a century from 1914 to 1965, only 613 tort cases came before the appellate courts.

The orthodox legal requirements under the law of torts and contracts forced the policy makers to craft specific legislation to protect consumers. As a result, the Consumer Protection Act of 1986 was enacted with the objective of providing cheap, simple and quick justice to Indian consumers.

5.2.1 Pre-Independence Era: Consumer protection legislations leading to consumer protection started in India during the late part of the nineteenth century. The various legislations enacted during different periods sought to protect consumers (i) against false weight and measures, [4] adulteration of food, drinks, drugs and other articles [5] and false property marks, [6] (ii) by laying down implied warranties and conditions to title, quantity of fitness of goods [7] and provides an exception in case goods are purchased under a trade or patent name, or purchased after examining the goods, [8] (iii) regulating the operation relating to dangerous drugs and contraband traffic in the abuse of dangerous drugs, [9] import, manufacture, distribution and sale of drugs, [10] by prescribing test or analysis by laboratories established by the Government, (iv) by prohibiting manufacture and sale of non-standard and misbrand drugs, [11] (v) by regulating the import possession and sale of poison, and (vi) by providing for the grading and marking of agricultural products. [12]

5.2.2 Post-Independence Era: In the post-Independence era, the consumer movement in India can be seen from various angles which led India to draw upon contemporary consumer movements elsewhere in the world.

After Independence, under various Articles such as 19(g), 21, 39, 43, 47, 48 (A) and 51 (G) of the Indian Constitution which provide a few safeguards for benefit of its citizens, the High Courts and Supreme Court extended their helping hands in protecting consumer interests and thus gave a new direction to the consumer movement. In Hamdard Dawakhana vs. Union of India [13] suit, the Supreme Court held that advertisement of prohibited drugs or commodities the sale of which was not in the interest of general public could not be considered "speech" within the meaning of "Freedom of Speech" envisaged in the Indian Constitution. Similarly in Zafar Mohammed vs. State of West Bengal [14] Hon'ble Supreme Court disapproved advertisement like 'New Life', 'New Vigour', 'New Wave'. It remarked if you want a cure, see today well known world famous experienced registered physician. Special diseases such as oldness, all sorts of defects in nerves such as weakness, laziness are treated with full responsibility" are objectionable advertisement and are prejudicial to consumer interest".

5.3 Legislative Protection

Indian Legislature, realising the need for providing safeguards to the user or consumer of free India, has enacted several legislations in this direction. Drug Control Act, 1950; Emblems and Names (Prevention of Improper Use) Act, 1950; Indian Standards Institution (Certification Marks) Act, 1952; Drug and Magic Remedies (Objectionable Advertisement) Act, 1954; Prevention of Food Adulteration Act, 1954; Essential Commodities Act, 1955; Trade and Merchandise Act, 1958; Monopolies and Restrictive Trade Practices Act, 1969; Water (Prevention and Control of Pollution) Act, 1974; Weights and Measures Act, 1976; and other like Acts indirectly provide protection to Indian consumers through their various provisions.

These Acts provide Indian consumer movement a new orientation. Other legislations which indirectly protect consumer interests are Essential Commodities Act, 1980; Essential Commodities (Special Provisions) Act, 1985, Multi-State Co-operative Societies Act, 1985; Standards of Weights and Measures (Enforcement) Act, 1985; Narcotic Drugs and Psychotropic Substances Act, 1986; Drugs and Cosmetics (amendment) Act, 1986; Agricultural Produce (Grading and Marketing) Amendment Act, 1986; and the last but not the least, Consumer Protection Act, 1986.

In interpreting these Acts, the judiciary added new dimensions to the consumer movement through some of its landmark judgments. To cite a few: in J.N. Srivastava vs. Rambeharilall [15] the Court held, wrong diagnosis of the patient by the doctor was actionable considering the patient as 'Consumer'. In Bangalore Water Supply vs. A. Rajjappa, [16] the Supreme Court held university as an industry and declared that absence of profit motive or gainful objective is irrelevant, be the venture in public, joint, private or other sector and hence, the "user" can claim benefit on this basis.

5.4 Impact of Movements in Other Countries

The consumer movement in India was also influenced by consumer movements of developed and developing countries. For example, Ralph Nader, the one-man consumer movement of 1960s, creation of Special Assistant for Consumer Affairs in 1971, National Consumer Protection Agency, Consumer Product Safety Commission, Better Business Bureau of USA, "Battle for Consumer" pamphlet of the Labour Party, appointment of Molony Committee giving birth to Consumer Council, Retail Trading Standards Association, creation of new Ministry known as Ministry for Consumer Protection, Fair Trading and Consumer Protection, Fair Trading and Consumer Protection Advisory Committee of Great Britain have also substantially influenced the acceleration of consumer movement in India.

Similarly, Institution of Consumer Ombudsman; Market Court and Public Complaint Board of Sweden; the Consumer Affairs Bureau and the Consumer Affairs Council of Australia; Better Business Bureau, Ottawa, Canada; Conciliation Consumer Commission of France; Consumer League of Holland; Consumer Federation, Fair Trade Commission and National Consumer Centre of Japan provided the necessary impetus for the consumer movement to grow and flourish in India. [17]

5.5 Indian Consumer Protection Act, 1986: New Legal Culture [18]

The Indian legal system experienced a revolution with the

enactment of the Consumer Protection Act of 1986 ["CPA"], which was specifically designed to protect consumer interests. It is intended to provide justice which is "less formal, [and involves] less paper work, less delay and less [expense]". CPA has received wide recognition in India as poor man's legislation, ensuring easy access to justice. However, the CPA simply gives a new dimension to rights that have been recognised and protected since the ancient days. It is rightly said that "the present-day concern for consumer rights...is not new and that consumer's rights like the right to have safe, unadulterated and defect-free commodities at appropriate prices has been recognised in India since ancient times".

More than two decades of experience with the operation of CPA shows its popular acceptance and the legal preference of injured consumers to enforce their rights under it. It commands the consumer's support because of its cost effectiveness and user-friendliness. In fact, CPA creates a sense of legal awareness among the public and at the same time, discourages them to approach traditional courts, especially on consumer matters. It has changed the legal mindset of the public and made them think first of their remedies under CPA, regardless of the nature of their case. In short, the CPA has instilled confidence among the "teeming millions" of impoverished litigants but the way in which the consumer fora are flooded with cases and the mode in which these cases are being disposed off creates an impression of "judicial populism" in the arena of consumer justice.

The uniqueness of CPA lies in its flexible legal framework, wider jurisdiction and inexpensive justice. One can find in the CPA, a mixture of the principles of torts and contracts. Basically, CPA liberalises the strict traditional rule of standing consumer groups—central or any state government are all empowered to lodge complaints under CPA. This clearly indicates that enough care has been taken to represent the cause of the weak, indifferent and illiterate consumers. The novelty of CPA is the inclusion of both goods and services within its ambit and consumers can bring suit for defective products as well as for deficiency in services. In the event of any deficiency, all services, whether provided by the government or private companies, can be questioned under CPA.

CPA also liberalised the rigid procedural requirements and introduced simple and easy methods of access to justice. To proceed under CPA, the consumer needs only to pay a nominal fee and need not send any notices to the opposite party.

A simple letter addressed to the consumer forum is enough to initiate legal action against the erring party. Another major flexibility is the option the consumer has in respect of securing the services of a lawyer. If the consumer prefers, he can represent himself. Such simple measures are of action good and encourage consumers to avail themselves of the benefits of CPA.

CPA initiated a legal revolution by ushering in the era of consumers and developing a new legal culture among the masses for redressal of their grievance.

The consumer disputes redressal agencies, the National Commission, the State Commission, and the District Fora are working together in a way that is revolutionary—challenging the prevailing traditional system of delivering justice. With easy access to the courts guaranteed by CPA, consumers now wage legal battles against unscrupulous traders or service providers without any hesitation.

The Indian government is also taking an active interest in protecting consumer rights and promoting effective consumer movements. In 2003, the Planning Commission of India identified "Consumer Awareness, Redressal, and Enforcement of the Consumer Protection Act of 1986" as a priority. As a result, a national action plan was formulated.

The consumer fora created by CPA have proven to be effective, disposing of thousands of cases with few legal formalities, and leading the way towards well-founded consumer jurisprudence in India. The traditional Indian legal system, in addition to a huge backlog of cases, is experiencing a litigation explosion in the area of consumer protection. According to National Consumer Disputes Redressal

Commission (NCDRC), total number of consumer cases pending with National Commission, State Commissions and District Forums stood at 3,69,082 as on 01.08.2014. Around 89,495 cases have been filed before the National Commission since its inception. At present, 11,725 cases are pending disposal. The huge backlog of consumer cases before consumer fora is compelling the Indian legal system to think of alternatives for speedy disposal of consumer cases. India, home to the majority of the world's consumers, is committed to working for the welfare of consumers through new legal innovations.

5.6 Some Important Consumer Organisations [19]

Consumer movement in India had its beginning in the early part of this Century. The first known collective body of consumers in India was set up in 1915 with the Passengers and Traffic Relief Association (PATRA) in Bombay. Women Graduate Union (WGU), Bombay was another organisation started in 1915. One of the earliest consumer co-operatives was the 'Triplicate Urban Co-operative Stores' started in late 1940s in Madras. It has about 150 branches all over the city. The Indian Association of Consumer (IAC) was set up in Delhi in 1956. This was an all-India Association for consumer interests with government support. However, even IAC did not make any headway.

The first organisation to really make an impact was the Consumer Guidance Society of India (CGSI), Bombay started by nine housewives in 1966 with Mrs. Leela Jog as its founder secretary. Instead of just holding conferences and meetings and raising issues and questions, it started testing and reporting the quality of items of daily use of foodstuffs and handling consumer complaints. It has 8 branches at various places carrying on publicity, exhibitions and education. It publishes a magazine called 'KEEMAT', in English, for consumer information.

The second consumer organisation which made quite an impact in making the cause of consumers known throughout the country is the 'Karnataka Consumer Services Society' (KCSS) formed in 1970. The driving force behind KCSS was Mrs. Mandana who spread the word of the movement throughout the country, especially among government circles at a time when the word 'consumer' was not familiar to many. It is based in Bangalore. It organised important seminars on consumers' education in schools and is represented on Prevention of Food and Drug Adulteration Committee and Karnataka Food and Civil Supplies Corporation.

Visaka Consumers Council (VCC), started in 1973 in Vishkhapatnam, Andhra Pradesh, is another pioneering consumer organisation which has made a significant contribution to the consumer movement. It represented the plight of the poor ration card holders and LPG gas users, who had to stand in long queues because of the callous attitude of the authorities concerned. Mr. V.K. Parigi with 20 members held meetings, survey of ration card holders and succeeded in achieving necessary changes in the fair price shop and public distribution system. Besides this, about 15 more organisations came up in Andhra Pradesh for taking up the task of solving problems of fair price shops and milk distribution in different parts of the state.

To wage a war against exploitation by the traders, some organisations came up with the novel idea of buying quality product of everyday use at wholesale rate and selling these to the consumers at much lower prices than that being sold by the merchants. These are Akhil Bhartiya Grahak Panchayat (ABGP) started in 1947 in Pune, Mumbai Grahak Panchayat (MPG) in 1979 in Mumbai and Grahak Panchayat in 1979 in Jamshedpur.

Another organisation which made a significant contribution to the cause of consumers is the Consumer Education and Research Centre (CERC), started in Ahmedabad in 1978. It added a new dimension to the consumer movement with Prof. Manubhai Shah as the managing trustee of CERC. The organisation used legal machinery to bring about changes and protect consumer rights. Its special focus and intervention is against the government and public corporations. It has a big library, a computer centre and a product testing laboratory. Recently, it has also launched a project on comparative testing in Ahmedabad where comparative testing, ranking and evaluation of consumer products are being undertaken with the object of publication of such findings for consumer education. Initially, to begin with, testing of food, pharmaceuticals and domestic appliances was taken up. Its findings were published and action initiated against unsafe products. CERC also undertakes internship training for consumer organisations, besides routine exhibitions, seminars and publications of the magazine 'Consumer Confrontation'.

The eighties of the present century saw the dawn of a new era in consumer movement in India. There was mushrooming of consumer organisations, many floated by politicians to earn additional income and capture a gullible vote bank. However, some associations were really committed to the cause of the consumers. One of these was 'Jagrut Grahak' in Baroda, Gujarat started in 1980 by ten retired professionals. It imparts consumer education through seminars and publication and runs a network of 45 complaint centres. 'Consumers Forum' is another important organisation started in 1980 in a small form in Udupi in South Karnataka. Under the leadership of Dr. P. Narayan Rao, it succeeded in bringing relief for many aggrieved consumers, chiefly from the bureaucrats.

VOICE (Voluntary Organisation in the Interest of Consumer Education), was founded by a band of energetic young students and teachers of the Delhi University in 1983 to fight against unfair trade practices. It gives consumers information about various products and brands and enables them to make informed choices. With Dr. Sri Ram Khanna as the managing trustee, it has launched comparative testing. Its first attempt was directed at comparative testing of well known brands of colour televisions.

Consumer Unity and Trust Society (CUTS) started in Jaipur, Rajasthan, in March 1984, made its impact by effectively making use of media and publicity. For example, to tackle problems of garbage, it announced prizes for photographs depicting the biggest heap of rubbish or the biggest pothole, and this galvanised the authorities into taking prompt action. Consumer Action Group (CAG) founded in 1985 in Madras concerns itself with issues of civic amenities, health and environment.

Besides organised efforts, some individual consumer activists have been at the forefront for augmenting the consumer causes in the country. Mr. R.R. Dollani, an old Gandhian, started a number of associations in Madras. He organises meetings and rallies on consumer issues and other public interest issues in various parts of the city. Mr. H.D. Shourie, Director, Common Cause Delhi, is a well known litigant in consumer circles.

This organisation has more than 5,000 members from all over the country keeping close touch with various consumer outfits and taking up cases on problems of electricity, hospitals, taxation and similar issues. Another activist who works primarily with his pen is Mr. R. Desikan of SMN Consumer Protection Council, Madras.

A fresh impetus was given to the consumer movement with the enactment of the Consumer Protection Act, 1986. It applies to the whole of India except Jammu & Kashmir. Suffice it to mention that the Act is unique in the sense that it provides for setting up of quasi-judicial bodies vested with jurisdiction concurrently with the established courts for redressal of consumer disputes at the district, state and national levels. The basic objective is to provide inexpensive justice to consumers.

The nineties saw fulfilment of efforts towards a unified approach. It had been always felt that there were benefits in collective and united approach. In March 1990, the Federation of Consumer Organisations (FEDCOT) was established in Tamil Nadu to bring together as many consumer groups as possible in the state under one umbrella. In 1992, consumer groups of Gujarat joined hands to from a federation—Gujarat State Federation of Consumer Organisation (GUSFECO). Now nine states in the country have federations, namely, Tamil Nadu, Gujarat, Kerala, Karnataka, Andhra Pradesh, Maharashtra, Rajasthan, Odisha and Uttar Pradesh. Besides, at the apex level, there are confederations of Indian Consumer Organisation (CICO), New Delhi, formed in February, 1991 and Consumer Coordination Council (CCC), New Delhi, formed in April, 1992. The idea behind these apex bodies is networking of consumer groups coming together for a common cause.

5.7 Achievements of the Consumer Movement [20]

Some interesting developments which are helping the consumer movement include, developments taking place in the field of consumer education and some noticeable changes that have taken place among business organisations and their associations or federations. Consumer protection is being incorporated in the syllabi at different levels in schools and colleges. Full-fledged courses have been introduced in served universities and management institutes.

A number of large organisations have set up consumer grievance cells as an in-house redressal mechanism. Life Insurance Corporation of India (LIC) has set up claims review committees at the zonal and central levels. Petroleum companies, railways, banks, and income tax departments have also initiated setting up of public grievance cells. The Government of India has set up a separate directorate called Directorate of Public Grievances in New Delhi. They deal with complaints relating to banks, railways, insurance, pensions and related matters. In the long run, they will cover all the ministries. The nationalised banks are observing 15th of every month as the 'Customer Grievance Day' where an aggrieved consumer can walk into the top managers' offices in their respective town, district or zone.

The Council of Fair Business Practices, of more than 20

years standing, is also trying to help in the redressal of complaints against business firms from individual consumers or groups. Federation of Indian Chambers of Commerce and Industry (FICCI) has set up a Consumer Business Forum which meets once a quarter in different cities of the country. All stock exchanges in the country have also set up similar cells. The Advertisement Standard Council of India (ASCI), Confederation of Indian Industry (CII) and FICCI have evolved a code of ethics towards this end.

Another significant achievement of the consumer movement has been the representation given to consumer organisations on the policy making bodies (regulatory machinery) of governments and advisory/welfare committees of big business organisations and the service sector. Central and State Government consumer protection councils, regulatory departments of Prevention of Food Adulteration, Supplies of Food and Drugs, Weights and Measures Department, quality control institutions like Bureau of Indian Standards (BIS) and AGMARK, Petroleum Product Department, Railway Commuters Welfare Committees, Regional Advisory Committees for Indian Airlines Services all these have representatives of various consumer organisations.

Thus, consumers at large get a chance to participate in policy making issues. It appears time has come when consumers in India can hope to be 'The King' in the market place very soon. The labour of dedicated individuals and groups who have fought relentlessly for consumers rights through the decades has not gone in vain after all.

5.8 Consumer Movement and Protection in Odisha

The State of Odisha is a political unit of the Indian Union with enormous potentialities of a long coastal line of 480 km., rich reserves of 57,183 sq. km. of forest wealth and seven major rivers with their branches and tributaries making a neat web. Though Odisha cannot be said to be an industrially developed state, yet it can boast of prestigious industries like Rourkela Steel Plant, Nalco Aluminium and Alumina

Complex, Paradeep Phosphates, Orissa Sponge Iron, etc. Along with about 2,327 small-scale industries employing a total work force of 1,18,83000 individuals with two major ports Paradip and Dhamra and two smaller ports Gopalpur and Chandbali, the state has immense potentialities for development.

Consumer protection in the State has been very similar to the developments in other States of India. While the Central authority provided the Parent Act in the form of the Consumer Protection Act, 1986, rules were framed by the state government under Section 30(2) of the Act named as "The Orissa Consumer Protection Rule, 1987" and promulgated on 24.3.1988.

As per the provisions of Section 9 of Consumer Protection Act, 1986, a state commission was constituted for the State of Odisha with its seat at Cuttack. Initially, 14 district forums were set up for the erstwhile 13 districts and when new districts were carved out, the number of districts rose to 30. But in reality, instead of 30, 31 forums were created, with 2 district forums for the district of Sundargarh, one stationed at Sundargrh and the other at Rourkela.

Earlier, forums were presided over by the respective district judges who devoted part time attention but consequent upon the Supreme Court's direction full time presidents have been appointed which enables the forums to function independent of the traditional judiciary.

The State Government has also formed the State Consumer Protection Council to promote and protect consumers' rights and consumer education. That apart, there are a few voluntary consumer organisations in the state who work in this field.

5.8.1 Leading Voluntary Consumer Organisations in Odisha [21]: These are as under:

1. Eastern Cuttack Consumer Welfare Association, Cuttack.
2. Committee for Legal Aid to Poor, Cuttack.
3. Orissa Consumer Association, Cuttack.
4. Anchalik Khauti Surakshya Society, Cuttack.

5. Suprativa, Cuttack.
6. Federation of Consumer Organisation, Bhubaneswar.
7. Consumer News of India, Jatni, Khurda.
8. State Consumer Protection League, Bhubaneswar.
9. Jankalyan Consumer Association, Khurda.
10. Centre for Youth and Social Development, Bhubaneswar.
11. Mousumi Social Charitable Organisation, Bhubaneswar.
12. National Institute for Community and Child Development, Khurda.
13. World of Mother, Bhubaneswar.
14. Orissa Multipurpose Development Centre, Bhubaneswar.
15. Sarbasena Janakalyan Society, Bhubaneswar.
16. F.M. Welfare Club, Puri.
17. Dhenkanal District Consumer Protection Association Dhenkanal.
18. Bhuban Consumer Protection Association, Bhuban, Dhenkanal.
19. "Research", Dhenkanal.
20. All Orissa Research Institute for Development of Women Movement, Talcher Thermal, Angul.
21. Jayadurga Mahila Samiti, Basala, Angul.
22. Ganjam District Consumer Protection Guild, Berhampur.
23. Khauti Surakhya Sangha, Rambha, Ganjam.
24. Gajapati District Consumer Association, Parlakhemundi, Gajapati.
25. Consumer Guidance Protection Forum, Balasore.
26. Upbhokta Surakhya Parishad, Balasore.
27. Gramin Consumer and Labourers Association, Bhadrak.
28. Dharmasala Khauti Surakshya Society, Jaraka, Jajpur.
29. Kendrapara District Consumer Grievance Association, Kendrapara.
30. Sahara, Kendrapara.
31. Sambalpur District Consumers Federation, Sambalpur.
32. Baragarh Consumer Association, Baragarh.
33. Nayagarh Sub-division Protection Cell, Nayagarh.
34. Agragami, Kasipur, Rayagada.

35. Bikash Niketan Muniguda, Koraput.
36. Kalahandi Consumer Welfare Organisation, Bhawanipatna, Kalahandi.
37. National Institute for People Development, Phulbani, Kandhamal.
38. Law Forum (Legal Aid to Weak Forum), Boudh.
39. Jatiya Seva Pratisthan, Baripada, Mayurbhanj.
40. Grama Seva Sanghathan, Sartpala, Mayurbhanj.
41. Research Academy for Rural Environment, (RARE), Sonepur.
42. Rourkela Consumer Forum, Rourkela, Sundergarh.
43. Consumer Protection Council, Rourkela.
44. Consumer Association, Jagatsinghpur.
45. Anchalik Khunti, Suraskhya, Sangha, Jagatsinghpur.
46. National Forum for Consumer Protection, Keonjhar.

Endnotes

1. Prasad, A.R., "Historical Evolution of Consumer Protection and Law in India: A Bird's Eye View", *Journal of Texas Consumer Law*, 2008, p. 132.
2. Ibid, pp. 132-134.
3. Ibid, pp. 134-135.
4. Indian Penal Code, Sections 264 to 267.
5. Ibid, Sections 272 to 276.
6. Ibid, Sections 478 to 489.
7. Proviso to Section 16(1) of Sale of Goods Act, 1930.
8. Proviso to Section 16(2) of Sale of Goods Act, 1930.
9. Dangerous Drugs Act, 1930; Drugs Act, 1940.
10. Drugs and Cosmetics Act, 1940.
11. Poisons Act, 1919.
12. Agricultural Product (Grading and Marking) Act, 1937.
13. 1960 (2) SCR 671.
14. 1976 (1) SCR 428.
15. AIR, 1982 MP 132.
16. AIR, 1978 SC 549.
17. Malik, J.K., "Consumer Movement in India: From Infancy to Maternity", in S.R. Bhansali (ed.), Consumer Protection and Law, Faculty of Law, University of Jodhpur, 1991, p. 358.
18. Op. cit., Prasad, A.R., pp. 134-135.

19. "Consumer Movement in India", Unit-6, Self Learning Material, Indira Gandhi National Open University, New Delhi, 2008, pp. 18-20.
20. Ibid, pp. 20-21.
21. Bakshi, P.M., "Consumer Protection Law", Ashoka Law House, New Delhi, 2004, pp. 1906-1908.

6

Pre-Independence Consumer Protection Legislations

6.1 Introduction

Protection of consumer has remained focal point of legislation in the country, responding whenever and wherever necessary by passing legislations. During the British period, the enactment of law on consumer protection was neither undertaken nor thought of. Perhaps, the reason for such a policy was that, at that time, Indians were consumers of goods manufactured by the British, whether in India or abroad. Accordingly, no attention was given to protect interests of the consumers. No doubt, the Indian Penal Code, 1860 [1] could extend some protection to the interest of consumers but, that too, indirectly, as the aims and objects of the Code were quite foreign to that of consumer protection.

The case law study of that period also reveals that the Courts did not decide any case on the subject under the provisions of the Code. However, the Britishers focused their attention on protection of the interest of consumers after the second decade of the twentieth century when Cotton Cloth Act, 1930; Petroleum Act, 1934 and Drugs and Cosmetics Act, 1940 were passed by them. But, no notable case was reported to have been decided by courts during the British period punishing offenders for violation of the provisions of these Acts. Perhaps, it was due to the fact that the beneficiaries of these Acts were, mainly Britishers and hence, they could not be tried and convicted for violation. Thus, during the British period, no substantial steps were taken or intended to be taken for consumer protection, as Britishers were busy in political activities rather than welfare activities. Even the aforesaid special Acts were aimed more at fetching revenue for the

Britishers and restricting natives to undertake trade and commerce in areas not covered by these Acts.

When India attained freedom from serfdom, a welfare State was set up. In order to boost the concept of a welfare State, among others, consumer protection was identified as an important area to work on. Accordingly, the first step to protect consumer interest was taken in 1950 by passing the Drugs Control Act, 1950, followed by Industries (Development and Regulation) Act, 1951, Indian Standards Institution (Certification Marks) Act, 1952 (since repealed), Food Adulteration Act, 1954, etc. Nevertheless, these Acts did not cater fully to the needs of consumers due to varied reasons. Hence, in 1986, influenced by the UN Guidelines on Consumer Protection, the Central Government passed the Consumer Protection Act, 1986. In this chapter, an attempt has been made to study some of the acts relating to consumer protection under law, i.e. Laws on Contract, Tort and Criminal Law.

6.2 Indian Penal Code, 1860

Under the Code, there are several provisions aimed at protecting the interest of the consumers, such as:

- **Fraudulent Use of False Instruments for Weighing:** Whoever fraudulently uses any instrument for weighing which he knows to be false, shall be punished with imprisonment of either description for a term which may extend to one year or with fine, or with both (Section 264).
- **Fraudulent Use of False Weight or Measure:** Whoever fraudulently uses any false weight or false measure of length or capacity as a different weight or measure shall be punished with imprisonment of either description for a term which may extend to one year or with fine, or with both (Section 265).
- **Being in Possession of False Weight or Measure:** Whoever is in possession of any instrument for weighing or of any weight, or of any measure of length or capacity

which he knows to be false, intending that the same may be fraudulently used, shall be punished with imprisonment of either description for a term which may extend to one year or with fine, or with both (Section 266).

- **Making or Selling False Weight or Measure:** Whoever makes, sells or disposes of any instrument for weighing or any weight or any measure of length or capacity which he knows to be false, in order that the same may be used as true shall be punished with imprisonment of either description for a term which may extend to one year or with fine, or with both (Section 267).
- **Adulteration of Food or Drink:** Intended for sale whoever adulterates any article of food or drink, so as to make such article noxious as food or drink, intending to sell such article as food or drink, or knowing it to be likely that the same will be sold as food or drink, shall be punished with imprisonment of either description for term which may extend to six months or with fine which may extend to thousand rupees, or with both (Section 272).
- **Sale of Noxious Food or Drink:** Whoever sells or offers or exposes for sale, as food or drink, any article, which has been rendered or has become noxious, or is in a state unfit for food or drink, knowledge or having reason to believe that the same is noxious as food or drink, shall be punished with imprisonment of either description for term which may extend to six months or with fine which may extend to one thousand rupees or with both (Section 273).
- **Adulteration of Drugs:** Whoever adulterates any drug or medical preparation in such a manner as to lessen the efficacy or changes the operation of such drug or medical preparation, or to make it noxious, intending that, it shall be sold or used, for or knowing it to be likely that it will be sold or to used, for any medicinal purpose, as if it had not undergone such adulteration, shall be punished with imprisonment of either description for a term which may extend to six months or with fine which may extend to one

thousand rupees, or with both (Section 274).

- **Sale of Adulterated Drugs:** Whoever knowing any drug or medicinal preparation to have been adulterated in such a manner as to lessen its efficacy, to change its operation, or to render it noxious, sells the same or offers or exposes it for sale, or issues it from any dispensary for medicinal purpose by any person not knowing of the adulteration, shall be punished with imprisonment of either description for a term which may extend to six months or with fine which may extend to one thousand rupees, or with both (Section 275).
- **Sale of Drug as a Different Drug or Preparation:** Whoever knowingly sells, or offers or exposes for sale or issues from a dispensary for medicinal purposes any drug or medicinal preparation as a different drug of medicinal preparation, shall be punished with imprisonment of either description for a term which may extend to six months or with fine which may extend to one thousand rupees, or with both (Section 276).

6.3 Indian Contract Act, 1872

The general principles of the law of contract as a means of protecting the consumer are of less applicability because of the principles of freedom of contract. Freedom of contract was one of the cornerstones of the nineteenth century laissez faire economics. [2] Freedom of contract means freedom of a party to enter into a contract with another on whatever terms he may consider advantageous to his interest.

6.3.1 Standard Form of Contract: Advancement of civilization and the economic development due to Industrial Revolution introduced the concept of the standard form of contract, [3] known as "contract adhesion". [4] According to Amos and Walton, the term "contracted adhesion" is employed to denote a type of contract of which the conditions are fixed by one of the parties in advance but is open to acceptance by any one. [5] This type of contract confronts every consumer—

whether a citizen or a non-citizen. Anson [6] has observed that any one, who travels in a bus or train, takes his clothes to the dry cleaner, receives gas, electricity or water from the municipal supply, deposits his luggage in a railway cloak-room or even, in some cases, takes a lease of flat, will receive a standard form of contract, devised by a dealer or a supplier. Taking advantage of this, crafty dealers and suppliers, even public or government undertakings, have been exploiting the weak and hapless consumers.

6.3.2 Exemption Clause: Such standard form of contract sometimes contains an exemption clause which provides that the imposing party will virtually not be rendered liable under any circumstances whatsoever. Not unnaturally, therefore, many vendors, both retailers and manufactures, attempt to exclude their liability under the Act by means of a printed form containing standard conditions of sale, resulting in the transformation of buyers' market to sellers' market.

One of the techniques adopted by the Courts to deal with the issue of oppressive exemption clause in standard form of contract was the doctrine of fundamental breach of contract. Under this doctrine, a contract was considered to fail altogether where the party in fault became unable to enforce the terms of the contract against the other party. When applied in a consumer context, the doctrine did serve to prevent reliance on exemption clause which might otherwise operate unfairly against consumers.

Thus, it became possible to invalidate a purported exclusion of liability of breach of the implied terms relating to the supply of consumer goods where the goods delivered were not in accordance with the contract description. In Karsales (Harrow) Ltd. vs. Wallis, [7] the supplier of a motor vehicle under contract of hire purchase, delivered a vehicle which was so badly damaged that it was incapable of independent movement. The contract contained a provision to the effect that there was no condition relating to, or warranty of, the condition or fitness of the goods supplied. It was considered that a motor vehicle which will not move cannot be described as a car with the result that there was a serious breach of condition relating to the description of the goods supplied. Applying the doctrine of fundamental breach, it was considered that no matter how extensive the exemption clause might be, it has no application if there has been a breach of the fundamental conditions.

6.3.3 Effect of Statements Made to a Consumer: Some of the statements may be made to a consumer directly by a retail trader, whereas others may be directed towards consumers through advertising media. The remedies available to a consumer will depend on the classification of such statements. Some contracts may amount to no more than a pre-contractual representation which will not give rise to remedies for breach of contract, but may allow for action for damages for misrepresentation.

6.3.4 Commendatory Puffs: Generally, advertising puffery, amounting to no more than commendatory praise of a product put on the market by a manufacturer, is unobjectionable. Such statements do not have any meaningful content to rely. Thus, a claim to the effect that a certain brand of beer refreshes the body which is not claimed by rival brands is merely intended to bring to the attention of consumer, a particular brand. However, the advertiser needs to be careful not to cross the line between puffery and misrepresentation. If an advertisement is credible as being factual, no liability for misrepresentation may be imposed. There appears to be a general reluctance to allow a commercial promoter to escape liability on the ground that his advertisements amount to nothing more than trade puffery. In such cases, the courts will try to judge the real intention of the advertiser. [8] Thus, where there is a very precise claim, for example, that a proprietary medicine can cure influenza, the statement is likely to be treated as a contractual term, thereby giving rise to a possible action for damages for breach of contract. [9]

6.3.5 Misrepresentation: A misrepresentation can cause a person to enter into a contract he would not otherwise have made. The standard remedy for misrepresentation is rescission of the contract, at the instance of the party misled, so as to restore the parties to the position they occupied before the misrepresentation was made; damages may also be awarded in the tort of deceit, where misrepresentation is made negligently. In theory, at least, where damages are awarded, the measures payable will differ since the objective of an award of damages for breach of contractual term should put the plaintiff into the position he would have been had the promise been fulfilled, whereas an award of damages for misrepresentation is intended to return the plaintiff to the position he was in before the false assurance was made to him. Sometimes rescission will not be allowed where one of the so-called bars to rescission applies. The bars are affirmation, lapse of time, the existence of third party rights and impossibility of restitution interregnum.

6.3.6 Manufacturer's Contractual Liability for Negligence: The manufacturer of a product is expected to exercise reasonable care in the preparation and putting of up his product so as to ensure the safety of the product he puts into circulation.

According to the principle, in Donoghue vs. Stevenson (1932), [10] a manufacturer of products, which he sells in such form as to show that he intends them to reach the ultimate consumer in the form in which they left him with no possibility of intermediate examination and with the knowledge that the absence of reasonable care in the preparation or putting up of the products will result in an injury to the consumer's life or property, owes a duty to the consumer to take reasonable care.

The rule is based on the notion of fault which must be proved by the consumer. Accordingly, it is not favourable to the consumer purchaser as the implied terms in contracts of supply imposes strict liability on the supplier. However, the duty of care owed by the manufacturer of a product does extend to anyone whom he can foresee as likely to be affected by his acts of omission and commission.

The term 'manufacturer' is given a very wide definition with the result that it includes not just the producer of an end product but also the supplier of a service and a retailer. A better way of stating the rule is that it covers any person who fails to take reasonable care when he puts a product into circulation.

Unlike the position of the retailer under the Sale of Goods Act, the manufacturer is liable to any person foreseeably affected by his defective product. There is no requirement that the person affected should have contracted to purchase the product. Accordingly, the rule will extend to cover a purchaser [11] or a borrower, [12] members of his family and invited guests. Similarly, a manufacturer may also owe a duty of care to a donee, [13] an employee of the purchaser [14] or even a mere by-stander. [15]

The rule in Donoghue vs. Stevenson has also been extended to clothing, [16] motor cars, [17] cleaning fluids, [18] hair dyes, [19] buildings, [20] and the packing in which products are supplied. [21]

6.4 Usurious Loans Act, 1918

Many a time, we come across loans carrying interest at usurious rate—the loans may be in money or in kind. Such loans are very harsh for the borrower and can be termed as unconscionable. The Usurious Loans Act, 1918 gives some powers to courts while they are dealing with such type of transactions.

Section 3 provides that where in any suit to which this Act applies, whether heard exparte or otherwise, the court has reason to believe that: (i) the interest rate is excessive, and (ii) the transaction was, as between the parties thereto, substantially unfair, the court may exercise all or any of the powers mentioned below. These are:

- reopen the transaction, take an account between the parties and relieve the debtor of all liability in respect of any excessive interest.

- notwithstanding any agreement, purporting to close previous dealings and to create a new obligation, reopen any account already taken between them and relieve the debtor of all liability in respect of any excessive interest, and if anything has been paid or allowed in account in respect of such liability, order the creditor to repay any sum which it considers to be repayable in respect thereof.
- set aside either wholly or in part or revise or alter any security given or agreement made in respect of any loan, and if the creditor, has parted with security, order him to indemnify the debtor in such manner and to such extent as it may deem just.

However, in exercise of these powers, the court shall not:

- re-open any agreement purporting to close previous dealings and to create a new obligation which has been entered into by the parties or any person from whom they claim at a date more than 12 years from the date of the transaction.
- do anything which affects any decree of a court. In this, which the court deems to be reasonable having regard to the risk recurred as it appeared or must be taken to have appeared to the creditor at the date of the loan.

In considering whether interest is excessive under this section, the court shall take into account any amounts charged or paid, whether in money or in kind, for expenses, in queries, fines bonus prima renewals or any other charges and if compound interest is charged, the periods at which it is calculated and the total advantage which may reasonably so be taken to have been expected from the transaction.

In considering the question of risk, the court shall take into account the presence or absence of security and the value thereof, the financial condition of the debtor and the result of any previous transactions of the debtor, by way of loan, so far as the same were known, or must be taken to have been known, to the creditor.

In considering whether a transaction was substantially unfair, the court shall take into account all circumstances materially affecting the relations of the parties at the time of the loan to tending to show that the transaction was unfair, including the necessities or supposed necessities of the debtor at the time of the loan so far as the same were known, or must so taken to have been known, to the creditor. Further, interest may itself be sufficient evidence that the transaction was substantially unfair.

This section shall apply to any suit whatever its form may be, if such suit is a substantial one for the recovery of a loan or for the enforcement of any agreement or security in respect of a loan or for the redemption of any such security.

Nothing in this section shall affect the right of any transferee for value which satisfies the court that the transfer to him was bonafide and that he had at the time of such transfer had no notice of any fact which would have entitled the debtor as against the lender for relief under this section.

6.5 Sale of Goods Act, 1930

The Sale of Goods Act, 1930 is the replica of the Sale of Goods Act, 1883 of England and hence, the same common law principles applied in the contract of sale of goods between the buyer and the seller. From the consumer protection angle, this Act rescues the consumer to a certain extent from rule of caveat emptor, i.e., let the buyer beware.

The three primary conditions laid down in the Act appear in Section 15, Section 16(1), and Section 16(2). In one sense, these three conditions, taken in that order, lay down a series of graduated duties upon the seller. In the first place, there is the implied condition that the goods must correspond with their description. This applies in far wider circumstances than those in which the two other conditions apply, but does not extend much protection to the buyer, especially where the description of the goods is not a detailed one.

The next implied condition is that the goods must be merchantable. [22] This does not apply in all the circumstances in which the first condition applies; on the other hand, it affords the buyer a greater degree of protection, since goods that correspond to their description may not be merchantable. Even, this may not suffice to protect the consumer, since goods may correspond to their description and may be merchantable, and yet they may still be unsuitable for the buyer's purpose. Hence, in certain circumstances, the consumer may be able to rely on the third implied condition, namely that the goods must be fit for the purpose for which they were sold.

The Sale of Goods Act, 1930 provides the buyer two implied warranties and six implied conditions.

The implied warranties relate to:

1. Warranty of quiet possession, [23] and
2. Warranty against encumbrances. [24]

The breach of these warranties gives rise to a consumer a right to claim damages.

The implied conditions relate to:

1. The seller has title to goods, [25]
2. The goods shall correspond to description, and
3. There is the implied condition for the seller that the goods are of merchantable quality. [26]

Further, there are three more implied conditions in sale by sample, namely:

1. Bulk should correspond to the sample in quality,
2. Buyer to have reasonable opportunity to compare, and
3. Condition of merchantability as regards latent defects. [27]

In a sale by sample as well as by description, there is an implied condition that the goods must correspond to the sample as well as with description. [28]

The seller owes an implied condition as to the quality and fitness for the purpose for which the buyer or consumer buys the goods. Regarding the quality of merchantability, the buyer has no right to return the goods if the following two conditions are satisfied:

- Goods are brought by description, and
- They must have been purchased from a seller who deals in goods of that description, whether a manufacturer or not.

As for fitness of purpose, the following conditions are to be satisfied:

- The buyer makes known to the seller the particular purpose for which the goods are required,
- The buyer relies on the seller's skill and judgment, and
- The goods are of a description dealt in by the seller, whether he is the manufacturer or not.

When the consumer is offered defective goods, the success of his action against the supplier will depend on whether his case fits Section 15 or Section 16 of the Sale of Goods Act, 1930.

Prima facie, the difference between the three provisions would appear to be simple to identify. Section 15 applies where the buyer has not received that which he contracted to buy and Section 16 applies where he got what he contracted for, but due to defects in the goods, he could not put them to their normal use or some special identified use.

6.6 Law of Tort

Rules of the law of tort have been adapted in a number of ways as a consumer protection technique. An obvious example is the adaptation of the tort of negligence in relation to the liability of manufacturers and producers for defective products and the liability of the supplier of service, but tortuous principles are also relevant in other respects. Though in India, the law of tort is not much developed, it has followed the common law principles when a question arises on tortuous liability.

6.6.1 Product Safety: The decision of the House of Lords in Donoghue vs. Stevenson represents a landmark judgment in the field of consumer protection—that a manufacturer owes a duty of care to consumers in respect of the safety of his product. Donoghue vs. Stevenson case [29] concerned a negligent act (the act of the manufacturer) which caused physical harm to the consumer. Later cases have raised the question whether a manufacturer owes any tortuous duty to a consumer who suffers economic loss, such as diminution in the value of the defective product itself. The position adopted in English law on the issue seems to be that, except in the most extreme cases, a producer will not owe a duty of care in respect of pure economic loss such as diminution in value, and that the consumer of such a product will be confined to an action for breach of contract, if one exists.

6.6.2 Defective Services: Although the supply of services will very often involve a contractual relationship between a consumer and the service provider, the tort of negligence can provide some assistance in circumstances in which services are supplied outside of contractual dealings. Doctors, lawyers, architects and surveyors are all required to exercise reasonable care in their dealings with both clients and others whom they may reasonably foresee as likely to be affected by their acts or omissions.

The principal difficulty encountered in applying negligence principles to non-contractual suppliers of service is that the proximity of relationship between the consumer and the service supplier may not be sufficiently close. In determining whether a duty of care is owed by the service provider to the consumer, it will be necessary to consider, in addition to the issue of foresight of harm, the proximity of relationship between the parties and whether it is just and reasonable to impose a duty of care in the particular circumstances of the case. It does not necessarily follow from this that the consumer must be known to the service supplier, but the consumer must fall into a group of people who could have been foreseen as likely to be affected by the 'negligence' provision of the service.

The tort of conversion may also play limited role in respect of the misuse of consumer goods. For example, if a consumer leaves his property with another for the purpose of repair or safe-keeping and the repairer wrongly disposes off the goods to another, the consumer may have an action for conversion. The same also applies where a consumer has temporary possession of goods belonging to the supplier, such as where a consumer hires a television set or acquires goods on hire purchase; such goods during the agreement period remain property of the finance company. In either event, a wrongful disposition of the goods subject to the contract of hire or hire purchase by the consumer might expose the consumer to liability for conversion.

6.6.3 Advertising Law: The principles of the law of tort have much significance in favour of consumer in case of a misleading advertisement. Where there is no contractual relationship between the advertiser and the consumer, but the consumer has incurred expenses through purchasing a product from a retail supplier, there may be a possibility of a negligent action arising out of an alleged negligent misstatement. Liability for such statement lies under the rule in Hedley Byrne and Co. Ltd. vs. Heller and Partners Ltd., [30] but recent explanation of the rule restricts the liability of the maker of the statement. Following the decision of the House of Lords in Caparo Industries Plc vs. Dickman [31], a duty of care will only be owed by the maker of a statement where three conditions are satisfied.

First, it must be foreseeable that the plaintiff will suffer damages as a result of relying on the statement. Secondly, there must be a close relationship of proximity between the maker of the statement and the person to whom it is communicated and thirdly, it must be just and reasonable to impose liability on the maker of the statement. Generally, advertising material is communicated to the world at large and there are strong reasons to apprehend whether a misleading advertisement will give rise to a successful action for damages. While it may be foreseeable that a consumer will suffer damage as a result of relying on a statement contained in advertising material, it does not necessarily follow that there will be a sufficiently close relationship of proximity between the consumer and the advertiser or that it will be just and reasonable to impose liability. [32]

It would appear that in deciding whether the maker of a statement is to be held liable for negligence for the consequences of the plaintiff's reliance on that statement, six criteria must be considered. [33] These are: (i) the purpose for which the statement was made, (ii) the purpose for which the statement was communicated, (iii) the relationship between the maker of the statement, the recipient of the information and any relevant third party, (iv) the size of any class to which the recipient of the information belongs, (v) the state of knowledge of the maker of the statement, and (vi) reliance by recipient of the information.

6.6.4 Product Quality: Because of the apparent defects in the law of contract emanating, in particular, from a strict application of the doctrine of privity of contract, the question has arisen whether the tort of negligence can be used to compensate these deficiencies. [34] The principal way in which this can be done is by enlarging the circumstance in which a duty of care is owed by a manufacturer to a consumer of a defective product.

The main problem with the issue of product quality is the consumer's complaint that the product is not worth as much as he expected when he made the purchase. The product loses value due to some inherent deficiency and it is this diminution in value which the consumer seeks to recover.

The House of the Lords in Anns vs. Merton London Borough Council [35] observed that in certain circumstances, economic loss such as the damage caused by a defective building was remediable if the defect of the building was such as to create immediate or imminent danger to the occupant of the building. By analogy, if a defective product gave rise to such a danger, damages covering the cost of rectifying the defect could be awarded.

6.7 Agricultural Produce (Grading and Marking) Act, 1937 (AGMARK)

It is well-known that agricultural commodities exhibit wide range of varieties in quality due to a number of factors like varying agro-climatic conditions of growth, different methods of processing, preparation, etc. The quality requirements for different uses of the same product also differ considerably. Thus, grading and standardisation play an important role in marketing of agricultural products. To this end, Agricultural Produce (Grading and Marking) Act was passed.

The Act confers powers on Government of India to prescribe grade standards for various processed and semi-processed agricultural commodities including livestock and horticultural products. It empowers Government to fix grade designation, indicating quality of the produce, define quality, specify grade designation marks, specify the manner in which the article shall be packed, sealed and marked and authorises person/s or body of persons to use grade mark under prescribed conditions. The entire programme of grading and quality control under AGMARK is implemented in two distinct spheres:

1. Compulsory grading for export.
2. Voluntary grading for products sold in India.

6.7.1 AGMARK Specification: These specifications are popularly known as 'AGMARK Standards' which signify agricultural marking standards with a statutory seal, ensuring quality and purity.

6.7.2 Purpose of Grading and Quality Control: Firstly, it protects the agriculturist from exploitation. Knowing the quality and grade of his product, he is in a better bargaining position against the trader.

Secondly, it serves as a means of describing the quality of commodities to be purchased or sold by buyers and sellers all over the country and also abroad.

Thirdly, it protects consumers' health by ensuring quality and standard of the product he is purchasing.

Fourthly, trading on the basis of accepted quality standard makes pricing more precise and equitable, thereby making the price reporting mechanism more meaningful.

6.7.3 Need for Revision in Grade Specifications: As a result of new inventions and development in the field of agriculture, new varieties of produce are being introduced. Due to introduction of new varieties and change in consumer preference, periodical revisions became necessary. Consultative committees have been framed for suggesting such revisions in the grade specifications of selected commodities.

The Central Agmark Laboratory at Nagpur provides technical guidance in testing methods and also in the methodology of drawing samples.

Under the Act, not only grades and grade standards are prescribed and the quality of each grade-designation defined, but the manner in which the produce is to be packed, sealed and marked have also been specified.

Only those traders who willingly adhere to the prescribed procedures and regulations are given "Certificate of Authorization" to become authorized packers.

Regular checking of packed and labelled packages can be done either at the packer's premises or in the market by senior officials.

6.8 Drugs and Cosmetics Act, 1940

A healthy body is the very foundation of all human activities. In a welfare State, therefore, it is the obligation of the State to ensure the creation and sustaining of condition congenial to good health. Attending to public health, therefore, is of high priority, perhaps the one at the top. The Constitution of India under Article 21, guarantees right to life and Supreme Court in several cases has interpreted the guarantee to cover life with normal amenities ensuring good living which include medical attention, life free from disease, and life having longevity of normal expectation. Article 47 has also laid stress on the improvement of public health and prohibition of drugs injurious to health as one of the primary duties of the State.

The main object of this Central Act is to regulate import, manufacture, distribution and sale of drugs and cosmetics. The problem of adulteration of drugs, production of spurious, misbranded and sub-standard drugs poses a serious threat to life.

6.8.1 Important Provisions: Some important provisions regulating the safety of consumers in the Act are:

1. The Act provides for the allopathic and homeopathic system and the indigenous systems such as ayurvedic and the unani systems of medicine. There is a separate technical advisory body for each of these systems.
2. Drug in the ordinary sense means a substance used as a medicine for curing disease. In the Act, it is defined as 'that which includes all medicines and substances for internal or external use of human being or animal or diagnosis, treatment, mitigation or prevention of disease or affecting the structure or function of the body'. [36] Cosmetic is defined as 'an article used for cleansing, beautifying, promoting attractiveness or altering appearance'. [37] Tobacco which is used for cleansing teeth has been held to be 'cosmetic' within the meaning of the Act. [38]
3. The Act creates an absolute liability and rules out intention as a constituent of offence. Thus, the knowledge of the purchaser about it is wholly immaterial as the object is to prohibit sale of adulterated drugs. [39]
4. Under the Act, a Drug Consultation Committee has been formed which advises Central Government, State Governments and the Drug Technical Advisory Board. [40] A person would be guilty of misbranding drug under the Act if drug found from his possession purports to be the product of a place or a country of which it is not truly a product.
5. The Act lays down standards of quality of drugs (Second Schedule) and prohibits the import of misbranded, spurious and adulterated drugs. [41] The Central Government has powers to prohibit such imports. [42]

6. A complainant can have drug or cosmetics analysed on payment at the Central Drug Laboratory. The report of the Government Analyst is a conclusive evidence but this does not prevent the complainant from getting it privately tested and attaching the report with a petition before a court.

The Supreme Court in Vincent Panekur Langare vs. Union of India [43] held that it was the manufacturer's obligation to disclose the formula and statutory warning or information in the national language and at least in one or two other languages keeping in view the place of manufacture of the drug and the area of its circulation.

Endnotes

1. Sections 264 to 267 deal with offences related to weights and measures; Sections dealing with some offences affecting public health.
2. Friedmen, "Law in a Chaning Society", 1972, 2nd edition, Penguin Books Ltd.
3. Treitel, "Law of Contracts", 8th edition, p. 196, Sweet and Maxell.
4. Iyer, T.S., "The Law of Contract", 4th edition.
5. "Introduction to French Law", 2nd edition, 1963, p. 152.
6. Anson, "Principles of the English Law of Contract", 25th edition, pp. 146-147.
7. 1956, 1 WLR 936.
8. Esso Petroleum Co. Ltd. vs. Commissioner of Customs and Excise, 1976, 1 WLR 1, 6 per Lord Simon.
9. Carlill vs. Carbolic Smokeball Co. Ltd., 1983, 1 QB 256.
10. 1932, AC 502, 599 per Lord Atkin.
11. Grant vs. Australian Knitting Mills Ltd., 1936, AC 85.
12. Griffiths vs. Arch Engineering Co. Ltd., 1968, 3 All ER 217.
13. Donoghue vs. Stevenson, 1932, AC 562.
14. Davie vs. New Merton Board Mills Ltd., 1957, AC 604.
15. Stennett vs. Hancock, 1939, 2 All ER 578.
16. Ibid., supra note 2.
17. Herchatal vs. Stewert and Araden Ltd., 1940, 1 KB 155.
18. Fisher vs. Harods Ltd., 1966, 1 Lioyd's Rep. 500.
19. Holmes vs. Ashford, 1950, 2 All ER 76.
20. Dutton vs. Bognor Regis Urban District Council, 1972, 1 QB 37.

21. Hill vs. James Crowe (Cases) Ltd., 1978, 1 All ER 812.
22. The Sale of Goods Act, 1930, Section 16(2).
23. Sale of Goods Act, 1930, Section 14(b).
24. Ibid., Section 14(c).
25. Ibid., Section 14(a).
26. Ibid., Sections 17(2)(c) and 16(2).
27. Ibid., Section 17.
28. Ibid., Section 15.
29. 1932, AC 562.
30. 1964, AC 465.
31. 1990, 2 AC 605.
32. 1990, 2 AC 617-618.
33. Markesinis, 1987, 103 LQR.
34. 1978, AC 728.
35. 1978, AC 728.
36. Drugs and Cosmetics Act, 1940, Section 36.
37. Ibid., Section 3.
38. Gopilal Agarwal vs. State of Orissa, AIR, 1973 Ori. 15.
39. Public Prosecutor vs. Soda Kondaya, AIR 1947, Mad. 184.
40. Ibid., Section 7.
41. Drugs and Cosmetics Act, 1940, Sections 9, 9-A, B, C and D.
42. Ibid., Section 10.
43. AIR, 1987 SC 990.

7

Post-Independence Consumer Protection Legislations

7.1 Prevention of Food Adulteration Act, 1954

Against this background, the Prevention of Food Adulteration Act, 1954 was enacted to curb the menace of adulteration. Laws existed in a number of States in India for the prevention of adulteration of food stuffs but they lacked in uniformity having been passed at different times without mutual consultation among the States—since the subject was under the State List. This warranted amendment to the Constitution, thereby transferring the subject from the State List to the Concurrent List.

The Act has been enacted to curb and remedy the evil of food adulteration and to ensure sale and supply of wholesome food to the people. It is intended to protect the public from using adulterated articles and therefore it has been made punishable to sell adulterated articles even if a purchaser purchases the article knowing it to be adulterated.

Adulteration of food articles is rampant in the country and has become a grave menace to the health and well-being of the community. It makes a heavy dent on the already low nutritional standards. The benefits of many health programmes, on which large sums of money are spent, are undermined as a consequence of uncontrolled adulteration. In view of the gravity of the problem and the danger posed to the health of the nation, it was necessary to enact a Central Act to prevent the menace of adulteration.

7.1.1 Salient Features of the Act: The salient features of this Act, stated below, would show that the provisions of this Act deal with safety of health and life of a consumer.

1. It intends to prevent adulteration and misbranding of food.
2. Secures purity of food to maintain public health.

3. Warns producers or manufacturers of food to ensure safety.
4. Ensures that food which the public buys is, inter alia, prepared, packed and stored under sanitary conditions so as not to be injurious to the health of the people.
5. Provides for adequate punishment of the adulterators.

7.1.2 Important Provisions: As per the provisions of the Act, it is not necessary for the complainant to prove the ulterior motive of the adulterator; it is sufficient to show that he has acted in contravention of the provisions of the law. [1]

1. Food has been defined to mean any food or drink that is used for human consumption. However, it does not include drugs as there is a separate law for the same.
2. Adulterated food means any food that is not of the quality demanded by the consumer or claimed by the supplier. If it contains something that affects the quality of food or is stored in conditions that have affected its quality, then to the food is rotten, contaminated or otherwise unfit for human consumption or if the article is obtained from a deceased animal, it is covered under the definition of adulterated food.
3. It is an offence to sell or offer for sale or expose for sale or manufacture for sale, any food which is below the standard prescribed by rules under the Act. [2]
4. If no statutory standard of purity is found in the Act, the only reasonable inference is that only articles of absolute purity have to be sold. Absence of rules in no way affects the liability of the accused for punishment. [3]
5. Consumer organisations can also have food analyzed. Earlier, only the food inspector and the purchaser were authorised to take samples of food alleged to be adulterated by the seller or anybody else and get them analysed by the public analyst. Now by virtue of the amendment made to the Act, a recognised consumer organization, whether the purchaser is a member thereof or not, is authorised to take samples subject to Section 11 and

get them analysed by a public analyst on payment of such fees as may be prescribed and receive reports of analysis.

6. A Central Committee for Food Standards under Section 2(i) is constituted to advise the Central and the State Governments on matters arising out of the administration of this Act. Section 10 lays down the powers of food inspectors, Section 11 lays down the procedure for collection of samples and Section 16 lays down the provision of punishment.

In case of adulteration, complaint can be made to the food inspector of the district, state health authorities or the director of health services, Government of India.

On receiving a complaint, it is the duty of the food inspector to investigate, inquire or inspect as may be necessary. If samples are required to be taken, he is to procure them and send for analysis. It is obligatory on the part of public analyst to deliver report to the health authority, who in turn is to send the report to the person who has taken the sample, who in turn can make an application to the magistrate. A court inferior to that of metropolitan magistrate/judicial magistrate cannot try an offence under the PFA Act. [4]

The Act punishes importing into India or manufacturing for sale or storing, selling or distributing any article of food which is adulterated or misbranded or the sale of which is contrary to the provisions of the Prevention of Food Adulteration Act or preventing a food inspector from taking sample or from exercising any other power; or being a manufacturer of food articles, possessing or keeping on premises occupied by him any material which may be employed for the purpose of adulteration. The punishment shall be imprisonment for a term not less than six months which may be extended to six years and fine not less than one hundred rupees. [5]

If the adulterated food which is distributed for sale, when consumed by human beings, is likely to cause death, the person from whose possession the article has been distributed is likely to be punished with life imprisonment. [6] If any person convicted of an offence under this Act repeats the crime afterwards, the court may cancel his license, besides getting the offender's name, address, nature of offence and the penalty imposed circulated through the print media. [7]

7.2 Drugs and Magic Remedies (Objectionable Advertisement) Act, 1954

In recent years there has been a great increase in the number of objectionable advertisements published in newspapers, magazines or otherwise, relating to claimed cures of various diseases. These are mainly related to venereal diseases, sexual stimulants and claimed cures of diseases and conditions peculiar to women. These advertisements tend to cause the ignorant and unwary to resort to self-medication of harmful drugs and appliances. People also rely on quacks who advertise magic treatments. In public interest, to put a stop to such undesirable advertisements, Drugs and Magic Remedies (Objectionable Advertisement) Act, 1954 was passed.

The basic object of the Act is to control advertisements of drugs and to prohibit advertisements of remedies for diseases for which no cure is normally possible. Also its aim is to prohibit advertisement of remedies which are supposed to be magical cures.

7.2.1 Important Provisions

1. As per the Act, 'advertisement' includes any notice, circular, label or wrapper. Even an announcement made orally by any means of producing or transmitting light, sound or smoke comes under its ambit. [8]
2. 'Drugs' include internal or external medicines, any substances or article other than food, which influences function of a human body. [9]
3. 'Magic remedy' is defined to include talisman, *mantra*, *kavacha* or any charm supposed to possess miraculous power to cure. [10]
4. The Act lists 54 diseases for which no cure can be

advertised. Among these are leucoderma, obesity, impotence, insanity, small-pox, sterility, cancer etc.

5. The Act prohibits a person from taking part in advertising a drug for cure of menstrual disorder, abortions, prevention of conception and diseases specified in the Second Schedule. [11] Taking part in advertisement for magic remedies for the specified diseases is also prohibited. [12]
6. There is certain exception too. The provisions of the Act do not apply to sign boards/notices displayed by registered medical practitioners on their premises or any treatise dealing with subject mentioned in Section 3. Advertisements published by the government or published with the previous sanction of the government are also exceptions.

A complaint can be filed for violation of provisions of the Act with a first class magistrate. Offence is cognizable and any Court within whose jurisdiction a newspaper or magazine carrying the advertisement has been sold or circulated has the jurisdiction to try the case. Offence in such cases is deemed to have been committed locally and the cause of action is local. [13]

7.3 Essential Commodities Act, 1955

It is the responsibility of any Government to ensure equitable supply of essential commodities to people at reasonable prices. Need for such control is necessary in case of inadequate supply and lack of competition. India started facing severe shortage of many commodities particularly before and during the II World War. Government of India, therefore, made certain rules to control production, supply and distribution of certain items under Defence of India Act, 1939. This provision continued up to 1946 when Essential Supplies (Temporary Powers) Act, 1946 was passed. This Act continued up to 26.1.1995. Since shortage continued, it was felt that a permanent measure for control of essential commodities was necessary. Hence, the Constitution was amended in 1954 by adding Entry No. 33 to List III of the

7th Schedule of the Constitution. After this, Essential Commodities Act, 1955 was passed which came into force on 1.4.1955. The Act has been amended from time to time. Under the Act, Government has the power to control production, supply and distribution of and trade and commerce in certain commodities. Essential commodities (Special Provisions) Act, 1981 was passed with provisions for Special Court to try offences.

The Act is designed to ensure that essential commodities are made available to common man at reasonable prices and distribution of the essential commodities is equitable.

7.3.1 Important Provisions

1. Essential Commodity as per Section 2(a) of the Act, means any of the following classes of commodities:

- Cattle fodder including oil cakes and other concentrates.
- Coal including coke and other derivatives.
- Groundnut, groundnut oil, oil cake thereof.
- Cotton and woollen textiles.
- Drugs (as defined in Drugs and Cosmetics Act).
- Foodstuffs, including edible oilseeds and oil.
- Iron and steel, including manufactured products of iron and steel.
- Paper including newsprint, paper-board, straw-board.
- Petroleum and petroleum products.
- Raw cotton whether ginned or un-ginned and cotton-seeds.
- Raw jute.
- Any other class of commodity which the Central Government may, by notified order, declare to be an essential commodity.

2. The powers of Government under ECA are:

- Power to issue order for regulating or prohibiting production, supply and distribution of essential commodities. [14]
- Power to fix prices for sale to Government. [15]
- Power to fix prices for sale to control rise in prices and prevent hoarding. [16]

- Fixing procurement price for food grains and edible oils. [17]
- Fixing prices of sugar to be paid to the producer. [18]
- Power to appoint controller. [19]

3. The Act has stringent provisions for punishments. Government authorities have also been given power to confiscate offending goods. [20]
4. Offence under ECA is a cognizable offence. [21]
5. The Act provides for punishment to any person contravening any order made under Section 3. [22]
6. The Act provides penalties for failure to keep records or supply information, the fine is up to ₹ 10,000 and imprisonment up to one year or both. [23]

7.4 Drugs (Control) Act, 1950

The Drugs (Control) Act, 1950 seeks to ensure easy availability of essential drugs and medicines at reasonable prices to consumers by controlling sale, supply and distribution of drugs. The Act safeguards interest of consumers by making it compulsory to give a cash memo if amount of purchase is not less than ₹ 5. [24] But in practice, often dealer would himself discourage the buyer from insisting upon cash memo saying he will have to pay additional sales tax which he could well save. By doing so, the buyer forfeits his right to protect his interest in case drug sold to him is sub-standard or spurious.

7.5 Indian Medical Council Act, 1956

The liability of a doctor for ill-treating a consumer (patient) whether civil or criminal, can arise under various laws. For safety of patients, Indian Medical Council Act, 1956 was passed which inter alia contains a code of medical ethics for all registered medical practitioners. Under this Act, Indian Medical Council and State Medical Councils are established. Thus, they are statutory and also autonomous bodies. Both are assigned and entrusted with high standards of academic, professional and ethical responsibilities.

Indian Medical Council Act, 1956 is concerned with post-graduate medical education in India, recognition of reciprocal standards criteria for admission to foreign and Indian medical institutions and establishment of uniform standards for medical education in Indian universities.

Indian Medical Council Act provides that a register of medical practitioners shall be maintained by Indian Medical Council. If a State Medical Council removes the name of a medical practitioner from its register, Indian Medical Council would also delete the name. It does not, however, entertain complaints of professional misconducts. This part is done by the State Medical Councils. Indian Medical Council and the State Medical Councils have formulated and published a code of ethics for all medical practitioners. This code of ethics generally prohibits solicitation of patients, advertisements or publicity by doctor of their professional skills, affiliations, appointments, honours received by them etc. Remuneration or fees charged by a doctor must be related to the services rendered to a patient and must be clearly told to the patient at the time of rendering the treatment.

7.5.1 Important Provisions: Under Indian Medical Council Act, the important duties imposed on medical practitioners with a view to governing the safety of consumers (patients) are:

1. Duty to exercise a reasonable degree of skill and knowledge as a medical practitioner.
2. Duty to attend to the case as long as it requires attention and to withdraw only after giving reasonable notice.
3. Duty to give proper and suitable medicines.
4. Duty to give proper and complete direction to the patients and/or their attendants regarding the use of medicine and diet.
5. Special duty towards treatment of children and incapacitated adults.
6. Duty to inform particulars of risks to state health

authorities.

7. Duty with regard to poisons or poisonous medicines.
8. Duty to give information of communicable diseases, births, deaths etc. to the public health authorities.
9. Duty to take proper operative and post-operative care in case of surgical operations.
10. Duty to advise for consultation with a specialist when the case is obscure or serious.
11. Duty to keep professional secrecy.

In the prescribed rules of conduct published by Medical Council of India and several State Councils, examples of acts which constitute infamous conduct of medical professions relating to health and safety of patients are:

1. Adultery.
2. Improper conduct or association with a patient or members of patient's family.
3. Withholding from health authorities, information of notifiable disease.
4. Performing, or enabling unqualified person to perform an abortion or any illegal operation.
5. Contravening provisions of Drugs Act.
6. Selling scheduled poison to public under cover of qualification of a doctor, except to patients in proper case.
7. Covering, i.e. assisting someone who has no medical qualification to attend, treat or perform an operation on some person in respect of matters requiring professional discretion or skill.

Every State Medical Council has a disciplinary committee to hear from anyone regarding misconduct by a medical practitioner. Apart from it, the Medical Council may itself initiate an inquiry against a doctor for the misconduct. The name of the erring doctor may be struck off the medical register, but there is no provision for grant of compensation to the patient.

Supreme Court in Parmanand Latera vs. Union of India [25] has directed all doctors and government hospitals to extend medical aid to the injured patient immediately without waiting for or insisting on completion of admission procedures, filling in of forms and similar technicalities. The decision is a landmark decision from the point of view of the code of ethics adopted by Medical Council of India.

7.6 Standard of Weights and Measures Act, 1976

Standard of Weights and Measures Act, 1976 was passed to establish standards of weights and measures, to regulate inter-state trade and commerce in weights, measures and other goods which are sold or distributed by weight, measure, number and to provide for matters connected therewith or incidental thereto.

The Act can be termed as a three-in-one Act as it is designed to:

- Standardize weights and measures,
- Control manufacture and sale of weights and measures to ensure accuracy, and
- Control over packaging commodities.

The Act specifies that metric system will be used for weights and measures for any unit. [26] The Act gives specifications of base units, i.e., meter (for length), kilogram (for mass), second (for time), ampere (for electric current), Kelvin (for thermodynamic temperature), Candela (for luminous intensity) and Mole (for amount of substance). The Act provides that derived, supplementary or other units will be prescribed by the Central Government. [27]

Use of non-standard weights or measures and non-standard number is prohibited. [28] Manufacture of non-standard weights and measures is also prohibited. [29] Non-standard weights and measures can be manufactured or inscribed only with permission of the Central Government for scientific investigation or exports. Use of such non-standard units in any notification, rule, contract, deed or instrument is prohibited. [30]

The Act provides for constitution of Department of Legal

Metrology. [31] The Act provides for power of inspection of premises where there is reason to believe that any offence punishable under the Act has been committed or is likely to be committed. The Act provides for seizure of weights, measures and other goods as evidence. [32] Every false or unverified weights or measures and false packages can be forfeited by the Central Government. [33]

Sections 50 to 67 of the Act provide penalty for offence under the Act. In some cases, penalty includes imprisonment as well as fine.

7.7 Bureau of Indian Standards Act, 1986

One of the important features of the right to safety is to be assured that goods purchased will be reasonably safe for use. Increasing affluence and range of complex nature of products has led to a situation in which unsafe products flow into market. Thus, there is a need for certain standards to be prescribed for composition, contents, design etc. leading to standardization, marking and quality certification of goods. For this purpose, the Bureau of Indian Standards Act, 1986 was enacted by the Parliament. The Indian Standards Institution (ISI) which has been performing the function for long, was made a statutory body and was renamed the Bureau of Indian Standards (BIS) with the enactment of the Bureau of Indian Standards Act, 1986.

Basically, standardization is a voluntary act. It is up to the producer to decide whether to opt for conforming with the prescribed standards and obtain certification marks or not.

This law has been framed for development of activities relating to standardization, marking and quality certification of goods which will ensure safety and quality of products. The Bureau is a statutory body comprising members nominated by the Government of India.

7.7.1 Important Provisions: It is provided under the Act that if the Central Government, in consultation with the BIS, thinks it necessary in public interest, it may:

- Notify any article or process to conform to Indian Standards.
- Direct the use of standard mark under licence as compulsory on such article/process. [34]

Thus, voluntary character of standardization has exceptions where products are of mass consumption or where safety from health-hazard is concerned. In such cases, standards have been made statutory and certification compulsory. These products are:

1. Food additives.
2. Milk products like milk powder.
3. Cement—ordinary and portland.
4. LPG cylinders.
5. Steel-tubes for water wells.
6. Vanaspati, vanaspati containers.
7. Pressure stoves, burners.
8. Dry cell batteries, electrical lamps, electrical appliances like irons, immersion water heaters, radiators, stoves, switches for domestic and similar purpose.

The important powers given to the Bureau are: [35]

1. To specify a standard and a mark to be called the Bureau of Indian Standards Certification Mark.
2. To grant, renew, suspend or cancel a licence.
3. To inspect articles and to take samples for examining whether it conforms to the standards.
4. To establish and recognize laboratories for the purpose of standardization and control of quality.
5. To establish, publish and promote the Indian Standards for articles or processes.
6. To search and seize in case of reasonable doubt about misuse of a standard mark.
7. Power to impose penalty on erring party and also power of forfeiture of property in case of misuse of standard marks by such party.

7.8 Railways Act, 1989

The main object of this Act is to consolidate the laws

relating to the Railways which undertake safe carriage and transportation of persons, animals and goods. Towards fulfilling this object, the Act has provided for construction of new railway lines and maintenance of the existing railway lines, property and services under ideal conditions.

7.8.1 Important Provisions

1. Railway authorities have power to refuse carrying a person suffering from an infectious disease for the safety of the rest of the passengers. In case permission is given, the infected person has to be taken separately. [36]
2. For the safety of female passengers travelling alone, an exclusive compartment or adequate number of berths, according to requirement, may be provided in every train. [37]
3. Carriage of dangerous or offensive goods is prohibited under the Act. [38] If under certain special conditions one carries such goods, it is obligatory for him to give notice to the authorities of the dangerous or offensive nature of the goods. Carrying of infectious animals is also prohibited. [39]
4. The Act provides for appointment of a chief commissioner of railway safety and other commissioners to:

- Inspect all new lines before opening.
- Make periodical inspection of any railway stock/stores.
- Conduct inquiries in cases of train accidents.
- Report to the Government regarding any condition which may endanger safety of the public.
- Make necessary recommendations to the Government in the interest of the railways.

5. In cases of accident causing loss of human life or serious injury and in cases of collision between trains, derailment of train etc., the railway servant in charge of the section is duty bound to give information about the accident to district magistrate and the superintendent of police. Thereafter an inquiry is to be held by the authority concerned. [40]

6. When an accident occurs, the railway administration is liable to pay compensation to the extent of loss or injury caused. It is immaterial whether there was any negligence on the part of the railway administration or not. [41]

7.9 Air (Prevention and Control of Pollution) Act, 1981

This Act was brought on the statute book for the following reasons:

- To provide for the prevention, control and abatement of air pollution.
- To establish Boards for carrying out the purposes given in.
- To confer on and assign to such Boards, powers and functions relating thereto.

Section 2 of the Act defines certain terms. Air pollution means any solid, liquid or gaseous substance including noise present in the atmosphere in such concentration as may be or tend to be injurious to human beings or other living creations or plants or property or environment. Air pollution means the presence in the atmosphere of any air pollutant. Emission means any solid or liquid or gaseous substance carrying out of my chimney, duct or fuel or any other outlet. Occupier, in relation to any factory or premises and includes in relation to any substance, the person in possession of the substance. Section 3 of the Act authorises the Central Pollution Central Board constituted under the Water (Prevention and Control of Pollution) Act, 1974 to exercise the powers and perform the functions of the Central Pollution Control Board for prevention and control of air pollution under this Act.

Similarly, if State Pollution Control Board has been constituted under the Act, it shall be deemed to be the State Board for the prevention of air pollution under this Act. Otherwise, the State Government shall constitute a State Board for prevention and control of air pollution. In the case of Union Territories, the central Board shall exercise the powers and perform the functions of a State Board.

Functions of the Central Board: Section 16 enumerates the

function of the Central Board. These are:

1. To advise the Central Government on any matter concerning improvement of the quality of air and prevention, control or abatement of air pollution.
2. To plan and cause to be executed a nation-wide programme for the prevention, control or abatement of air pollution.
3. To co-ordinate the activities of the State Board and resolve disputes among them.
4. To provide technical assistance and guidance to the State Board, carry out and sponsor investigations and research relating to problems of air pollution and prevention, control or abatement of air pollution.
5. To perform such of the functions of any State Boards as may be specified in an order made under Section 18(2).
6. To plan and organise the trainings of persons engaged or to be engaged in programmes for the prevention, control and abatement of air pollution on such terms and conditions as the Central Board may specify.
7. To organise, through mass media, a comprehensive programme regarding the prevention, control or abatement of air pollution.
8. To collect, compile and publish technical and statistical data relating to air pollution and the measures devised for its effective prevention, control and abatement and to prepare manuals, codes or guidelines relating to prevention, control or abatement of air pollution.
9. To lay down standards for the quality of air.
10. To collect and disseminate information in respect of matters relating to air pollution.
11. To perform such other functions as may be prescribed.

Section 17 enumerates the functions of a State Board. These are:

- To plan a comprehensive programme for the prevention, control, abatement of air pollution and to secure the execution thereof.

- To advise the State Government on any matter concerning the prevention, control or abatement of air pollution.
- To collect and disseminate information relating to air pollution.
- To collaborate with Central Board in organising the training of the persons engaged or to be engaged in programmes relating to prevention control or abatement of air pollution and to organise mass education programme relating thereto.
- To inspect, at all reasonable times, any control equipment, industrial plant or manufacturing process and to give by order, such directions to such persons as it may consider necessary to take steps for prevention, control or abatement of air pollution.
- To inspect air pollution control areas at such intervals as it may think necessary, assess the quality of air therein and take steps for prevention, control or abatement of pollution in such areas.
- To advise the State Government with respect to the suitability of any premises or location for carrying on any industry which is likely to cause air pollution.
- To perform such other functions as may be prescribed or as may from time to time, be entrusted to it by the Central or State Government.
- To do such other things and to perform such other acts, as it may think necessary, for the proper discharge of its functions and generally for the purpose of carrying into effect the purposes of this Act.

Section 19 empowers the State Government to declare any or areas within the State as air pollution control areas for the purposes of this Act.

Section 20 provides that with a view to ensure that standards for emission of air pollution from automobiles, laid down by the State Board, are complied with, the State Government shall give such instructions as may be deemed necessary to the concerned authority in charge of registration of motor vehicles under the Motor Vehicles Act, 1988.

Section 21 provides that no person shall, without the consent of the State Board, establish or operate any industrial plant in any air pollution control area.

Section 22 provides that no person operating any industrial plant, in any air pollution control area, shall discharge or cause or permit to be discharged the emission of any air pollution in excess of the standards laid down by the State Board.

Section 23 A empowers the Board to make application to court for restraining persons from causing air pollution.

Section 23 provides as follows: where in any area, the emission of any air pollution into the atmosphere, in excess of the standards laid down by the State Board, occurs or is apprehended to occur due to accident or other unforeseen act or event, the person in charge of the premises from where such emission occurs or the premises from where such emission occurs or is apprehended to occur shall, forthwith intimate the fact of such occurrence or the apprehension of such occurrence to the State Board. On receipt of information, the State Board shall as early as practicable, cause such remedial measures to be taken as are necessary to mitigate the emission of such air pollutants. Expenses, if any, incurred by the State Board, authority or agency with interest (at such reasonable rate, as the State Government, by order, fix) from the date when a demand for the expenses is made until it is paid, may be recovered from the person concerned, as arrears of land revenue or of public demand.

Section 26 empowers a State Board to take for the purpose of analysis, samples of air or emission from any chimney, flue or duct or any other outlet.

Section 27 provides the reports of the result of analysis of samples taken under Section 26.

Section 31A provides that a Board may issue any directions in writing to any person, officer authority. This power includes authority to direct: (a) the closure, prohibition or regulation of any industry, operation or process, or (b) the stoppage or regulation of supply of electricity, water or any other service.

Section 37 provides for imprisonment and fine in case of failure to comply with certain provisions.

Section 38 makes certain acts to be punishable with imprisonment with fine or with both.

Section 39 provides penalty for contravention of certain provisions of this Act.

Section 40 makes provisions as regards offence by companies.

Section 41 is concerned with offence by government departments.

7.10 Hire Purchase Act, 1972

A hire purchase agreement is a hybrid transaction which, starting as a contract of hire may culminate in on out and out sale. It is an agreement for hire with an option to the hirer to purchase the goods.

Sections 3, 4 and 22 stipulate that the hirer understands the true nature and implications of the agreement in real sense. Furthermore, he has a right to obtain, from time to time, the current state of his account in relation to the agreement.

Section 6 implies that every hire purchase agreement does contain certain conditions and warranties in favour of the hirer. It makes provision for two implied warranties and reads as follows:

"Notwithstanding anything contained in any contract, in every hire purchase agreement there shall be an implied warranty: (i) that the hirer shall have and enjoy quiet possession of the goods, and (ii) that the goods shall be free from any charge or encumbrance in favour of any third party at the time when the property is to pass".

Section 9 deals with purchase at any time with rebate.

Section 10 deals with termination of agreement at any time.

Sections 15 and 16 provide obligation of hirer in respect of use of goods and to give information as to whereabout of goods respectively.

Section 17 ensures the rights of hirer in case of seizure of goods by the owner.

Section 20 puts a restriction on owner's right to recovery, possession of goods otherwise than by proceeding through court of law after a specified proportion of hire purchase price has been paid or tendered. From these provisions, it is obvious that this Act has extended special protection to a hirer (i.e. the consumer).

7.11 Code of Criminal Procedure, 1973

This Code protects the consumer to some degree or so.

Section 153 entitles any officer in charge of a police station to enter, without warrant, any place within the limits of such station for the purpose of inspecting or searching for any weights or measures or instruments for weighing, used or kept therein. Further, whenever there is a reason to believe that in such a place, weights, measures or instruments for weighing are false, he may seize the same and send information of such seizure to a magistrate having the jurisdiction.

Section 406 empowers the Supreme Court to direct transfer of cases and appeals from High Court to another criminal court of equal or superior jurisdiction subordinate to another High Court. The court is to be satisfied that the order of transfer is necessary for the ends of justice i.e. to protect the interest of the litigants.

Section 407 empowers a High Court to transfer: (i) cases and appeals if it is made to appear to it that a fair and impartial enquiry or trial cannot be had in any criminal court subordinate there to, or (ii) that some question of law of unusual difficulty is likely to arise, or (iii) that an order under this section is required by any provision of the Code or will tend to the general convenience of the parties or witnesses or is expedient for the ends of justice. Then the court may order: (i) that any offence be inquired into or tried by any court not qualified under Sections 177 to 185 (both inclusive) but in other respects competent to inquire into or try such offence,

(ii) that any particular case or appeal, or class of cases or appeals, be transferred from a criminal court subordinate to its authority to any other such criminal court of equal or superior jurisdiction, (iii) that any particular case be committed for trial to a court of session, or (iv) that any particular case or appeal be transferred to and tried before itself.

Section 408 empowers the session judge to transfer cases and appeals. It provides that whenever it is made to appear to a session judge that an order under the sub-section is expedient for the ends of justice, he may order that any particular case be transferred from one criminal court to another criminal court in session division. The session judge may act either on the report of the lower court, or on the application of a party interested in, or on his own initiative.

Section 409 provides for withdrawal of cases and appeals by a session judge. A session judge may withdraw any case or appeal from or recall any case or appeal which he had made over to, any assistant session judge or chief judicial magistrate subordinate to him. Section 410 empowers the chief judicial magistrate to withdraw cases from any magistrate subordinate to him and may enquire himself or refer it for enquiry to any other magistrate subordinate to him.

Section 482 saves the inherent powers of the High Court from all the provisions of code, to make such orders as may be necessary to give effect to any order under this Code, or to prevent abuse of the process of any court or otherwise to secure the ends of justice.

7.12 Environment (Protection) Act, 1986

The objective of the Act is to provide for the protection and improvement of environment and for matters connected therewith. The Act came into force with effect from 19th November, 1986. This Act is in addition to the two allied Acts viz. Water and Air (Prevention and Control of Pollution). The genesis of the Act is in Article 48A and 51A of the Indian Constitution.

This Act is the most comprehensive piece of legislation relating to environment as it: (i) contains a very wide definition of environment, (ii) empowers the Central Government to take strict actions, and (iii) provides for penalties for various offences.

Section 3 empowers the Central Government to take all such measures as it deems necessary or expedient for the specific purposes which are:

- Protecting and improving the quality of the environment, and
- Preventing, controlling and abating environment pollution.

This Act empowers the Central Government to initiate an authority and delegate the following powers to it.

1. Such of its power and functions under this Act, as may be mentioned in the order.
2. Power of Central Government to issue directions.
3. The power to take fourteen measures as enumerated in Section 3.

Section 11 empowers the Central Government or any officer empowered by it on this behalf, to take for the purpose of analysis, samples of air, water, soil or other substance from any factory, premises or other place in such manner as may be prescribed.

Section 12 empowers the Central Government to: (a) establish one or more laboratories, (b) recognise one or more laboratories or institutions as environmental laboratories to carry out the functions entrusted to an environmental laboratory under this Act.

Section 16 provides for penalty in case of offences by companies. Section 17 provides for penalty when an offence under this Act is committed by any department of Government.

In March 1992, Rule 14 was introduced in Environment (Protection) Rules, 1992. Every person carrying on an industry, operation or process requiring consent under Section 25 of the Water (Protection and Control of Pollution) Act, 1981, or both or authorisation under the Hazardous Wastes (Management and Handlings) Rules, 1989 issued under the

Environment Audit Report for the financial year ending 31st March in Form V to the concerned State Pollution Control Board on or before 15th day of May every year, beginning 1993.

7.13 Export Quality (Control and Inspection) Act, 1963

Under this Act, a certificate of export worthiness is issued to commodity by the export inspection agency. The Central Government is empowered to notify the commodities, which are prohibited from export unless they are accompanied by certificates issued by export inspection agencies.

When the decision to subject a product to quality control, or inspection or both is made, a notification is issued under Section 6. This notification has to specify the type of quality control and it has to establish, adopt or recognise one or more standard specifications for a notified commodity.

Under Section 17 of the Act, rules are framed which lets a standard for the export of products which are subject to quality control under the Act.

7.14 Protection of Civil Rights Act, 1955

This legislation was enacted with the objective of protecting the civil rights of *Harijans* by prohibiting enforcement of any religious disability at any religious place like a temple and social and in public places and restaurants. Thus, they are equally entitled to the enjoyment of and use of wells, water taps, public conveyance, education institutions, hotels, hospitals, parks, shops etc. Anyone denying these rights to *Harijans* will attract penalty under the Act.

Section 4 Provides that an enforcement of any disability against any person with regard to the following would attract penalty under the Act: (i) access to any shop, public restaurant, hotel or place of public entertainment, or (ii) the use of any utensils and other articles kept in any public restaurant, hotel, *dharamshala*, *sarai*, or *musafirkhana* for the use of general public or of any section thereof, or (iii) the practice of any profession or the carrying on of any occupation, trade or business or employment in any job, or (iv) the use of, or access to, any river, stream, spring, well, tank, cistern water tap or other watering place or any bathing ghat, burial or cremation ground, any sanitary convenience, any road, or passage or any other place of public resort which other members of the public, or persons professing the same religion or belonging to the same religious denomination or any section thereof, as such have a right to use or have access to, or (v) the use of, or access to, any place used for a charitable or public purpose maintained wholly or partly out of state funds or dedicated to the use of the general public, or any section thereof, or (vi) the enjoyment of any benefit under a charitable trust created for the benefit of the general public or of any section thereof, or (vii) the use of, or access to any public conveyance, or (viii) the construction, acquisition or occupation of any residential premises in any locality, whatsoever, or (ix) the use of any *dharamshala*, *sarai* or *musafirkhana*, which is open to the general public or to any section thereof, or (x) the observance of any social or religious custom, usage or ceremony or taking part in, or taking out, any religious, social or cultural procession, or (xi) the use of jewellery and finery.

Section 6 provides that any refusal to sell any goods or any refusal to render any service to any person, at the time and place and on the same terms and conditions at or on which such goods are sold or services rendered to other persons (i.e. non-*Harijans*) in the ordinary course of business, on the ground of untouchability, will attract penalty.

7.15 Prevention of Black Marketing and Maintenance of Supplies of Essential Commodities Act, 1980

The Essential Commodities Act, 1955 could not deal effectively with certain malpractices indulged in and try unscrupulous elements like black marketers, hoarders, profiteers. Hence, it was felt necessary to supplement the Act with a legislation i.e., the Prevention of Black Marketing and Maintenance of Supplies of Essential Commodities Act, 1980.

Section 3 provides for ordering a person to be detained with the object of preventing him from acting in a manner which might be prejudicial to maintenance of supplies of commodities considered essential to the community.

The power to make detention orders have been conferred on the Union as well as State Government, district magistrate and commissioners of police. The detention orders are to be executed at any place within India in the manner prescribed for execution of warrants of arrest under the Criminal Procedure Code, 1973. Section 5 empowers the appropriate government to regulate the place and conditions of detention. Section 8 provides for disclosure of grounds of detention in order to the person affected there by. Sections 9 and 10 provide that the appropriate government shall place before the advisory board, the grounds of the detention order and any representation, if so made, by the detained person. Section 11 sets out the procedure of the advisory board. The board is required to submit its report to the appropriate government, specifying therein, its opinion the action to be taken on the report of the board about the detention. Accordingly, the appropriate government may confirm the order of detention or the order be revoked and the detained person to be forthwith released.

7.16 Trade and Merchandise Marks Act, 1958

This Act provides a comprehensive law in tune with consumer protection relating to registration and better protection of trade marks in the country.

This Act provides for the registration of trade marks. Once a person gets a trade mark registered, he acquires certain rights under the Act. If his trade mark is infringed, he has certain remedies. A trade mark is registered by the competent authority only if it is not likely to injure the public interest.

However, the registration of a trade mark could be attacked on the ground of invalidity of registration or the defendant could establish honest concurrent user, or acquiescence on the part of the registered, then the plaintiff has to establish that the defendant's mark is deceptively similar, i.e., the similarity is such as to be likely to deceive or cause confusion in the minds of the public. This may not be very easy for the plaintiff to establish. In the case of unregistered marks and marks which are not registrable, no protection under the Act is provided to the owner thereof. However, an action for passing off may be maintained by the plaintiff if he proves sufficient use of the mark so as to create a valuable goodwill of the business connected with the goods bearing the mark.

One of the functions of the trade mark is to give an indication of the source of goods. Thus, the public in general will associate a particular trade mark on certain goods with a particular manufacture. The law provides for the prevention of the use of fraudulent marks on merchandise in the public interest.

7.16.1 Deceptive Similarity: A mark shall be deemed to be deceptively similar to another mark if it so nearly resembles that other mark as to be likely to deceive or cause confusion.

Section 96 lays down an implied warranty on sale of marked goods. It provides that on the sale or in the contract for sale of any goods to which a trade mark or mark or trade description has been applied, there shall be deemed to be an implied warranty on the part of the seller that the mark is a genuine mark and not falsely applied, or that the trade description is not a false trade description unless the contrary is expressed in some writing signed by or on behalf of the seller and delivered at the time of contract to sell and accepted by the buyer.

Section 76 provides that a person shall be deemed to apply a trade mark or mark or trade description to goods who: (a) applies to the goods themselves, or (b) applies it to any package in or with which the goods are sold, or exposed for sale, or had in possession for sale or for any purpose of trade or manufacture, or (c) places, encloses or annexes any goods which are sold, or exposed for sale or it had in possession for sale or for any purpose of trade description has been applied, or (d) uses a trade mark, or mark or trade description in any manner reasonably likely to lead to the belief that the goods in connection with which it is used are designed and described by that trade mark or mark or trade description, or (e) in relation to the goods, uses a trade mark or trade description, in any sign, advertisement, invoice, catalogue, business letters, business papers, price list, or other commercial document and goods are delivered to a person in pursuance of a request or order made by reference to the trade mark or trade description as so used.

Further, a trade mark or mark or trade description shall be deemed to be applied to goods whether it is woven in or impressed on, or otherwise worked into, or annexed or affixed to, the goods or to any package or other thing.

Section 77 provides that:

1. When is a person deemed to falsify a trade mark? A person shall be deemed to falsify a trade mark who, either: (a) without the assent of the proprietor of the trade mark applies that trade or a deceptively similar mark, or (b) falsify any genuine trade mark, whether by alteration, addition effacement or otherwise.
2. When a person is deemed to falsely apply to goods a trade mark? A person shall be deemed to falsely apply to goods a trade mark who, without the assent of the proprietor of the trade mark:

- Applies such trade mark or a deceptively similar mark, to goods or any package containing goods.
- Uses any package bearing a mark which is identical with deceptively similar to the trade mark of such proprietor, for the purpose of packing, filling, or wrapping therein any goods other than the genuine goods of the proprietor of the trade mark.

7.16.2 Penalty: Under the Act, penalties are provided for the following:

1. For applying false trade marks, trade description etc. (Section 78).

2. For selling goods to which false trade marks is applied.
3. For removing piece goods (Section 80).
4. For falsely representing a trade mark as registered (Section 81).
5. For falsely representing a trade mark as registered (Section 81).
6. For offences by companies (Section 88).

7.17 Specific Relief Act, 1963

Under this Act, enactment underlines the various reliefs to be granted by the Civil Court. Section 4 clearly postulates that specific relief can be granted only for the purpose of enforcing individual civil right and not for the mere purpose of enforcing a penal law.

Section 5 lays down that a person entitled to the possession of specific immovable property may recover it in the manner provided by the Code of Civil Procedure, 1908. Immovable property can be recovered under Order 21 and Rules 35 and 36 in execution of a decree providing for the delivery of the property. Such a decree can be passed in an ejectment suit. A plaintiff suing for ejection can succeed only on the basis of his own title.

Furthermore, Section 6 of the Act provides that if any person is dispossessed without his consent of immovable property otherwise than in due course of law, he or any person claiming through him may by suit, recover possession thereof, notwithstanding any other titles that may be set up in such suit. However, such suit shall be brought within six months from the date of dispossession. It is a summary and speedy remedy since a right of possession receives protection from the statute. The question of ownership or title to the property is irrelevant in a suit of this kind. Even if the defendant has a superior title, he must first put the plaintiff back in possession and later file his own suit on the basis of title.

Recovery of specific movable property is provided under Section 7.

Specific performance of any contract may in the discretion of the Court, be enforced under Section 10 when there exists no standard for ascertaining the actual damage caused by the non-performance of the act agreed to be done or when the act agreed to be done is such that the compensation in money for its non-performance would not afford adequate relief.

Specific performance of part of a contract has been enshrined in Section 12 of the Act as under:

1. Except as otherwise herein after provided in this section, the court shall not direct the specific performance of a part of a contract.
2. Where a party to a contract is unable to perform the whole of it, but the part which must be left unperformed bears only a small proportion to the whole in value and admits of compensation in money, the court may at the suit of either party, direct the specific performance of so much of contract as can be performed, and award compensation in money for the deficiency.
3. Where a party to a contract is unable to perform the whole of this part, and the part which must be left unperformed either:

- forms a considerable part of the whole through admitting of compensation in money, or
- does not admit of compensation in money, he is not entitled to obtain a decree for specific performance; but the court may at the suit of the other party, direct the party in default to perform specifically so much of his part of the contract as he can perform, if the other party:

➢ in a case falling under clause (a), pays or has paid the agreed consideration for the whole of the contract reduced by the consideration for the part which must be left unperformed and in a case falling under clause (b) pays or has paid, the consideration for the whole of the contract without any abatement; and

➢ in either case, relinquishes all claims to the performance of the remaining part of contract and all right to compensation either for the deficiency or for the loss or damage sustained by him through the default of the defendant.

4. When a part of a contract which, taken by itself, can and ought to be specifically performed, stands on a separate and independent footing from another part of the same contract which cannot or ought to be specifically performed, the Court may direct specific performance of the former part.

Explanation-For the purpose of this section, a party to a contract shall be deemed to be unable to perform for the whole or his part of it if a portion of its subject-matter existing at the date of the contract has ceased to exist at the time of its performance.

Specific performances of contracts which cannot be specifically enforced as enshrined in Section 14 are:

- A contract for the non-performance of which compensation in money is an adequate relief.
- A contract which runs into such minute or numerous details or which is so dependant on the personal qualification or volition of the parties, or otherwise from its nature is such, that the court cannot enforce specific performance in its material terms.
- A contract which in its nature is determinable.
- A contract the performance of which involves the performance of a continuous duty which the court cannot supervise.

Save as provided by the Arbitration Act, 1940 (10 of 1940), no contract to refer present or future differences to arbitration shall be specifically enforced; but if any person who has made such a contract (other than arbitration agreement to which the provisions of the said Act apply) and has refused to perform it, sues in respect of any subject which he has contracted to refer, the existence of such contract shall bar the suit.

Notwithstanding anything contained in clause (a) or clause

(d) of sub-section (I), the Court may enforce specific performance in the following cases:

- Where the suit is for the enforcement of a contract:
  - to execute a mortgage or furnish any other security for securing the repayment of any loan which the borrower is not willing to repay at once.

Provided that where only a part of the loan has been advanced, the lender is willing to advance the remaining part of the loan in terms of the contract, or

  - to take up and pay for any debentures of a company.
- Where the suit is for:
  - the execution of a formal deed of partnership. The parties having commenced to carry on the business of the partner in a firm.
- Where the suit is for the enforcement of contract for the construction of any building or execution of any other work on land:

Provided that the following conditions are fulfilled, namely:

  - the building or other work is described in the contract in terms sufficiently precise to enable the court to determine the exact nature of the building or work,
  - the plaintiff has substantial interest in the performance of the contract and the interest is of such a nature that the compensate in money for non-performance of contract is not an adequate relief, and
  - the defendant has, in pursuance of the contract obtained possession of the whole or any part of the land on which the building is to be constructed or other work is to be executed.

The Court has been vested with powers under Section 22 to grant relief in a case of a specific performance of a contract for transfer of immovable property for possession or partition and separate possession of such property or any other relief including refund of any earnest money or deposit paid in case the relief of specific performance is declined.

Any person entitled to any legal character, or to any rights as to any property if defined, apprehends to be denied the same, may invoke Section 34 to seek a decree of declaration to that effect.

The relief of preventive nature in the form of injunction is available at the discretion of the court under Section 36. In common parlance, it is called 'stay'. The order may be temporary or perpetual. In the former case, it continues till a specified time or till further orders of the court while the latter can only be granted by the decree on merits whereby the defendant is perpetually restrained from infringing on the rights of plaintiff.

In case defendant is to be compelled to do certain acts, then positive directions are issued by the court in the form of mandatory injunctions provided under Section 39. Damages may also be awarded in addition to or as an alternate relief of injunction under Section 40. However, the court cannot grant an injunction in the following cases enshrined under Section 41:

- To restrain any person from prosecuting any judicial proceeding pending at the institution of the suit in which injunction is sought, unless such restrain is necessary to prevent a multiplicity of proceedings.
- To restrain any person from instituting or prosecuting any proceeding in a court not subordinate to that from which the injunction is sought.
- To restrain any person from applying to any legislative body.
- To restrain any person from instituting or prosecuting any proceedings in a criminal matter.
- To prevent the breach of contract the performance of which would not be specifically enforced.
- To prevent on the ground of nuisance, an act of which it is not reasonably clear that it will be a nuisance.
- To prevent a continuing breach in which the plaintiff has acquiesced.
- When equally efficacious relief can certainly be obtained

by any other usual mode of proceeding except in case of trust.

- When the conduct of the plaintiff or his agents has been such as to disentitle him to be of the assistance of the Court.
- When the plaintiff has no personal interest in the matter.

7.18 Monopolies and Restrictive Trade Practices Act, 1969

Monopolies and Restrictive Trade Practices Act (MRTP Act or MRTP), 1969 was passed with the objective of implementing Directive Principles of State Policy as enshrined in the Constitution of India—the underlying idea being that the State shall direct its policy towards securing ownership and control of material resources and their equitable distribution so as to serve the common good. The idea that the operation of the economic system should not result in concentration of wealth and means of production with a few to the detriment of the many had also a role to play. The Act also provides for the control of monopolies and prohibition of monopolistic, restrictive and unfair trade practices for protection of consumer interest.

The Act, amended in 1974, 1980, 1984, 1988 and lastly in 1991 places many restrictions on companies having assets over ₹ 100 crore in respect of new projects, expansion, diversification, mergers and even appointment of directors. In 1988, by an amendment, a new chapter was added by inserting Section 36(A) defining unfair trade practice which in practice protects consumers directly, whereas the other two practices protect consumers indirectly by imposing restriction on the traders.

The functions of MRTP Commission are: [42]

- Relating to restrictive trade practices;
- Relating to unfair trade practices;
- Relating to monopolistic trade practices; and
- Relating to concentration of economic power to the detriment of the consumer.

In any one of the following ways, MRTP Commission can inquire into restrictive/unfair trade practices:

- Upon receiving a complaint from any trade association or from a consumer or a registered consumer association, of which the consumer is a member or not, or [43]
- Upon a reference to it by the Central Government or a State Government, or [44]
- Upon an application made to it by the director general of investigation and registration appointed under MRTP Act, or [45]
- Upon its own knowledge or information. [46]

A monopolistic trade practice is essentially a trade practice which represents abuse of market power in the production or marketing of goods or in providing services by eliminating potential competitors from the market and taking advantage of the control over the market by charging unreasonably high prices, preventing or reducing competition, deteriorating product quality or by adopting unfair or deceptive practices.

In an attempt to maximize profits and market power, traders often attempt to indulge in certain trade practices which tend to obstruct the flow of capital (resources) into the stream of production. It may also bring about manipulation of prices or conditions of delivery or affect the flow of supplies in the market so as to impose unjustified prices. [47] If a trade practice merely regulates and thereby promotes competition, it should not fall within the definition of restrictive practices. These are:

- An agreement expressly authorized by or under law being in force.
- An agreement to which the Government is a party or which has the approval of the Central Government.

7.18.1 Deemed Restrictive Trade Practices: Section 33(1) of the Act gives illustration of some restrictive trade practices. Supreme Court in Voltas Ltd. vs. Union of India [48] has held that these are deemed to be restrictive trade practices and per se bad. MRTP Commission can issue 'cease and desist' order in respect of these practices only if these are against 'public interest'. The deemed restrictive trade practices are as follows:

1. **Restriction on Buying/Selling:** This means restricting person or persons in respect of certain goods to be sold or bought, [49] viz. chemists' association asking its members not to deal in goods of a particular manufacturer. [50]
2. **Tie-in Sales or Full Line Forcing:** This means requiring a person to purchase some other goods compulsorily along with goods he wants to purchase. [51]
3. **Exclusive Dealing Agreement:** Not to deal in goods other than those of the sellers. [52]
4. **Collective Price Fixation and Tendering:** This means a collective agreement to purchase or sell or to tender only at agreed prices and terms only. [53]
5. **Discriminatory Dealings:** This means allowing concessions, discount, benefits, allowances, rebate etc. based on purchase of certain goods from a dealer. [54]
6. **Resale Price Maintenance:** This means not to allow resale below certain price or not to sell above a certain price. [55]
7. **Restrictions on Output or Supply:** This means an agreement to limit, withhold or restrict the output or supply of any goods or allocate any market or areas for disposal of goods. [56]
8. **Restriction on Manufacturing Process:** This means an agreement not to use a particular method, machinery or process in the manufacture of goods. [57]
9. **Boycott from Association:** This means, to exclude from trade association, any person carrying on trade in good faith. [58]
10. **Price Control Arrangement:** This means an agreement to sell goods with a view to eliminating competition or competitors. [59]
11. **Restriction on Buying:** To restrict a class or a number of wholesalers, producers or suppliers from whom goods may

be bought. [60]

12. **Collective Bidding:** This means an agreement as to bids to be offered at auction or agreement not to bid at auction. [61]
13. Agreement declared by Government to be restrictive. [62]
14. Agreement to enforce any of the aforesaid agreements. [63]

7.18.2 Unfair Trade Practices: Unfair trade practices refer to any of the five trade practices mentioned in the Act [64] which are adopted for the purpose of promoting sale, use or supply of any goods or for the provision of any services which causes loss or injury to the consumer. They are:

1. False or misleading representation:

- False representation about standard, quality etc. of goods; [65]
- False representation about quality, grade etc. of services; [66]
- Representing old goods as new goods; and
- False representation about sponsorship or approval of goods or services. [67]

2. Bargain sale, bait and switch selling: Advertising goods for bargain sale without real intention of offering at bargain prices, or offering at bargain prices only for unreasonably limited time is an unfair trade practice. [68]
3. Offering free gifts and promotional contents: Offering gifts or prizes with the intention of or giving an impression that something is being given free or at subsidised rate though really its price is covered partly or fully in the transaction as a whole. [69]
4. Not following product safety standards. [70]
5. Hoarding or destruction of goods. [71]

7.19 Consumer Protection Act, 1986

As pointed out in the earlier paragraphs, there was no exclusive legislation on consumer matters till 1986. In 1986, the Indian Parliament by enacting Consumer Protection Act, (hereinafter referred to as Act), 1986 opened a new era by conferring certain rights on consumers. There is a thrust for rights and justice to consumers in this Act's objectives and the legal framework for the same has been designed with that spirit. Authors responsible for its drafting had taken due care to include all the issues relating to consumer grievances. Indian legislation has all such legal components which any consumer legislation is expected to possess. They are:

- Easy accessibility by allowing a number of persons to lodge a complaint.
- Informal quasi-judicial mechanism.
- Covering more ground relating to consumer matters in the jurisdiction.
- Inclusion of broader spectrum of services.
- Adoption of simple procedures.
- Greater care to eliminate or restrict frivolous claims.
- Power to award different legal reliefs.

In addition to these general perceptions, the Act has certain salient features which provide easy and effective access to justice. They are:

1. No court fee nor stamp duty is payable on complaint, appeal or revision;
2. Complaint can be written in English, Hindi or even in the local languages;
3. No need to serve notice to opposite party before filing complaint;
4. Consumer is empowered to plead his own case before the Forum; and
5. Statutory mandate to dispose of cases within a stipulated time.

Endnotes

1. Bhagwan Das Jagdish Chandra vs. Delhi Administration, AIR, 1975 SC 1309, 1315; J.L. Roy vs. Amrit Lal Roy, 1980 Cr. L.J. 24,28.
2. Karnidan Sarada vs. Emperor, AIR, 1935 Pat. 525.
3. Public Prosecutor vs. Sannidhi Sriranga, AIR, 1949 Mad. 629

and Braham Dass vs. State of H.P., AIR, 1988 SC 1989.

4. Section 20(2), PFA Act, 1954.
5. Ibid., Section 16(1-A).
6. Ibid., Section 16(1-A).
7. Ibid., Section 16(1-D).
8. Drugs and Magic Remedies (Objectionable Advertisements) Act, 1954, Section 2(a).
9. Ibid., Section 2(b).
10. Ibid., Section 2(c).
11. Ibid., Section 3.
12. Ibid., Section 5.
13. Ibid., Section 9-A.
14. Essential Commodities Act, 1955, Section 3(1).
15. Ibid., Section 3.
16. Ibid., Section 3(A).
17. Ibid., Section 3(B).
18. Ibid., Section 3(C).
19. Ibid., Section 3(4).
20. Ibid., Section 6A.
21. Ibid., Section 10 A.
22. Ibid., Section 7(1)(a)(i).
23. Ibid., Section 7(1)(a)(ii).
24. The Drugs (Control) Act, 1950, Section 9.
25. AIR, 1989, SC 2039.
26. The Standards of Weights and Measures Act, 1976, Section 4 (1).
27. Ibid., Section 12.
28. Ibid., Section 21.
29. Ibid., Section 22.
30. Ibid., Section 80.
31. Ibid., Section 28.
32. Ibid., Section 29.
33. Ibid., Section 30.
34. Bureau of Indian Standards Act, 1986, Section 14.
35. Ibid., Section 10.
36. The Railways Act, 1989, Section 56.
37. Ibid., Section 58.
38. Ibid., Section 67.
39. Ibid., Section 68.
40. Ibid., Sections 113, 114 and 115.

41. Ibid., Section 124.
42. Monopolies & Restrictive Trade Practices Act, 1969, Sections 12, 12-A, 12-B, 12-C, 13-A, 13-B.
43. Ibid., Section 10(i).
44. Ibid., Section 10(ii).
45. Ibid., Section 10(iii).
46. Ibid., Section 10(iv).
47. Ibid., Section 10(0).
48. 1995, 3 CTJ 49 SC: AIR, 1995 SC 1881.
49. Ibid., Section 33 (1) (a).
50. All Chemist and Druggist Association, In re (1984) 1 Comp. LJ 281 and All India Organization of Chemist and Druggist, In re (1996) 21 CLA 322.
51. Monopolies and Restrictive Trade Practices Act, 1969, Section 33(1)(b); See for instance Chanakya and Sidhartra Gas Co., In re RTPE 11/1985.
52. Ibid., Section 33(1)(c); see for instance Bharatia Cutler Hammer Ltd., In re, (1997) 24 CLA 104 (MRTPC); DGIR vs. Studs Accessories Pvt. Ltd., RTPE 231/1988; Vadilal Enterprises Ltd., In re, (1998) 91 Comp. Cas 824.
53. Ibid., Section 33(1)(d); see Union of India vs. Hindustan Development Corporation, 1993, 3 SCC 499.
54. Ibid., Section 33(1) (e); see Seraikela Glass Works Pvt. Ltd., In re, (1993) 2 Comp. LJ 385; DGIR vs. Rajashree Cement, 1995, 16 CLA 325 (MRTPC).
55. Ibid., Section 33(1)(f) ; see Re India Cements Ltd., RTP Enquiry 48/1985.
56. Ibid., Section 33(1)(g); see Megaware Computers Ltd., In re, (1994) 79 Comp, Cas. 84.
57. Ibid., Section 33(1)(h); see DGIR vs. Mundipharma AG (1985) 18 CLR 272 (MRTPC).
58. Ibid., Section 33 (1)(i).
59. Ibid., Section 33(1)(j); see Modern Food Industries, In re, (1996) 4 CTJ 81 (MRTPC).
60. Ibid., Section 33(1)(ja).
61. Ibid., Section 33(1)(jb).
62. Ibid., Section 33(1)(k).
63. Ibid., Section 33(1)(l).
64. Ibid., Cla. (1) to (5) of Section 36A.
65. Hindustan Lever Ltd. vs. Colgate Palmolive (India) Ltd., (1999)

32 CLA 483.

66. DGIR vs. Indian Institute of Entrepreneurship and Management, (1997) 5 CTJ 271 (MRTPC).
67. DGIR vs. Indian School of Labour Education, (1997) 5 CTJ 273 (MRTPC).
68. Ibid., Section 36(A)(2).
69. Ibid., Section 36(A)(3), see DGIR vs. Usha International Ltd. (1997) 89 Comp. Cas. 648; Jay Engg. Works Ltd. vs. Khaitan India Ltd. (1992) Comp. LJ 196 (MRTPC); DGIR vs. Hero Honda Motor (1998) 29, CLA 324 (MRTPC); Godrej G.E. Applliances vs. Whirlpool India Ltd. (1999) 33 CLA 324 (MRTPC).
70. Ibid., Section 36(A)(4).
71. Ibid., Section 36(A)(5).

8

Consumer Protection Act (CPA), 1986: Provisions and Enforcement

8.1 Introduction

Consumer Protection Act can be described as common man's civil court. The Act is designed to make available inexpensive and speedy remedy to the consumers. Basically, Sale of Goods Act is driven by the principle of 'caveat emptor', i.e., 'buyer beware'. Accordingly, buyer is supposed to take care before buying any goods. He is supposed to be knowledgeable and well informed. This was true about a century ago, when both buyers and sellers were on equal footing. In many cases, tracing seller after the sale was difficult. However, as organised manufacturing activity increased, sellers became larger and better organised, while buyers despite their numerical growth, continued to be unorganised and weak. In the modern marketing scene, an average buyer can be easily misled and duped. It is now realised that a common consumer is neither knowledgeable nor well informed. He needs protection from unscrupulous sellers. Once duped, a common consumer is not in a position to approach the civil court. There was a growing realisation that quick, inexpensive and speedy justice to the genuine complaints of the consumers is essential.

Realising the importance of consumer protection world over, the United Nations adopted guidelines for protection of consumers on April 9, 1985. All countries were expected to take suitable legislative measures. Accordingly, 'Consumer Protection Act, 1986' was enacted in India with this view in mind.

8.2 Main Objectives of CPA

The main object of the Act (as per the preamble to the Act) is to provide for better protection of interests of consumers.

Consumer councils and other authorities are provided for settling the consumers' disputes and other matters.

Rights of Consumer: The Act is intended to protect the following rights of the consumers (Section 6):

1. Right of protection from marketing of goods and services which are hazardous to life and property.
2. Right to be informed about the quality, quantity, purity, standard and price of the goods or services, so that consumers are protected from the unfair trade practices.
3. Right to have access to variety of goods and services at competitive prices.
4. Right to be heard and to be assured that consumer interests receive its due consideration.
5. Right to stop unfair trade practices, restrictive trade practices and exploitation of consumers.
6. Right to consumer education.
7. Right to speedy and simple redressal to consumer disputes.

8.3 Procedure under CPA

The Act envisages setting up of 'Consumer Disputes Redressal Agency' at local i.e. district level, state level and national (Central) level. District forums have jurisdiction to decide consumer disputes where value of goods or services and the compensation claimed does not exceed ₹ 20 lakh. State commission has jurisdiction to decide the cases where value of goods and services plus compensation is over ₹ 20 lakh but not over ₹ 100 lakh. In addition, it decides appeals filed against the orders of district forum.

National Commission with its headquarters in New Delhi, has original jurisdiction where the matter is over ₹ 100 lakh. It also has appellate jurisdiction over state commissions. Appeal against the orders of state commissions can be filed only in case of an original order by a state commission i.e. when matter was over ₹ 20 lakh. No appeal can be filed to National Commission in case where state commission has passed order in appeal against the original order of district forum.

Appeal against the order of National Commission lies with Supreme Court, only in matters where it exercises original jurisdiction, i.e., when the matter is over ₹ 100 lakh. There is no provision of appeal in cases where National Commission decides under its appellate jurisdiction, i.e., when it decides appeal against order of state commission.

Thus, in all' cases, only one appeal has been provided. However, revision petition to National Commission, which is a second appeal by back door, can be filed.

Complaint can be filed by a consumer, a voluntary consumer association or Central/State Government. Class action i.e., some consumers filing complaint on behalf of many consumers is also permitted. Fee is required to be paid along with the complaint. Complaint must be filed within two years from the 'cause of action'. This period can be extended on showing a sufficient cause. Appeal against the order of district forum/state commission/National Commission must be filed within 30 days from the date of order.

Penalty up to ₹ 10,000 can be imposed on a complainant, if it is found that he has made frivolous (bogus) complaint. Persons not complying with the order of redressal authorities can be punished with imprisonment up to three years and/or fine up to ₹ 10,000.

On receipt of a complaint with prescribed fees, it has to be admitted or refused within 21 days. If complaint is admitted, a copy is sent to the 'opposite party' by the district forum i.e., the party against whom a complaint is made. He is expected to reply within 30 days. Granting personal hearing is not mandatory at district forum level. However, such personal hearing is normally given.

Each redressal agency is headed by a President. The president must be from judicial discipline. Other members are selected from the society. Such members should be persons of ability, integrity and standing and should have experience relating to economics, law commerce, accountancy, industry, public affairs or administration. They must be graduates and over 35 years of age. One of the members must be a woman.

The members sit in benches—with at least two members in case of district forum. The bench can be a single member bench or multi-member bench in case of state/National Commission. President must be a member of the bench of district forum but this is not essential in case of state commission or National Commission. Matters are expected to be decided by district forums within a period of three months where laboratory testing is not required; and within five months where laboratory testing and analysis is required. Appeal is expected to be decided within 90 days.

Provisions are made for enforcement of order and imposition of penalty in case order of consumer forum is disobeyed.

In addition to the redressal procedure, the Act makes provisions for Central Consumer Protection Council at the National level, State Consumer Protection Councils at the State level and District Council at the district level. These councils are in advisory capacity only. They should meet periodically and promote steps to protect rights of consumers.

The Act extends to whole of India except Jammu and Kashmir [Section 1(2)]. However, separate Act for J&K has been passed by the J&K Assembly.

8.4 Complaint to Consumer Forum

Section 12(1) provides that a complaint in relation to any goods sold or delivered or to be sold or delivered or any service provided or agreed to be provided may be filed with the consumer forum.

District forum, state commission and National Commission are consumer forums, termed as consumer dispute redressal agencies. It is necessary to understand the meaning of 'complaint' and who can file the same.

Meaning of 'complaint': Section 2(1)(c) of the Consumer Protection Act defines that "complaint" means any allegation in writing made by a complainant that:

1. An unfair trade practice or a restrictive trade practice has been adopted by any trader or service provider.
2. The goods bought by him or agreed to be bought by him suffer from one or more defects.
3. The services hired or availed of or agreed to be hired or availed of by him suffer from deficiency in any respects.
4. A trader or the service provider, as the case may be, has charged for the goods or for the services mentioned in the complaint, a price in excess of the price: (a) fixed by or under any law for the time being in force; (b) displayed on the goods or any package containing such goods; (c) displayed on the price list exhibited by him by or under any law for the time being in force; and (d) agreed between the parties;
5. Goods which will be hazardous to life and safety when used, being offered for sale to the public: (a) in contravention of any standards relating to safety of such goods as required to be complied with, by or under any law for the time being in force; and (b) if the trader could have known with due diligence that the goods so offered are unsafe for the public.
6. Services which are hazardous or likely to be hazardous to life and safety of the public when used, are being offered by the service provider which such person could have known with due diligence to be injurious to life and safety, with a view to obtaining any relief provided by or under this Act.

Thus, the intention of filing 'complaint' is with a view to obtain relief provided in the Act. Section 14(1) states what reliefs can be granted. Here, it may be noted that definition of 'trader' is quite wide and it includes manufacturer also. Goods has same meaning as per the Sale of Goods Act [Section 2(1)(i)].

Section 2(7) of the Sale of Goods Act defines 'goods' as every kind of movable property other than actionable claims and money; and includes stocks and shares, growing crops, grass and things attached to or forming part of the land, which are agreed to be served from land before sale, or under contract of sale. Things like patent, copyright, trade mark, water, gas, electricity, ships etc. are goods.

The word 'defect' means any fault, imperfection or shortcoming in the quality, quantity potency, purity or standard that is required to be maintained by or under any law for the time being in force or under any contract, express or implied, or as is claimed by the trader in any manner whatsoever in relation to any goods [Section 2(1)(f) of the Consumer Protection Act].

'Consumer dispute' means a dispute where the person against whom a complaint has been made, denies or disputes the allegations contained in the complaint [Section 2(1)(e)]. Obviously, if the person against whom a complaint is made agrees to the complaint, there is no 'consumer dispute'. Interestingly, if he agrees, there is no 'consumer dispute'. However, Section 12(1) which provides for filing of complaint, does not talk of 'consumer dispute' at all. It only talks of filing of complaint. Hence, this definition does not seem to be of much relevance.

Consumer protection rules made by State Governments provide that where opposite party admits the allegations made by the complainant, the district forum shall decide the complaint on the basis of merit of the case and documents presented before it.

8.4.1 Who Can File A Complaint? As per Section 12(1), a complaint in relation to any goods sold or delivered or agreed to be sold or delivered or any service provided or agreed to be provided may be filed with a district forum by:

1. The consumer to whom such goods are sold or delivered or agreed to be sold or delivered or such service provided or agreed to be provided.
2. Any recognised consumer association whether the consumer to whom the goods sold or delivered or agreed to be sold or delivered or service provided or agreed to be provided is a member of such association or not.

3. One or more consumers, where there are numerous consumers having the same interest, with the permission of the district forum, on behalf of, or for the benefit of, all consumers so interested.
4. Central Government or the State Government, as the case may be, either in its individual capacity or as a representative of interests of consumers in general.

Thus, 'class action' is permissible. Voluntary consumer associations can also file a complaint. This provision is particularly useful in case of complaint against unfair trade practices, higher prices charged by trader and/or sale of hazardous goods.

Class action—when there are numerous consumers, one or more consumers can file a complaint on behalf of, or for benefit of, all interested consumers. Such class action can be filed only with permission of the consumer forum. In case of class action, (persons making a complaint on behalf of numerous consumers), an order passed is binding on all persons, on whose behalf the complaint was filed. Provisions of Rule 8 of First Schedule of CPC will apply in such cases [Section 13(6)].

8.4.2 Who is a Complainant? Section 2(1)(b) of the CPA defines that "complainant" means: (i) a consumer, or (ii) any voluntary consumer association registered under the companies Act, or under any other law for the time being in force; or (iii) the Central Government or any State Government, who or which makes a complaint; or (iv) one or more consumers, where there are numerous consumers having the same interest; or (v) in case of death of a consumer, his legal heir or representative, who or which makes a complaint.

Section 2(1)(d) defines the word "consumer" as follows. Consumer means any person who:

1. Buys any goods for a consideration which has been paid or promised or partly paid and partly promised, or under any system of deferred payment and includes any user of such goods other than the person who buys such goods for

consideration paid or promised or partly paid or partly promised, or under any system of deferred payment when such use is made with the approval of such person, but does not include a person who obtains such goods for resale or for any commercial purpose; or

2. Hires or avails of any services for a consideration which has been paid or promised or partly paid and partly promised, or under any system of deferred payment and includes any beneficiary of such services other than the person who hires or avails of the services for consideration paid or promised, or partly paid and partly promised, or under any system of deferred payment, when such services are availed of with the approval of the first mentioned person but does not include a person who avails of such services for any commercial purpose.

Explanation: For the purpose of this clause, "commercial purpose" does not include use by a person of goods bought and used by him and services availed by him exclusively for the purpose of earning his livelihood by means of self-employment [Section 2(1)(d)].

Thus, definition of consumer covers: (a) one who buys goods for a consideration for personal use, (b) one who uses such goods with permission of buyer of goods, (c) one who obtains goods on hire purchase or lease, (d) one who hires or avails of any services for a consideration, (e) one who uses the services with permission of person who has hired the service, (f) one who obtains services on deferred payment basis, i.e. hire purchase or lease, and (g) one who buys goods or avails services exclusively for the purpose of earning his livelihood through self-employment.

Though definition of consumer is wide, only a consumer to whom goods are sold or delivered or agreed to be sold or delivered or service provided or agreed to be provided can file a complaint as per clear provisions of Section 12(1)(a).

Who is not a 'Consumer'—The word "consumer" does not include:

1. One who buys goods or avails services for commercial purposes.
2. One who has not bought the goods. Thus, an individual cannot complain unless he has actually bought the goods or availed the services. However, this condition is not applicable in case of complaints by voluntary consumer associations or by the Government. It may be noted that the voluntary consumer association need not be registered with any authority.

Trader: Complaint can be lodged against a trader in case of goods and against a service provider in case of service. 'Trader' includes manufacturer.

Trader means a person who sells or distributes any goods for sale and includes the manufacturer thereof, and where such goods are sold or distributed in package form, including the packer thereof [Section 2(1)(q)]. Complaint can also be lodged against the 'trader' who sells the goods.

8.4.3 What is a Service? Complaint can be lodged against a service provider if there is a deficiency in service or if he charges higher prices or provides services which are hazardous or where service provider follows unfair or restrictive trade practice. Hence, it is necessary to understand the meaning of 'service' and 'deficiency'.

Section 2(1)(o) defines that 'service' means service of any description, which is made available to potential users and includes, but not limited to, the provision of facilities in connection with banking, financing, insurance, transport, processing, supply of electrical or other energy, boarding or lodging or both, housing construction, entertainment, amusement or the purveying a news or other information, but does not include rendering of any service free of charge or under a contract of personal service. However, complaint for deficiency in service cannot be filed if service received is for commercial purpose.

8.4.4 Deficiency in Service: 'Deficiency' means any fault, imperfection or shortcoming in the quality, quantity, potency, purity or standard, which is required to be maintained by or under any law for the time being in force or has been undertaken to be performed by a person in pursuance of a contract or otherwise in relation to any service [Section 2(1)(g) of CPA].

No Jurisdiction in Case of a Special Law: If there is a special law, jurisdiction of Consumer Protection Act is barred.

Jurisdiction in respect of complaints on account of deficiency in service due to loss, destruction, damage, deterioration or non-delivery of goods entrusted to railways lies exclusively with the 'Railway Claims Tribunal'. Thus, consumer forums have no jurisdiction to entertain complaints in these matters.

8.5 Restrictive and Unfair Trade Practices in CPA

Restrictive and unfair trade practices are covered under Consumer Protection Act (CPA). It is interesting to note that though these provisions were incorporated in Consumer Protection Act in 1993, there seems to be hardly any case pertaining to these issues.

8.5.1 Restrictive Trade Practice: Section 2(1)(nnn) of CPA as amended by Amendment Act, 2002, defines restrictive trade practice as one which tends to bring about manipulation of price or its conditions of delivery or to affect flow of supplies in the market relating to goods or services in such a manner so as to impose on the consumers, unjustified costs or restrictions and shall include: (a) delay beyond the period agreed to by a trader in supply of such goods or in providing the services which has led or is likely to lead to a rise in the price; and (b) any trade practice which requires a consumer to buy, hire or avail of any goods or, as the case may be, services as condition precedent to buying, hiring or availing of other goods or services.

The section gives only two illustrations: (a) delay in supply of goods and services, and (b) tie-up sales i.e. full line forcing. However, the definition of 'restrictive trade practice' is 'inclusive'. It means that any trade practice which tends to bring about manipulation of price or its conditions of delivery or to affect flow of supplies in the market relating to goods or service in such a manner so as to impose on the consumers unjustified costs or restrictions will be 'restrictive trade practice' and definition is not restricted to two illustrations given.

Delay in Supply of Goods or Provision of Services: This will normally be treated as a 'restrictive trade practice'. However, it will be so only if it is a 'practice' that is regularly done. If it is occasionally done or happens due to reasons beyond the control of trader or service provider, it is not a 'trade practice' and hence obviously will not be a restrictive trade practice. Moreover, it will be a restrictive trade practice only if it imposes unjustified costs on consumer and it has led to or is likely to lead to rise in prices.

Tie-in Sales or Full Forcing: This means requiring a person to purchase or hire goods or avail of services compulsorily along with goods he wants to have or service he wants to avail of [Section 2(1)(nnn)(b)]. This provision is comparable to Section 33(1)(b) of the MRTP Act.

It is called a tie-in sale or full line forcing. For example, a company has two products A and B out of which A is popular, but B is not. It may say that A will not be given unless B is also purchased, e.g. forcing dealers to purchase tooth brush (which is not very popular) along with a tooth paste (which is popular). Some of the examples of restrictive trade practice are: (a) compelling consumers to buy a gas stove from the dealer while giving a gas connection; (b) asking a person to keep some amount as a fixed deposit before allotting him a locker in a bank. The MRTP Act covers various other practices as restrictive trade practice. However, Consumer Protection Act covers only one type of restrictive trade practice.

Rule of Reason: There will always be some restrictions. These are permissible as long as these are 'reasonable'. This is termed as 'rule of reason'. The Court should be satisfied that considering the balance between circumstances and its probable effect, the restrictions are reasonable.

Most important case in respect restrictive trade practice is

Telco vs. Registrar of Restrictive Trade Agreement. [1] Honourable Supreme Court had stated that any agreement that restrains and binds persons or place or prices, per se would be bad.

The question is whether the restraint is such as to regulate and thereby promote competition or suppresses competition. It will be bad if it destroys competition. Hence: (a) facts particular to business, (b) condition before and after the restraint, and (c) probable effects of restraint, have to be considered and this is the 'rule of reason'.

8.5.2 Unfair Trade Practice: Unfair Trade Practice is defined under Section 2(1)(r) of the Consumer Protection Act, as follows, "unfair trade practice" means a trade practice which, for the purpose of promoting the sale, use or supply of any goods or for the provision of any service, adopts any unfair method or unfair or deceptive practice including any of the following practices, namely:

(1) The practice of making any statement, whether orally or in writing or by visible representation which:

(i) Falsely represents that the goods are of a particular standard quality, quantity, grade, composition, style, or model;

(ii) Falsely represents that the services are of a particular standard, quality or grade;

(iii) Falsely represents any re-built, second-hand, renovated, reconditioned or old goods as new goods;

(iv) Represents that the goods or services have sponsorship, approval, performance, characteristics, accessories, uses or benefits which such goods or services do not have;

(v) Represents that the seller or the supplier has a sponsorship or approval or affiliation which such seller or supplier does not have;

(vi) Makes a false or misleading representation concerning the need for, or the usefulness of, any goods or services;

(vii) Gives to the public any warranty or guarantee of the performance, efficacy or length of life of a product or of any goods that is not based on an adequate or proper test thereof.

Provided that where a defence is raised to the effect that such warranty or guarantee is based on adequate or proper test, the burden of proof of such defence shall lie on the person raising such defence;

(viii) Makes to the public a representation in a form that purports to be: (i) a warranty or guarantee of a product or of any goods or services, or (ii) a promise to replace, maintain or repair an article or any part thereof or to repeat or continue a service until it has achieved a specified result, if such purported warranty or guarantee or promise is materially misleading or if there is no reasonable prospect that such warranty, guarantee or promise will be carried out;

(ix) Materially misleads the public concerning the price at which a product or like products or goods or services, have been or are, ordinarily sold or provided, and, for this purpose, a representation as to price shall be deemed to refer to the price at which the product or goods or services has or have been sold by sellers or provided by suppliers generally in the relevant market unless it is clearly specified to be the price at which the product has been sold or services have been provided by the person by whom or on whose behalf the representation is made;

(x) Gives false or misleading facts disparaging the goods, services or trade of another person.

Explanation: For the purpose of clause (1), a statement that is: (a) expressed on an article offered or displayed for sale, or on its wrapper or container; or (b) expressed on anything attached to, inserted in, or accompanying, an article offered or displayed for sale, or on anything on which the article is mounted for display or sale; or (c) contained in or on anything that is sold, sent, delivered, transmitted or in any other manner whatsoever made available to a member of the public shall be deemed to be a statement made to the public by, and only by, the person who had caused the statement to be so expressed, made or contained.

(2) Permits the publication of any advertisement whether

in any newspaper or otherwise, for the sale or supply at a bargain price, of goods or services that are not intended to be offered for sale or supply at the bargain price, or for a period that is, and in quantities that are, reasonable, having regard to the nature of the market in which the business is carried on, the nature and size of business, and the nature of the advertisement.

Explanation: For the purpose of clause (2), "bargaining price" means: (a) a price that is stated in any advertisement to be a bargain price, by reference to an ordinary price or otherwise, or (b) a price that a person who reads, hears or sees the advertisement, would reasonably understand to be a bargain price having regard to the prices at which the product advertised or like products are ordinarily sold.

(3) Permits: (a) the offering of gifts, prizes or other items with the intention of not providing them as offered or creating an impression that something is being given or offered free of charge when it is fully or partly covered by the amount charged in the transaction as a whole; (b) the conduct of any contest, lottery, game of chance or skill, for the purpose of promoting, directly or indirectly, the sale, use or supply of any product or any business interest.

(3A) Withholding from the participants of any scheme offering gifts, prizes or other items free of charge, on its closure, the information about final results of the scheme.

(4) Permits the sale or supply of goods intended to be used, or are of a kind likely to be used, by consumers, knowing or having reason to believe that the goods do not comply with the standards prescribed by competent authority relating to performance, composition, contents, design, construction, finishing or packaging as are necessary to prevent or reduce the risk of injury to the person using the goods.

(5) Permits the hoarding or destruction of goods, or refuses to sell the goods or to make them available for sale or to provide any service, if such hoarding or destruction or refusal raises or tends to raise or is intended to raise, the cost of those

or other similar goods or services.

(6) Manufacture of spurious goods or offering such goods for sale or adopting deceptive practices in the provision of services.

False or misleading representation is required, mere deficiency of service is not an unfair trade practice. If there was no allegation or evidence of any false or misleading representation, party cannot be said to be guilty of unfair trade practice. Mere deficiency in service is not unfair trade practice. [2] Illustrations of Unfair Trade Practice given in the Consumer Protection Act are classified as:

- False or misleading statements—Section 2(1)(r)(1) of the CP Act.
- Bargain sales—Section 2(1)(r)(2) of the CP Act.
- Free gifts and prizes—Section 2(1)(r)(3) of the CP Act.
- Not publishing results of gift or prize scheme—Section 2(1)(r)(3A) of the CP Act.
- Selling goods not as per prescribed standards—Section 2(1)(r)(4) of the CP Act.
- Hoarding or destruction of goods—Section 2(1)(r)(5) of the CP Act.
- Manufacture/supply of spurious goods/deceptive practices in offering services—Section 2(1)(r)(6) of the CP Act.

Spurious Goods and Services: As per Section 2(1)(oo), "spurious goods and services" mean such goods and services which are claimed to be genuine but they are actually not so.

This insertion of definition has been made as definition of unfair trade practice which specifically provides that the manufacturer of spurious goods or offering spurious goods for sale or adopting deceptive practices in the provision of services will be an unfair trade practice [Section 2(1)(r)(6)].

Information about Scheme of Gifts and Prizes: If a seller, trader or service provider announces some scheme of gifts and prizes to allure consumers, he is required to disclose final results of the scheme. If he does not do so, it will be an unfair trade practice. This has been provided by amending/inserting sub-clause (3A) to Section 2(1)(r) in the definition of unfair trade practice, which provides that withholding from the participants of any scheme offering gifts, prizes or other items free of charge, on its closure the information about final results of the scheme will be an unfair trade practice.

As per the explanation to this sub-clause, the participants of a scheme shall be deemed to have been informed of the final results of the scheme where such results are within a reasonable time period, published prominently in the same newspapers in which the scheme was originally advertised [Section 2(1)(r)(3A)].

Thus, results of any scheme of gifts and prizes will be required to be announced in the same newspapers where the scheme was advertised.

8.6 Consumer Forums under CPA

The Consumer Protection Act Provides for a three tier structure for redressal of complaints under the Act. The consumer disputes redressal agencies (CDRAs) are established at district, state and national level.

Sections 12, 13 and 14 which are in respect of district forum have been made applicable to State commissions and National Commission also. Hence, the common provisions are discussed first.

Time Limit for Filing Complaint: A complaint must be filed within two years from the date on which the cause of action arose.

However, the district forum, State commission or National Commission can entertain complaint after the date, on showing sufficient cause. Reasons should be recorded for condoning the delay [Section 24 A].

Penalty for Frivolous or Vexatious Complaints: If the complaint is found to be frivolous or vexatious, district forum, State commission or National Commission may order that the complainant to pay to the opposite party, costs which shall not exceed ₹ 10,000 (Section 26 of CPA). This section is to discourage bogus complaints or complaints only with a view to harass someone.

Powers of Redressal Agencies: The redressal agencies, namely district forums, State commissions and National Commission have all the powers of civil court such as: (a) summoning and enforcing attendance of witnesses and examining the witnesses on oath, (b) discovery and production of any document or other material as evidence, (c) receiving evidence on affidavits, (d) requisitioning report of test or analysis from concerned laboratory, (e) issuing commission for examination of witnesses, and (f) any other matter that may be prescribed by the Central or State Government by rules [Section 13(4)].

Power to Order Production of Documents etc.: As per Rule 10(1) of the Consumer Protection Rules, 1987, the consumer disputes redressal agencies (district forums and State/National Commission) have the power to require a person to produce before them, books of account, documents or commodities. They can also ask a person to furnish to a specified order, information required under the Act. They are also authorised to seize a person's books of account, documents or commodities required for under the purposes of Act, or where there is reason to believe that such books etc. may be destroyed, altered, falsified etc. [Rule 10(2)].

Proceedings before the redressal agencies are deemed to be judicial proceedings within the meaning of Sections 193 (punishment for giving false evidence) and 228 (punishment for intentional insult or interruption to public servant, sitting in judicial proceeding) of the Indian Penal Code. A district forum, State commission or National Commission is deemed to be a civil court for the purposes of Section 195 and Chapter XXVI of the Code of Criminal Procedure (i.e. punishment for contempt of lawful authority of public servant, giving false evidence, etc.) [Section 13(5)].

After conducting proceedings as per Section 13, if the redressal agency is satisfied that the goods complained against, suffer from defects or that allegations regarding deficiency in service are proved, it shall issue an order to other party directing him to do any one or more of the following things [Section 14(1)].

- To remove the defects pointed by laboratory [Section 14(1)(a)].
- To replace goods with new goods free of defect [Section 14(1)(b)].
- To return the price of goods or charge of services paid by the complainant [Section 14(1)(c)].
- Compensation for loss or injury suffered by consumer due to negligence of opposite party. In addition, punitive damages can also be granted [Section 14(1)(d)].
- To remove defects in goods or deficiencies in services in question [Section 14(1)(e)].
- To discontinue the unfair trade practice or the restrictive trade practice or not to repeat them [Section 14(1)(f)].
- Not to offer the hazardous goods for sale [Section 14(1)(g)].
- To withdraw hazardous goods from being offered for sale [Section 14(1)(h)].
- To cease manufacture of hazardous goods and to desist from offering services which are hazardous in nature [Section 14(1)(ha).
- To pay such sum as may be determined by it, if it is of the opinion that loss or injury has been suffered by a large number of consumers who are not identifiable conveniently, provided that the minimum amount of sum so payable shall not be less than five percent of the value of such defective goods sold or service provided, as the case may be, to such consumers. Further, the amount so obtained shall be credited in favour of such person and utilized in such a manner as may be prescribed. If such large number of consumers cannot be conveniently identified, the amount of fine shall be deposited in Consumer Welfare Fund constituted under Section 12C of the Central Excise Act [Rule 10A of Consumer Protection Rules,1987] [Section 14(1)(hb)].

- To issue corrective advertisement to neutralize the effect of misleading advertisement at the cost of the opposite party responsible for issuing such misleading advertisement [Section 14(1)(hc)].
- To provide for adequate costs to parties [Section 14(1)(i)].
- Consumer redressal agencies have no powers to issue any order other than that mentioned in Section 14. [3]

8.7 Establishment of Consumer Disputes Redressal Agencies [4]

There shall be established for the purpose of this Act, the following agencies, namely:

(a) A consumer disputes redressal forum to be known as "district forum" established by the State Government in each district of the State by notification. The State Government may, if it deems fit, establish more than one district forum in a district.

(b) A consumer disputes redressal commission to be known as the "state commission" established by the State Government in the State by notification; and

(c) A National Consumer Disputes Redressal Commission be established by the Central Government by notification.

8.7.1 Consumer Disputes Redressal Forum: The district forum: Sections 10 to 15; composition (Section 10). Each district forum shall consist of: [5]

(a) A person who is, or has been, or is qualified to be a district judge, shall be its president;

(b) Two other members, one of whom shall be a woman and who shall have the following qualifications namely:

(i) be not less that 35 years of age,

(ii) possess a bachelor's degree from a recognized university,

(iii) be persons of ability, integrity and standing, and have adequate knowledge and experience of at least 10 years in dealing with problems relating to economics, law, commerce, accountancy, industry, public affairs or administration.

Further, a person shall be disqualified for appointment as a member, if he:

(a) has been convicted and sentenced to imprisonment for an offence which, in the opinion of the State Government, involves moral turpitude; or

(b) is an undischarged insolvent; or

(c) is of unsound mind and stands so declared by a competent court; or

(d) has been removed or dismissed from the service of the Government or a body corporate owned or controlled by the Government; or

(e) has, in the opinion of the State Government, has financial or other interest as is likely to affect pre-judicially the discharge by him of his functions as a member; or

(f) has such other disqualifications as may be prescribed by the State Government [This clause has been substituted by Consumer Protection (Amendment) Act, 2002].

Every appointment shall be made by the State Government on the recommendation of a selection committee consisting of the following, namely:

(i) President of the state commission—chairman.

(ii) Secretary, Law department of the state—member.

(iii) Secretary in charge of the department dealing with consumer affairs in the State—member.

Where the president of the State Commission is, by reason of absence or otherwise, unable to act as chairman of the selection committee, the State Government may refer the matter to the Chief Justice of the High Court for nominating a sitting judge of that High Court of act as chairman.

Term of Office: Every member of the district forum shall hold office for a term of 5 years or up to the age of 65 years, whichever is earlier. He shall not be eligible for re-appointment. However, a member shall be eligible for re-appointment for another term of 5 years or up to the age of 65 years, whichever is earlier, subject to the condition that he fulfils the qualifications and other conditions for appointment and such re-appointment is also made on the basis of the recommendation of the selection committee.

Resignation: A member may resign his office in writing under his hand addressed to the State Government. On such resignation being accepted, his office shall become vacant. The vacancy so caused may be filled by appointment of a person processing the qualifications mentioned above in relation to the category of the member who has resigned.

Salary and Terms of Conditions of Service: The salary or honorarium and other allowances and payable to, and the other terms and conditions of service of, the members of the district forum shall be prescribed by the State government. However, the appointment of a member on whole time basis shall be made by the State government on the recommendation of the president of the State commission taking into consideration such factors as may be prescribed including the work load of the district forum [Inserted by the Consumer Protection (Amendment) Act, 2002].

Jurisdiction (Section 11): The district forum shall have jurisdiction to entertain complaints where the value of the goods of services and the compensation, if any, claimed does not exceed ₹ 20,00,000. This is however subject to other provisions of this Act.

A complaint shall be instituted in a district forum within the local limits of whose jurisdiction:

(a) The opposite party (i.e., the person who answers complaint or claim) or each of the opposite parties, where there are more than one, at the time of the institution of the complaint, actually and voluntarily resides or carries on business or has a branch office, or personally works for gain, or

(b) Any of the opposite parties, where there are more than one, at the time of the institution of the complaint, actually and voluntarily resides, or carries on business or has a branch office, or personally works for gain. But in such a case either the permission of the district forum is given, or the opposite parties who do not reside, or carry on business or have a branch office, or personally work for gain, as the case may be, must acquiesce in such institution; or

(c) The case of action, wholly or in part, arises.

Manner in Which Complaint Shall be Made: [Section 2 as substituted by the Consumer Protection (Amendment) Act, 2002].

A complaint, in relation to any goods sold or delivered or agreed to be sold or delivered or any service provided or agreed to be provided, may be filed with a district forum by:

(a) The consumer to whom such goods are sold or delivered or agreed to be sold or delivered or such service provided or agreed to be provided.

(b) Any recognized consumer association, whether the consumer to whom the goods sold or delivered or agreed to be sold or delivered or service provided or agreed to be provided, is a member of such association or not.

(c) One or more consumers, where there are numerous consumers having the same interest, with the permission of the district forum, on behalf of, or for the benefit of, all consumers so interested.

(d) The Central Government or the State Government, as the case may be, either in its individual capacity or as a representative of interests of the consumers in general.

Every complaint shall be accompanied with such amount payable in such manner as may be prescribed.

On receipt of a complaint, the district forum may, by order, allow the complaint to be proceeded with or rejected. However, a complaint shall not be rejected unless an opportunity of being heard has been given to the complainant.

The admissibility of the complaint shall ordinarily be decided within 21 days from the date on which the complaint was received.

Where a complaint is allowed to be proceeded with, the district forum may proceed with the complaint in the manner provided under this Act. However, where a complaint has been admitted by the district forum, it shall not be transferred to any other court or tribunal or any authority set up by or under any other law for the time being in force.

Procedure on Admission of Complaint: [Section 13 as amended by the Consumer Protection (Amendment) Act, 2002].

Complaint Relating to Goods-Reference of complaint to opposite party: The district forum shall, on admission of a complaint, if it relates to any goods, refer a copy of the complaint to the opposite party mentioned in the complaint. Further it shall direct the opposite party to give his version of the case within a period of 30 days. This period may be extended by a further period not exceeding 15 days as may be granted by the district forum.

Denial of Allegation etc. by Opposite Party: Where the opposite party on receipt of a complaint referred to him denies or disputes the allegations contained in the complaint, or omits or fails to take any action to represent his case within the time given by the district forum, the district forum shall proceed to settle the consumer dispute in the following manner:

1. Reference of sample to laboratory where the complaint alleges a defect in the goods which cannot be determined without proper analysis or test of the goods. In such a case, the district forum shall obtain a sample of the goods from the complainant, seal it and authenticate it and refer the sample so sealed to the appropriate laboratory for an analysis or test whichever may be necessary. The direction for such analysis or test shall be made with a view to find out whether such goods suffer from any defect alleged in the complaint or suffer from any other defect. The laboratory shall report its findings to the district forum within a period of 45 days of the receipt of the reference or within such extended period as may be granted by the district forum.
2. Before any sample of the goods is referred to any appropriate laboratory for analysis or test, the district forum may require the complainant to deposit to the credit of the forum such fees as may be specified. Such fees are meant for payment to the appropriate laboratory for

carrying out the necessary analysis or test in relation to the goods in question.

3. Remission of fees to laboratory and forwarding of report to opposite party: The district forum shall remit the amount of fee deposited to its credit to the appropriate laboratory to enable it to carry out the analysis or test. On receipt of the report from the appropriate laboratory, the district forum shall forward a copy of the report along with such remarks as the district forum may feel appropriate to the opposite party.
4. Objections by any of the parties: If any of the parties disputes the correctness of the findings of the appropriate laboratory, or disputes the correctness of the methods of analysis or test adopted by the appropriate laboratory, the district forum shall require the opposite party or the complainant to submit in writing his objections in regard to the report made by the appropriate laboratory.
5. Reasonable opportunity to parties of being heard and issue of order: The district forum shall give a reasonable opportunity to the complainant as well as the opposite party of being heard as to the correctness or otherwise of the report made by the appropriate laboratory and also as to the objection made in relation thereto. Thereafter, it shall issue an appropriate order under Section 14.

Complaint Relating to Services-Reference of claim to opposite party: If the complaint admitted by the district forum relates to any services (or to goods in respect of which the procedure specified above cannot be followed), the district forum shall refer a copy of such complaint to the opposite party directing him to give his version of the case within a period of 30 days or such extended period not exceeding 15 days as may be granted by the district forum.

Denial etc. of Allegation by the Opposite Party: The opposite party may, on receipt of a copy of the complaint, deny or dispute the allegations contained in the complaint, or omit or fail to take any action to represent his case within the time given by the district forum.

Settlement of Dispute: In case of denial etc. of the allegation by the opposite party, the district forum shall proceed to settle the consumer dispute:

1. Ex-parte on the basis of evidence brought to its notice by the complainant and the opposite party, where the opposite party denies or disputes the allegations contained in the complaint, or
2. Ex-parte on the basis of evidence brought to its notice by the complainant where the opposite party omits or fails to take any action to represent his case within the time given by the forum, or
3. Where the complainant fails to appear on the date of hearing before the district forum, the district forum may either dismiss the complaint for default or decided it on merits.

Proceedings of the District Forum Final: The proceedings complying with the procedure laid down above cannot be called in question in any court on the ground that the principles of natural justice have not been complied with.

Death of a Complainant: In the event of death of a complainant who is a consumer or of the opposite party against whom the complainant has been filed, the provisions of Order XXII of the First Schedule to the Code of Civil Procedure, 1908 shall apply, subject to the modification that every reference therein to the plaintiff and the defendant shall be construed as reference to a complainant or the opposite party, as the case may be.

Period: Every complaint shall be heard as expeditiously as possible and endeavour shall be made to decide the complaint within a period of 3 months from the date of receipt of notice by opposite party where the complaint does not require analysis or testing of commodities and within 5 months, if it requires analysis or testing of commodities.

No adjournment shall be ordinarily granted by the district forum unless sufficient cause is shown and the reasons for grant of adjournment have been recorded in writing by the forum.

The district forum shall make such orders as to the costs occasioned by the adjournment as may be provided in the regulations made under this Act.

In the event of a complaint being disposed of after the period so specified, the district forum shall record in writing, the reasons for the same at the time of disposing of the said complaint.

Where during the pendency of any proceedings before the district forum, it appears to it necessary, it may pass such interim order as is just and proper in the facts and circumstances of the case.

Powers of the District Forum: The district forum shall have the same powers as are vested in a civil court under the Code of Civil Procedure, 1908, while trying a suit in respect of the following matters, namely:

1. The summoning and enforcing attendance of any defendant or witness and examining the witness on oath.
2. The discovery and production of any document or other material object producible as evidence.
3. The reception of evidence on affidavits.
4. The requisitioning of the report of the concerned analysis or test from the appropriate laboratory or from an, other relevant source.
5. Issuing of any commission for the examination of any witness.
6. Any other matter which may be prescribed.

Every proceeding before the district forum shall be deemed to be a judicial proceeding within the meaning of Sections 193 and 228 of the Indian Penal Code, 1860 and the district forum shall be deemed to be a civil court for the purposes of Section 195, and Chapter XXVI of the Code of Criminal Procedure, 1973.

Where the complainant is a consumer, the provisions of Rule 8 of Order 1 of the First Schedule to the Code of Civil Procedure, 1908 shall apply subject to the modification that every reference therein to a suit or decree shall be construed as a reference to a complaint or the order of the district forum thereon.

Appeal (Section 15): Any person aggrieved by an order made by the district forum may prefer an appeal against such order to the State commission within a period of 30 days from the date of the order. The State commission may entertain an appeal after the expiry of this period of 30 days if it is satisfied that there was sufficient cause for not filing the appeal within that period. But no appeal by a person, who is required to pay any amount in term of an order of the district forum, shall be entertained by the State commission unless the appellant has deposited in the prescribed manner, 50 percent of that amount or ₹ 25,000 whichever is less.

8.7.2 Consumer Disputes Redressal Commission [The State Commission-Sections 16 to 19]: Composition [Section 16 as amended by the Consumer Protection (Amendment) Act, 2002]. Each State commission shall consist of:

(a) A person who is or has been a judge of a High Court, appointed by the State Government, shall be its President. However, no appointment under this clause shall be made except after consultation with chief justice of the High Court.

(b) Not less that 2 and not more that such number of members as may be prescribed and one of whom shall be a woman who shall have the following qualifications, namely:

(i) Be not less than 35 years of age;

(ii) Possess a bachelor's degree from a recognized university; and

(iii) Be person of ability, integrity and standing and have adequate knowledge and experience of at least 10 years in dealing with problems relating to economics, law, commerce, accountancy, industry, public affairs or administration.

However, not more than 50 percent of the members shall be from amongst persons having a judicial background.

The expression "persons having a judicial background" shall mean persons having knowledge and experience for at least a period of 10 years as presiding officer at the district level court or any tribunal at equivalent level.

Further, a person shall be disqualified for appointment as a member, if he:

1. Has been convicted and sentenced to imprisonment for an offence which, in the opinion of the State Government, involves moral turpitude; or
2. Is an undischarged insolvent; or
3. Has been removed or dismissed from the service of the Government or a body corporate owned or controlled by the Government; or
4. Has, in the opinion of the State Government, such financial or other interest, as is likely to affect prejudicially the discharge by him of his functions as a member; or
5. Has, such other disqualifications as may be prescribed by the State Government.

Every appointment under Section 16 shall be made by the State Government on the recommendation of a selection committee consisting of the following members, namely:

1. President of the State commission—chairman.
2. Secretary of the Law Department of the State—member.
3. Secretary in charge of the department dealing with consumer affairs in the State—member.

Where the president of the State commission is, by reason of absence or otherwise, unable to act as chairman of the selection committee, the State Government may refer the matter to the chief justice of the High Court for nominating a sitting judge of that High Court to act as chairman.

1. The jurisdiction, powers and authority of the State commission may be exercised by benches thereof.
2. A bench may be constituted by the president with one or more members as the president may deem fit.
3. If the members of a bench differ in opinion on any point, the points shall be decided according to the opinion of the majority—if there is a majority—but if the members are equally divided, they shall state the point or points on

which they differ, and make a reference to the president who shall either hear the point or points himself or refer the case for hearing on such point or points by one or more of the other members and such point or points shall be decided according to the opinion of the majority of the members who have heard the case, including those who first heard it.

The salary or honorarium and other allowances payable to, and the other terms and conditions of service of, the members of the State commission shall be prescribed by the State Government. However, the appointment of a member on whole-time basis shall be made by the State Government on the recommendation of the president of the State commission taking into consideration such factors as may be prescribed including the work load of the State commission.

Every member of the State commission shall hold office for a term of 5 years or up to the age of 67 years, whichever is earlier.

A member shall however be eligible for re-appointment for another term of 5 years or up to the age of 67 years, whichever is earlier, subject to the condition that he fulfils the qualifications and other conditions for appointment and it is made on the basis of the recommendation of the selection committee.

Further, a person appointed as the president of the State commission shall also be eligible for re-appointment in the manner discussed above.

Further, a member may resign from his office in writing addressed to the State Government and on such resignation being accepted, his office shall become vacant and may be filled by appointment of a person possessing any of the qualifications mentioned earlier in relation to the category of the member.

Every member of the State commission shall hold office for a term of 5 years or up to the age of 67 years, whichever is earlier and shall not be eligible for re-appointment.

Jurisdiction [Section 17(1)]: The State Commission shall have jurisdiction:

(a) To entertain: (i) complaints where the value of the goods or services and compensation, if any, claimed exceeds ₹ 20 lakh but does not exceed ₹ 1 crore; and (ii) appeals against the orders of any district forum within the State; and

(b) To call for the records and pass appropriate orders in any consumer dispute which is pending before or has been decided by any district forum within the State where it appears to the State commission that such district: (i) has exercised a jurisdiction not vested in it by law, or (ii) has failed to exercise a jurisdiction so vested, or (iii) has acted in exercise of its jurisdiction illegally or with material irregularity.

A complaint shall be instituted in a State commission within the limits of whose jurisdiction:

(a) The opposite party or each of the opposite parties, where there are more than one, at the time of the institution of the complaint, actually and voluntarily resides, or carries on business or has a branch office or personally works for gain; or

(b) Any of the opposite parties where there are more than one, at the time of the institution of the complaint, actually and voluntarily resides or carries on business of has a branch office or personally works or gain, provided that in such case either the permission of the State commission is given or the opposite parties who do not reside or carry on business or have a branch office or personally work for gain, as the case may be, acquiesce in such institution; or

(c) The cause of action, wholly or in part, arises [inserted by the Consumer Protection (Amendment) Act, 2002].

Transfer of Cases [Section 17-A as inserted by the Consumer Protection (Amendment) Act, 2003]: On the application of the complainant or of its own motion, the State commission may, at any stage of the proceeding, transfer any complaint pending before the district forum to another district forum within the State if the interest of justice so requires.

Circuit Benches [Section 17-B as inserted by the Consumer Protection (Amendment) Act, 2002]: The State commission shall ordinarily function in the State Capital but may perform its functions at such other place as the State Government may, in consultation with the State commission, notify in the official gazette, from time to time.

Procedure (Section 18): The provision of Sections 12, 13 and 14 and the rules made there under for the disposal of complaints by the district forum shall, with such modifications as may be necessary, be applicable to the disposal of disputes by the State commission.

Appeal (Section 19): Any person aggrieved by an order made by the State commission may prefer an appeal against such order to the National Commission within a period of 30 days from the date of the order. The National Commission may entertain an appeal after the expiry of this period of 30 days if it is satisfied that there was sufficient cause for not filing the appeal within that period.

Further, no appeal by a person who is required to pay any amount in terms of an order of the State commission, shall be entertained by the National Commission, unless the appellant has deposited in the prescribed manner, 50 percent of the amount or ₹ 35,000 whichever is less.

Hearing of Appeal [Section 19-A inserted by the Consumer Protection (Amendment) Act, 2002]: An appeal filed before the State Commission or the National Commission shall be heard as expeditiously as possible and an endeavour shall be made to finally dispose of the appeal within a period of 90 days from the date of its admission.

No adjournment shall be ordinarily granted by the State commission or the National Commission as the case may be, unless sufficient cause is shown and the reasons for grant of adjournment have been recorded in writing by such Commission.

Further the State commission or the National Commission, as the case may be, shall make such orders as the costs occasioned by the adjournment as may be provided in the regulations made under this Act.

Also that in the event of an appeal being disposed of after

the period so specified, the State commission or the National Commission, as the case may be, shall record in writing the reasons for the same at the time of disposing of the said appeal.

8.7.3 National Consumer Disputes Redressal Commission (National Commission-Sections 20 to 23) [6] Composition [Section 20 as amended by the Consumer Protection (Amendment) Act, 2002]: The National Commission shall consist of:

(a) A person who is or has been a judge of the Supreme Court, to be appointed by the Central Government, who shall be its president. However, no appointment under this Clause shall be made except after consultation with the Chief Justice of India;

(b) Not less than 4 and not more than such number of members, as may be prescribed and one of whom shall be a woman who shall have the following qualifications, namely:

(i) be not less than 35 years of age;

(ii) possess a bachelor's degree from a recognized university; and

(iii) be persons of ability, integrity and standing and have adequate knowledge and experience of at least 10 years in dealing with problems relating to economics, law, commerce, accountancy, industry, public affairs or administration.

However, not more than 50 percent of the members shall be from amongst the persons having a judicial background.

The expression "persons having a judicial background" shall mean persons having knowledge and experience for at least a period of 10 years as a presiding officer at the district level court or any tribunal at equivalent level.

Further, a person shall be disqualified for appointment, if he:

(a) Has been convicted and sentenced to imprisonment for an offence which, in the opinion of the Central Government, involves moral turpitude; or

(b) Is an undercharged insolvent; or

(c) Is of unsound mind and stands so declared by a

competent court; or

(d) Has been removed or dismissed from the service of the Government or a body corporate owned or controlled by the Government; or

(e) Has, in the opinion of the Central Government, such financial or other interest as is likely to affect prejudicially ,the discharge by him of his functions as a member; or

(f) Has such other disqualifications as may be prescribed by the Central Government.

Every appointment referred to above shall be made by the Central Government on the recommendations of a selection committee consisting of the following, namely:

(a) A person who is a judge of the Supreme Court to be nominated by the Chief Justice of India—chairman.

(b) The secretary in the Department of Legal Affairs in the Government of India—member.

(c) Secretary of the Department dealing with Consumer Affairs in the Government of India—member.

The jurisdiction, powers and authority of the National Commission may be exercised by benches thereof.

A bench may be constituted by the president with one or more members as the president may deem fit.

If the members of a bench differ in opinion on any point, the points shall be decided according to the opinion of the majority, if there is a majority, but if the members are equally divided they shall state the point or points on which they differ, and make a reference to the president who shall either hear the point or points himself or refer the case for hearing on such point or points by one or more of the other members and such point or points shall be decided according to the opinion of the majority of the members who have heard the case, including those who first heard it.

Every member of the National Commission shall hold office for a term of 5 years or up to the age of 70 years, whichever is earlier. However, a member shall be eligible for re-appointment for another term of 5 years or up to the age 70 years, whichever is earlier, subject to the condition that he fulfils the qualifications and other conditions for appointment and such re-appointment is made on the basis of the recommendation of the selection committee.

The salary or honorarium and other allowances payable to and the terms and conditions of service of the members of the National Commission shall be prescribed by the Central Government.

Place of the National Commission: The office of the National Commission shall be located in the Union Territory of Delhi (Rule 5 of the Consumer Protection Rules, 1957).

Jurisdiction (Section 21): Subject to the other provisions of this Act, the National Commission shall have jurisdiction:

1. To entertain: (i) complaints where the value of the goods or services and compensation, if any, claimed exceeds ₹ 1 crore, and (ii) appeals against the orders of any State commission; and
2. To call for the records and pass appropriate orders in any consumer dispute which is pending before or has been decided by any State commission where it appears to the National Commission that such State commission: (i) has exercised a jurisdiction not vested in it by law, or (ii) has failed to exercise a jurisdiction so vested, or (iii) has acted in the exercise of its jurisdiction illegally or with material irregularity.

Appeal (Section 23): Any person, aggrieved by an order made by the National Commission in exercise of its powers, may prefer an appeal against such order to the Supreme Court within a period of 30 days from the date of the order. The Supreme Court may entertain an appeal after the expiry of this period of 30 days if it is satisfied that there was sufficient cause for not filing the appeal within that period.

Further, no appeal by a person who is required to pay any amount in terms of an order of the National Commission shall be entertained by the Supreme Court unless that person has deposited in the prescribed manner, 50 percent of that amount or ₹ 50,000, whichever is less.

Finality of Orders (Section 24): Every order of a district forum, the State commission or the National Commission shall, if no appeal has been preferred against such order under the provisions of this Act, be final.

Sections 24-A and 24-b which have been inserted by the Consumer Protection (Amendment) Act, 2002, deal with "limitation period" and "administrative control" respectively.

Enforcement of Orders of the District Forum, the State Commission or the National Commission [Section 25 as substituted by the Consumer Protection (Amendment) Act, 2002]: Where an interim order made under this Act is not complied with, the district forum or the State commission or the National Commission, as the case may be, may order the property of the person, not complying with such order to be attached.

No such attachment shall remain in force for more than 3 months at the end of which, if the non-compliance continues, the property attached may be sold and out of the proceeds thereof, the district forum or the State commission or the National Commission may award such damages as it thinks fit to the complainant and shall pay the balance, if any, to the party entitled thereto.

Where any amount is due from any person under an order made by the district forum, State commission or the National Commission, the person entitled to the amount may make an application to the district forum, the State commission or the National Commission, and such district forum or the State commission or the National Commission may issue a certificate for the said amount to the collector of the district by whatever name called.

Dismissal of Frivolous or Vexatious Complaints (Section 26): Where a complaint instituted before the district forum, the State commission or, the National Commission is found to be frivolous or vexations, it shall dismiss the complaint and make an order that the complainant shall pay to the opposite party such cost, not exceeding ₹ 10,000 as may be specified in the order.

8.8 Consumer Protection Councils [7]

8.8.1 Central Consumer Protection Council (Sections 4 to 6); Establishment (Section 4): The Central Government shall establish, by notification, a council to be known as the Central Consumer Protection Council (referred to as the Central Council).

Membership: The Central Council shall consist of the following members, namely:

(a) The Minister in charge of the Consumer Affairs in the Central Government, who shall be its chairman, and

(b) Such number of other official or non-official members representing such interest as may be prescribed.

According to Rule 3 of the Consumer Protection Rules, 1987, the Central Council shall consist of the following 150 members, namely:

(a) The Minister in charge of Consumer Affairs in the Central Government, who shall be the chairman of the Central Council;

(b) The Minister of State (where he is not holding independent charge) or Deputy Minister in the Department of Civil Supplies who shall be the vice-chairman of the Central Council;

(c) The Ministers of Food and Civil supplies or Minister in charge of Consumer Affairs in States;

(d) 8 Members of Parliament, 5 from the Lok Sabha and 3 from the Rajya Sabha;

(e) The Commissioner for Schedule Castes and Schedule Tribes;

(f) Representatives of the Central Government Departments, autonomous organisations concerned with consumer interests, not exceeding 20;

(g) Representatives of the Consumer Organisations or consumers—not less than 35;

(h) Representatives of women—not less than 10;

(i) Representatives of farmers, trade and industries—not exceeding 20;

(j) Persons capable of representing consumer interests not specified above—not exceeding 15;

(k) The Secretary in the Department of Civil Supplies shall be the member secretary of the Central Council.

The term of the council shall be 3 years.

Any member may, by writing under his hand to the chairman of the Central Council, resign from the Council. The vacancies, so caused or otherwise shall be filled from the same category by the Central Government. The person shall hold office so long as the member whose place he fills would have been entitled to hold office, if the vacancy had not occurred.

Procedure for Meetings of the Central Council (Section 5): The Central Council shall meet as and when necessary, and at least one meeting of the Council shall be held every year. It shall meet at such time and place as the chairman may think fit and shall observe such procedure in regard to the transaction of its business as may be prescribed.

Objects of the Central Council (Section 6): The objects of the Central Council shall be to promote and protect the rights of the consumers such as:

(a) The right to be protected against the marketing of goods and services which are hazardous to life and property;

(b) The right to be informed about the quality, quantity, potency, purity, standard and price of goods or services so as to protect the consumer against unfair trade practices;

(c) The right to be assured, wherever possible, access to a variety of goods and services at competitive prices;

(d) The right to be heard and to be assured that consumers' interests will receive due consideration at appropriate forums;

(e) The right to seek redressal against unfair trade practices or unscrupulous exploitation of consumers; and

(f) The right to consumer education.

The Central Council shall give wide publicity to the rights of the consumers and the consumer dispute redressal agencies and procedure of filing complaints therein through television, radio, newspapers and magazines to give impetus to consumer movement in the country.

8.8.2 State Consumer Protection Councils (Sections 7 and 8): Establishment (Section 7): The State Government shall by notification, establish with effect from such date as it may specify in such notification, a Council to be known as the Consumer Protection Council (referred to as the State Council).

Membership: The State Council shall consist of the following members, namely:

(a) The minister in charge of consumers' affairs in the State Government who shall be its chairman;

(b) Such number of other official or non-official members representing such interests as may be prescribed by the State Government;

(c) Such number of other official or non-official members, not exceeding 10, as may be nominated by the Central Government.

Meetings: The State Council shall meet as and when necessary but not less than 2 meetings shall be held every year.

Time and Place of Meetings and Procedure: The State Council shall meet at such time and place as the chairman may think fit and shall observe such procedure in regard to the transaction of its business as may be prescribed by the State Government.

Objects of the State Council (Section 8): The objects of every State Council shall be to promote and protect within the State the rights of the consumers as laid down in Section 6.

8.8.3 District Consumer Protection Council [Section 8A as inserted by the Consumer Protection (Amendment) Act, 2002].

The State Government shall establish for every district, by notification, a council to be known as the District Consumer Protection Council with effect from such date as it may specify in such notification.

The District Consumer Protection Council (hereinafter referred to as the District Council) shall consist of the following members, namely:

(a) The collector of the district (by whatever name called), who shall be its chairman; and

(b) Such number of other official and non-official members representing such interests as may be prescribed by the State Government.

The District Council shall meet as and when necessary but not less than 2 meetings shall be held every year.

The District Council shall meet as such time and place within the district as the chairman may think fit and shall observe such procedure in regard to the transaction of its business as may be prescribed by the State Government.

Objects of the District Council: [Section 8B inserted by the Consumer Protection (Amendment) Act, 2002]: The objects of every District Council shall be to promote and protect within the district the rights of the consumers as laid down in Clauses (a) to (f) of Section 6.

Endnotes

1. 1977, 47 Comp. Cas. 520 (SC), AIR 1977 SC 973, (1977) 2 SCC 55.
2. KLM Royal Dutch Airlines vs. DGIR (2008) 88 SCL 153 (SC).
3. Datey, V.S., "Taxman's Supplement to Business and Corporate Laws", Taxmann Allied Services (P) Ltd., New Delhi, 2010, pp. 1-7.
4. Choudhari, V.R., "Law of Consumer Protection", Premier Publishing Company, Allahabad, 2008, pp. 882-889.
5. Bakshi, P.M., "Consumer Protection Law", Ashoka House, New Delhi, 2004, pp. 1262-1310.
6. Kapoor, N.D., "Elements of Mercantile Law", Sultan Chand & Sons, New Delhi, 2005, pp. 555-557.
7. Ibid., pp. 543-545.

9

Service Sector Redressal and Consumer Protection

9.1 Introduction

The expression 'service' as defined in the Consumer Protection Act connotes service of any description which is made available to potential users and includes, but not limited to the provision of facilities in respect of banking, insurance, railways, housing, telephone, medical, electricity, etc. It does not include any service provided free of charge or under a contract of personal service. The deficiency in service, as stated above may be divided into three parts: (i) inclusive, (ii) illustrative, and (iii) exclusionary. Deficiency in service is one of the grounds for filing complaint under the Act. At present, majority of complaints before these adjudicatory bodies relate to deficiency in service of various service providers. The term 'deficiency' has also been defined in Section 2(1)(g) of the Act. It means any fault, imperfection, shortcoming or inadequacy in quality, nature and manner of performance, which is required to be maintained by or under law in force or has been undertaken to be performed by a person in pursuance of a contract or otherwise in relation to any service.

Services as contemplated in the definition include public utility services such as insurance, power, post, telecommunication, airways, etc. Of course, the Government has diluted its stand on monopoly in these sectors—thanks to the New Economic Policy, paving way for liberalization, globalisation and privatisation. The services provided by these state-owned monopolies in the public utilities are not up to mark since more and more cases are filed in the consumer forums for deficiency in these services. Earlier, consumers were provided redressal under civil law which was not only time consuming but also cumbersome and an expensive affair. With the enactment of the Consumer Protection Act, consumers can now file complaints against these public utility services for speedy redressal. Against this backdrop, an attempt has been made to make an empirical study of the cases filed in consumer fora selecting eight service providers, most of which are under the State monopoly. They are:

1. Airlines.
2. Indian Railways.
3. Banking.
4. Insurance.
5. Telecommunication.
6. Housing.
7. Electricity.
8. Medical.

9.2 State Commissions/District Forums in India

Table 9.1 contains information regarding the functional and non-functional status of the State Commissions and the District Forums in the country as on 01.08.2014. From the said table, it can be observed that at present, the State Commissions are functional in all the States and Union Territories of the country.

As far as the district fora are concerned, out of the total 644 fora, 618 are functional and the remaining 26 are non-functional. This means about 4 percent of district fora in the country are non-functional. The highest number of non-functional district fora is in the state of Chattisgarh where out of the total of 27 district fora, 18 are functional and 9 are non-functional. This represents a huge 33 percent of fora as non-functional in the State. Chattisgarh is followed by the states of U.P. and Tamil Nadu where, out of 79 and 30 district fora, 4 each are non-functional respectively. Similarly, states like Arunachal Pradesh, Assam, Jharkhand and Uttarakhand have got 3, 2, 2 and 2 fora as non-functional out of their respective share of 16, 23, 22 and 13 fora. This clearly depicts the gross negligence of the administration towards consumerism.

Table 9.1: Functional/Non-Functional State Commissions (SCs)/Districts Forums (DFs) (as on 01.08.2014)

S. No.	Name of State/UT	Whether SC F* or NF**	No. of DF	F*	NF**	As on
1.	Andhra Pradesh	Yes	29	29	0	30.06.2014
2.	A&N Islands	Yes	1	1	0	31.03.2006
3.	Arunachal Pradesh	Yes	16	13	3	31.03.2014
4.	Assam	Yes	23	21	2	31.03.2014
5.	Bihar	Yes	38	38	0	31.12.2012
6.	Chandigarh	Yes	2	2	0	31.12.2013
7.	Chattisgarh	Yes	27	18	9	30.06.2014
8.	Daman and Diu	Yes	2	2	0	31.03.2011
9.	Delhi	Yes	10	10	0	30.06.2014
10.	Goa	Yes	2	2	0	30.06.2014
11.	Gujarat	Yes	30	30	0	31.08.2013
12.	Haryana	Yes	21	21	0	31.03.2014
13.	Himachal Pradesh	Yes	12	12	0	30.06.2014
14.	Jammu and Kashmir	Yes	2	2	0	31.03.2009
15.	Jharkhand	Yes	22	20	2	30.09.2013
16.	Karnataka	Yes	31	31	0	30.06.2014
17.	Kerala	Yes	14	14	0	31.12.2010
18.	Lakshadweep	Yes	1	1	0	31.03.2014
19.	Madhya Pradesh	Yes	48	48	0	31.03.2014
20.	Maharashtra	Yes	40	40	0	30.06.2014
21.	Manipur	Yes	9	9	0	31.12.2008
22.	Meghalaya	Yes	7	7	0	31.10.2012
23.	Mizoram	Yes	8	8	0	31.12.2010
24.	Nagaland	Yes	8	8	0	31.12.2011
25.	Odisha	Yes	31	31	0	30.09.2013

Contd...

26.	Pondicherry	Yes	1	1	0	31.12.2012
27.	Punjab	Yes	20	20	0	31.03.2014
28.	Rajasthan	Yes	37	37	0	31.05.2014
29.	Sikkim	Yes	4	4	0	30.06.2014
30.	Tamil Nadu	Yes	30	26	4	30.06.2014
31.	Tripura	Yes	4	4	0	30.06.2014
32.	Uttar Pradesh	Yes	79	75	4	31.12.2013
33.	Uttarakhand	Yes	13	11	2	30.04.2014
34.	West Bengal	Yes	21	21	0	30.06.2014
35.	Darda & Nagar Haveli	Yes	1	1	0	31.03.2011
Total			**644**	**618**	**26**	-

F* = Functional; NF** = Non-functional
Source: NCDRC.

9.3 Consumer Complaints Filed/Disposed of at Different Levels

Table 9.2 shows the total number of complaints filed and/or disposed of in the National Commission, State Commission and District Fora respectively since their inception till August 1, 2014 under consumer protection law. The table discerns that a total of 89,495 cases have been filed before the National Consumer Dispute Redressal Commission, out of which 77,770 cases have already been disposed off and 11,725 cases are still subjudice. The percentage of total disposal by the Hon'ble National Commission stands at 86.90 percent which cannot be considered satisfactory. Further, it is observed that out of 6,45,486 cases filed before the State Commissions across the country since enactment of CPA, 5,54,341 have been disposed off. The percentage of disposal by the State Commissions is about 85.88 percent and 91,145 numbers of cases are still pending.

As far as district fora across the country are concerned, since inception 34,42,730 number of cases have been filed, out of which 31,76,518 cases have been disposed off at the rate of

92.27 percent and 2,66,212 cases are still pending and awaiting disposal.

Table 9.2: Consumer Complaints Filed/Disposed of since Inception under Consumer Protection Law (as on 01.08.2014)

S. No.	Name of Agency	Cases Filed since Inception	Cases Disposed of since Inception	Cases Pending	% of Total Disposal
1.	National Commission	89,495	77,770	11,725	86.90
2.	State Commissions	6,45,486	5,54,341	91,145	85.88
3.	District Forums	34,42,730	31,76,518	2,66,212	92.27
Total		41,77,711	38,08,629	3,69,082	91.17

Source: NCDRC

The total figure of cases filed in the three tier CPA fora since inception stands at 41,77,711 out of which 38,08,629 cases have been disposed off at the rate of 91.17 percent and 3,69,082 cases are yet to be disposed off. In a country like India having a population of more than 1.2 billion the number of cases filed under CPA remains negligible. Stated otherwise, when consumer negligence and cheating has become a common practice, such a few number of cases filed under CPA clearly indicate the lack of awareness among the population regarding the speedy and inexpensive justice of CPA. Another weakness of the CPA is that justice is inordinately delayed against the avowed objective of speedy and inexpensive justice for the consumers.

9.4 Cases Filed/Disposed of/Pending in the National Commission and State Commissions

Table 9.3 depicts the statement of cases filed/disposed of/pending since inception with the National Commission and State Commissions across the country as on 01.08.2014. The table shows that amongst the States and Union Territories, the highest number of disputes have been filed before the State Consumer Disputes Redressal Commission of Uttar Pradesh i.e. 70,955 cases have been filed out of which 43,262 have been disposed of @ 60.97 percent and 27,693 cases are still pending.

Table 9.3: Cases Filed/Disposed of/Pending in the National Commission and State Commissions (as on 01.08.2014)

S. No.	Name of State/UT	Cases Filed since Inception	Cases Disposed of since Inception
	National Commission	**89,495**	**77,770**
1.	Andhra Pradesh	30,778	29,563
2.	A & N Islands	42	38
3.	Arunachal Pradesh	68	66
4.	Assam	2,687	2,318
5.	Bihar	17,332	12,087
6.	Chandigarh	13,292	13,186
7.	Chattisgarh	9,710	8,950
8.	Daman, Diu, DNH	25	20
9.	Delhi	37,666	34,714
10.	Goa	2,524	2,481
11.	Gujarat	49,089	44,684
12.	Haryana	44,443	43,848
13.	Himachal Pradesh	8,550	8,405
14.	Jammu and Kashmir	6,727	6,170
15.	Jharkhand	5,271	4,774
16.	Karnataka	47,408	43,622
17.	Kerala	27,053	25,353
18.	Lakshadweep	18	16
19.	Madhya Pradesh	45,448	39,105
20.	Maharashtra	61,594	48,510

Contd...

11.	Gujarat	4,405	91.03	30.06.2014
12.	Haryana	600	98.65	30.06.2014
13.	Himachal Pradesh	145	98.30	30.06.2014
14.	Jammu and Kashmir	557	91.72	31.03.2013
15.	Jharkhand	497	90.57	31.12.2013
16.	Karnataka	3,786	92.01	30.06.2014
17.	Kerala	1,700	93.72	30.06.2014
18.	Lakshadweep	2	88.89	31.05.2014
19.	Madhya Pradesh	6,343	86.04	31.05.2014
20.	Maharashtra	13,084	78.76	30.06.2014
21.	Manipur	43	69.06	30.09.2008
22	Meghalaya	87	66.79	31.10.2012
23.	Mizoram	5	97.61	31.05.2014
24.	Nagaland	19	24.00	31.12.2011
25.	Odisha	6,324	71.72	30.09.2013
26.	Puducherry	18	98.16	31.05.2014
27.	Punjab	3,639	88.62	31.05.2014
28.	Rajasthan	5,165	90.67	31.05.2014
29.	Sikkim	3	94.34	30.06.2014
30.	Tamil Nadu	2,317	90.94	30.06.2014
31.	Tripura	56	96.46	30.06.2014
32.	Uttar Pradesh	27,693	60.97	31.01.2014
33.	Uttarakhand	925	81.86	30.04.2014
34.	West Bengal	3,031	85.71	30.06.2014
Total		**91,145**	**85.88**	

Source: NCDRC

The State Commission of U.P. is followed by the State Commission of Maharashtra where since inception, 61,594 numbers of cases have been filed and out of which 48,510 were disposed off at the rate of 78.76 percent and 13,084 cases are still pending. The State Commission of Rajasthan comes third with 55,338 cases filed since inception and 50,173 cases were disposed of (90.67 percent) and 5,165 cases are still pending for disposal. Interestingly among all the State Commissions though Uttar Pradesh tops the bill in terms of highest number of consumer cases instituted, the disposal rate of cases is very abysmal (60.97 percent). In fact, it is juxtaposed, that is, the state is being discredited for least number of disposal cases during the said period. This implies that the State Commission of Uttar Pradesh, has miserably failed in redressing the plights of the hapless consumers.

On the other hand, Chandigarh (99.20 percent) occupies the first position in terms of disposal of cases followed by Haryana (98.65 percent), Goa (98.30 percent), Himachal Pradesh (98.30 percent), Puducherry (98.16 percent) and Arunachal Pradesh (97.06 percent) etc. in that order. The position of the State Commission for Redressal of Consumer Disputes (SCRCD), Odisha is far low. As far as filing of cases is concerned, since inception 22,360 cases have been filed out of which 16,036 have been disposed of and 6,324 cases are still subjudice. The rate of disposal by the State Commission of Odisha works out to 71.72 percent. This disposal rate seems to be quite poor in comparison to the performance of other State Commissions as cited above. However, a few States namely Nagaland (24.00 percent), Uttar Pradesh (60.97 percent), Meghalaya (66.79 percent) and Manipur (69.06 percent) are lagging behind Odisha. If compared to the 35 states and Union Territories, the position of the State Commission of Odisha, as far as rate of disposal is concerned, seems to be quite dismal.

As against the rate of disposal of 71.72 percent achieved by it, the overall aggregate rate of disposal of all the State Commissions of the country stands as high as 85.88 percent. This means on an average out of 100 cases filed, around 86 cases are disposed of by State Commissions. The rate of disposal of the NCDRC stands at 86.90 percent. This clearly is a pointer that efforts should be made by the State Commission to reach a disposal rate of more than 80 percent to give a semblance of respectability to the figures. In other words, speedy disposal of cases for which CPA comes into being must be the guiding factor for the State Commission.

9.5 Cases Filed/Disposed of/Pending in the District Fora

Table 9.4 comprises the aggregate number of cases filed/disposed of/pending in district fora of States and Union Territories of the country as on 01.08.2014. The District Fora of Uttar Pradesh is far ahead of the rest of their counterparts in terms of cases filed since inception.

Table 9.4: Cases Filed/Disposed of/Pending in District Fora: State-wise (as on 01.08.2014)

S. No.	Name of State/UT	Cases Filed since Inception	Cases Disposed of since Inception
1.	Andhra Pradesh	1,97,847	1,91,535
2.	A and N Islands	330	301
3.	Arunachal Pradesh	408	350
4.	Assam	13,704	11,976
5.	Bihar	94,345	81,161
6.	Chandigarh	49,379	48,218
7.	Chattisgarh	39,917	36,829
8.	Daman, Diu, DNH	162	144
9.	Delhi	2,49,505	2,34,740
10.	Goa	6,691	6,245
11.	Gujarat	1,87,240	1,76,132
12.	Haryana	2,31,459	2,17,895
13.	Himachal Pradesh	59,931	56,919
14.	Jammu and Kashmir	20,792	18,855

Contd...

15.	Jharkhand	35,437	31,628
16.	Karnataka	1,69,253	1,59,489
17.	Kerala	1,89,937	1,80,500
18.	Lakshadweep	77	65
19.	Madhya Pradesh	1,98,331	1,83,829
20.	Maharashtra	2,73,203	2,49,210
21.	Manipur	1,037	1,012
22.	Meghalaya	847	750
23.	Mizoram	3,466	2,819
24.	Nagaland	290	266
25.	Odisha	96,218	88,912
26.	Puducherry	3,002	2,772
27.	Punjab	1,66,164	1,62,493
28.	Rajasthan	3,15,509	2,85,122
29.	Sikkim	323	299
30.	Tamil Nadu	1,07,549	1,00,663
31.	Tripura	3,071	2,944
32.	Uttar Pradesh	5,95,574	5,19,542
33.	Uttarakhand	36,602	33,901
34	West Bengal	95,130	89,002
	TOTAL	**34,42,730**	**31,76,518**

Contd...

S. No.	Name of State/UT	Cases Pending	Percent of Disposal	As on
1.	Andhra Pradesh	6,312	96.81	30.06.2014
2.	A and N Islands	29	91.21	31.03.2006
3.	Arunachal Pradesh	58	85.78	31.05.2014
4.	Assam	1,728	87.39	31.08.2010
5.	Bihar	13,184	86.03	31.12.2013
6.	Chandigarh	1,161	97.65	31.03.2014

7.	Chattisgarh	3,088	92.26	30.06.2014
8.	Daman, Diu, DNH	18	88.89	31.03.2011
9.	Delhi	14,765	94.08	31.12.2012
10.	Goa	446	93.33	30.06.2014
11.	Gujarat	11,108	94.07	30.06.2014
12.	Haryana	13,564	94.14	30.06.2014
13.	Himachal Pradesh	3,012	94.97	30.06.2014
14.	Jammu and Kashmir	1,937	90.68	31.12.2007
15.	Jharkhand	3,809	89.25	30.11.2013
16.	Karnataka	9,764	94.23	30.06.2014
17.	Kerala	9,437	95.03	30.06.2014
18.	Lakshadweep	12	84.42	31.05.2014
19.	Madhya Pradesh	14,502	95.69	31.15.2014
20.	Maharashtra	23,993	91.22	30.06.2014
21.	Manipur	25	97.59	30.09.2008
22.	Meghalaya	97	88.55	31.10.2012
23.	Mizoram	647	81.33	31.12.2010
24.	Nagaland	24	91.72	31.12.2011
25.	Odisha	7,306	92.41	30.09.2013
26.	Puducherry	230	92.34	31.05.2014
27.	Punjab	3,671	97.79	31.05.2014
28.	Rajasthan	30,387	90.37	31.05.2014
29.	Sikkim	24	92.57	30.06.2014
30.	Tamil Nadu	6,886	93.60	30.06.2014
31.	Tripura	127	95.86	31.05.2014
32.	Uttar Pradesh	76,032	87.23	31.01.2014
33.	Uttarakhand	2,701	92.62	30.04.2014
34.	West Bengal	6,128	93.56	30.06.2014
Total		**2,66,212**	**92.27**	

Source: NCDRC

In the District Fora of Uttar Pradesh, since inception, 5,95,574 cases have been filed in aggregate out of which 5,19,542 have been disposed of and 76,032 are still pending. The overall rate of disposal achieved by them is 87.23 percent.

Rajasthan comes 2nd where, since inception, 3,15,509 cases have been filed, while 2,85,122 have been disposed of at the rate of 90.37 percent and 30,387 cases are still pending. Maharshtra occupies 3rd position having 2,73,203 number of cases being filed since inception out of which 2,49,210 cases have been disposed at the rate of 91.22 percent and 23,993 cases are yet to be disposed of followed by Delhi and Haryana etc. where 2,49,505 and 2,31,459 cases were filed out of which 2,34,740 and 2,17,895 were disposed of at the rate of 94.08 percent and 94.14 percent respectively.

As far as disposal rate is concerned, Punjab (97.79 percent) occupies the top position, followed by Chandigarh (97.65 percent), Manipur (97.59 percent), Andhra Pradesh (96.81 percent), Tripura (95.86 percent), Kerala (95.03 percent), Himachal Pradesh (94.97 percent) and Haryana (94.14 percent) in that order.

In district fora of Odisha, since inception, 96,218 cases have been filed out of which 88,912 cases have been disposed of at the rate of 92.41 percent and 7,306 cases are still awaiting disposal. As compared to other states, the State of Odisha is lagging behind as far as disposition of cases under CPA. Though the state's disposal rate is more than 92 percent, it is comparative to the national average of about 92 percent, however, as compared to other states and UTs like Punjab, Chandigarh, Manipur, Andhra Pradesh, Kerala and Himachal Pradesh, the state is lagging behind. This is a major cause of worry.

10

Consumer Protection Act: Appraisal, Conclusions and Suggestions

The aim of the present study is to critically examine the merits as well as the deficiencies of the social welfare legislation i.e. The Consumer Protection Act, 1986. As examined in the earlier chapters, the various mechanisms and practices of Consumer Protection Act have to a great extent fulfilled the long felt needs of the hapless consumers in the ever changing Indian market place.

10.1 Appraisal of Consumer Justice, Consumer Protection, Consumerism and Consumer Movement

Consumer justice aims at consumer protection which is co-extensive with the growth of consumerism and consumer movement. Consumerism, consumer movement and consumer protection are the concepts which arose out of the exploitation of the consumers by business houses in the market place.

Consumerism is the social movement seeking to promote, preserve and protect the rights and powers of the consumers in relation to the sellers in the market place. Even today there is a lack of complete awareness regarding the rights of the consumers. Advancement of civilisation, industrialisation and establishment of big business houses are responsible for the metamorphosis of buyers' market into sellers' market, rendering the consumer sovereignty a myth. Consumer who was once sovereign has now become a pathetic victim of exploitation by big business houses—national and multinational.

Consumer movement started in all the civilised countries to combat the evil of exploitation of the masses. In India, most of the consumers are innocent, ignorant and illiterate. The movement spearheaded by a few voluntary organisations was not enough to combat the evil of massive exploitation. Even today, most of the consumers are ignorant about their rights as a result of which business houses, big and small, continue to fleece them. Voluntary organisations are discernible more in urban areas than in the rural areas and even in those places, such organisations barring a few, have little concern for the consumers. A majority of such organisations are taken more as pass time avocation trying to gain recognition for themselves than to genuinely serve the consumer community. In this scenario, Consumer Protection Act was passed in India in 1986. This no doubt marked a good beginning but it has its fair share of shortcomings as in the case of most social welfare legislations. The objects of the Act are no doubt laudable but the execution and implementation is left entirely to the mercy of people with humanitarian outlook.

The Act has provided two tier protection councils to motivate the executive to implement the provisions of the Act and to make consumers aware of their rights. The number of councils—national and state—are grossly inadequate to promote and protect the interest of millions of consumers. The number of members as fixed is so high that it has become unwieldy and as a result, such councils have failed to convene the minimum number of annual meetings as required by the law. The councils, the State and National have therefore, not been able to achieve anything tangible so far in safeguarding consumer interest.

10.1.1 Constitutional Basis of Consumer Protection: Though the word 'consumer' does not appear in the Constitution of India, it peeps through the Preamble, the chapters on Fundamental Rights and Directive Principles of State Policy. The Constitution is committed to the establishment of a welfare State catering to the economic and social justice of the people, inclusive of the consumers.

The Consumer Protection Act does not deal with substantive law but expressly deals with the existing law relating to consumer protection. The Act provides for two types of mechanism viz.: (i) two tier protection councils—

State Consumer Protection Councils and Central Consumer Protection Councils for promotion of consumer rights, and (ii) three tier consumer dispute redressal agencies—district forum, State commission and National Commission for vindication of consumer rights inclusive of administration of consumer justice by applying the existing substantive law relating to consumer protection.

10.1.2 Consumer Forums: Unlike the MRTP Act which provided only one tribunal for the entire country, the Consumer Protection Act, 1986 created three tier consumer dispute redressal agencies— a district forum for each district, a State Consumer Dispute Redressal Commission for each State and a National Commission for the entire country. These adjudicatory bodies, the district forum, the State commission and the National Commission are bodies created to provide inexpensive and expeditious remedies to the consumers. These tribunals have to be constituted by a notification by the government. Their composition is broad based. Each district forum and State commission shall consist of three members of whom one will be the president.

The president of the district forum shall be a person who is, or has been or is qualified to be a district judge while the president of the State commission shall be a person who is or has been a judge of a High Court. The other two members of each tribunal shall be persons of ability, integrity and standing and have adequate knowledge or experience of or have proven ability in dealing with problems relating to accounts, law, commerce, accountancy, industry, public affairs or administration, one of whom shall be a women. The National Commission shall consist of president and four other members, the president shall be a person who is or has been judge of the Supreme Court and the other members shall have similar qualifications required for the appointment as members of the other two tribunals of whom one shall be a woman.

The salary and other allowances payable and other terms and conditions of service of the members of the district forum and State commission shall be fixed by the State Government and those of the members of the National Commission shall be fixed by the Central Government. Age limit of 65 years and 67 years have been prescribed for members of the district forum and State commission and 75 years age limit is prescribed for members of the National Commission and district forum till superannuation which ever is earlier. All the three CDRAs, namely district forum, State commission and National Commission are invested with original jurisdiction based on the pecuniary value of the subject matter involved in the dispute. Further, the State and National Commissions have also been conferred appellate and original jurisdictions. The enforcement of the provisions of the Act is exclusively entrusted to the hierarchy of this body of three tier tribunals unlike the MRTP Act.

Modern social welfare legislations not only generally establish tribunals but also prescribe special procedure, sometimes supplementing and at others, substituting the general procedural law. The Consumer Protection Act, 1986 not only established the above three tier tribunals called CDRA but also prescribed the procedure similar to that provided by the Civil Procedure Code for jurisdiction and trial of suits. The territorial jurisdiction is based on similar lines as of Civil Procedure Code and the procedure requires evidence to be taken and witnesses to be examined and cross-examined. There are provisions relating to the summoning and enforcing attendance of the opposite parties or the witnesses, examining the witnesses on oath, discovery and production of documents or other material objects prescribed as evidence and receipt of evidence on affidavits, the requisitioning of the report of the analysis test from appropriate laboratory or from any other relevant source, issuing of any commission for the examination of witnesses and other allied matters.

In consonance with the principles of natural justice, adequate opportunity is to be afforded to the parties to prove and defend themselves in the dispute. These redressal agencies have been empowered only to grant one or more reliefs provided under Section 14 of the Consumer Protection Act, 1986. They do not to have inherent powers like the civil court to pass any order granting other reliefs even if the tribunals deem other reliefs appropriate in the circumstance of the case.

10.2 Conclusions

The broad conclusion from the present study can be deduced hereunder.

(a) The Consumer Protection Act, 1986 is one of the social welfare legislations passed with the pious intention of protecting a large number of consumers at the market place who are the victims of exploitation. The necessity of passing the Act in 1986 was guided by many factors—changing practices by the businessmen in the market place, liberalised industrial licensing system adopted by the government in the interest of increasing industrialisation, mass propaganda by sophisticated means of advertisements by the business world etc., which more or less perplexed the consumers in their choice of purchasing. All these factors widened the inequality of the bargaining power of the consumer with that of the seller in the market place. Consequently, in consonance with legislations adopted in many advanced countries, the government was compelled to come to the rescue of the helpless and exploited consumers through legislative intervention. This is certainly a good beginning and most of the literature on the subject shows that it has made a good progress, aptly described as a boon to the consumer and hailed as a 'consumer charter'.

(b) However, an objective assessment of the CPA against its implementation clearly indicates that it is just a beginning and the success achieved is nothing compared to what is yet to be done. The problem of consumer protection in a country like India is really gigantic. It concerns a huge mass of unorganised people scattered throughout the length and breadth of this vast country, the majority of whom are illiterate and poor. The Act aims to protect them from commercial exploitation by well organised, rich, greedy and cunning business people including organised retailers, producers and big business houses, national and multinational companies.

Further, one of the inherent difficulties of the protection agency or legislation in consumer protection is that in a majority of cases, the victims are not aware of their rights and the nature of the damages they are put to. Thus, it is absolutely essential that consumer in general must be made aware of this problem. This needs to be done by educating them to be a part of the voluntary organisations. Consumer movement to be effective and successful has to be four dimensional, namely government, business houses, voluntary organisations and consumers. Since in almost all the cases, consumers are the victims, consumer education in the matter of consumer protection is highly essential. The government, both Central and State, should put their best efforts to build a strong consumer movement.

Similarly, one national consumer protection council and one consumer protection council for each state are too grossly insufficient to carry out the objects for which they are constituted. Moreover, their composition is so unwieldy that they are not able to meet even the prescribed minimum number of times in a year.

Though representation is provided to the registered consumer associations in the councils, the associations themselves are neither adequate nor as active as they ought to be. There are hardly five hundred voluntary organizations in the country having a population of over 1.2 billion. Even at the modest estimation of one association per one lakh population, it requires approximately ten thousand voluntary associations, actively engaged in consumer protection, education and awareness. Therefore, not only there must be sufficient number of voluntary organisations but there must also be a good number of them committed to serious work.

Even the existing insignificant number of associations, exist only in metro, urban and semi-urban areas. The rural and hinterland population who are mostly illiterate and poor remains untouched by any such associations or organisations. A deeper investigation clearly reveals that mostly such organisations are formed to acquire self-recognition in the society rather than vindicating the rights of the member consumers or even educating them. Unless the government evinces keen interest in this matter and boosts the voluntary organisations, they will never able to tackle a problem of such gigantic proportion. Just as the growth of law on the protection of consumers has been haphazard and piecemeal, the rise of voluntary organizations is sparse and sporadic.

As a matter of fact, the protection councils at the centre and the state have not been able to achieve any of the objects set before them by the Act though more than two and half decades has passed since the passing of CPA.

The inadequate number of three tier consumer redressal agencies has failed to achieve the purposes for which they were established. Consumer dispute redressal agencies (CDRAs) constituted under the Act cater to the needs only of a segment of the urban consumers, ignoring a vast majority of rural as well as urban consumers.

Even when the awareness of the consumers is at a low ebb, the CDRAs are not able to cope up with the work as is evident from the fact that only a few cases are disposed of within the stipulated timeframe of 90 days and 150 days prescribed by the Act. The tribunals do not have the power to grant reliefs deemed appropriate by them as their power of granting relief is circumscribed by limits of Section 14 of the Consumer Protection Act.

Though the Act entrusted the implementation of its provisions to the State and the Central Governments, they have not been evincing any active interest in its implementation.

The appointment of the members of the tribunals is to be made by the government but a number of posts of presidents and members of the consumer tribunals remain unfilled for long, thereby delaying justice. Besides, the remuneration offered for them is not proportionate to the work expected of them. The want of infrastructure is evident from the fact that there are no adequate buildings for accommodation either for the office or the staff.

(c) The Act applies the existing laws relating to consumer protection in various segments of civil and criminal laws of the country and does not enact by itself any substantive law.

(d) The substantive law to be administered and applied by the consumer dispute redressal agencies includes various social welfare legislations passed by the Parliament from time to time of which the MRTP Act, 1969, designed to control monopolistic and restrictive trade practices, is a novelty. The MRTP Act was amended in the year 1984 to regulate the newly emerging trade practices with ever changing techniques in the market place. The MRTP Act in due course of time lost its original objective of controlling monopolies due to the trend of liberalisation policies adopted by the government in its industrial licensing system. The omnibus concept of restraining unfair trade practice embracing most of the evil practices employed by the business houses to exploit the consumer was inserted by the Amendment Act, 1984. In view of its utility, it was bodily lifted from MRTP Act and incorporated in the Consumer Protection Act, 1986 by an amendment in 1993. Thus, the Consumer Protection Act adds one more string to the bow of the consumers and provided teeth to the gamut of the existing law.

The Act inserting the provisions relating to hazardous goods in 1993 has introduced the concept of product liability in the field of consumer justice in India in sync with modern trends in business practices at the market place as in U.S.

10.3 Suggestions

Twenty eight years is neither a short period nor a long period for assessing the gains and setbacks of any national level social movement converted to a legislation, but it is a matter of considerable satisfaction that the consumer movement has taken palpable roots in this country taking into account the vast population and their wide diversities. In order to attain this object of spreading awareness among the population at large, both the government and the consumer protection agencies must work hand in hand for the achievement of the same. Besides, to ensure consumer protection under the legal regime of the Consumer Protection Act, suggestions stated hereunder be given serious consideration at appropriate levels.

10.3.1 Spreading Awareness among Consumers

(a) In addition to the existing Central consumer protection council, State consumer protection councils and district consumer protection council, village consumer protection councils, *mandal/tehsil* consumer protection councils, must first be established to ensure that the spirit of consumerism percolates from the urban to the rural level. Such councils may gradually be withdrawn as and when effective voluntary organisations are formed in the rural areas.

(b) Until such councils are constituted at the grass root level, functionaries and operatives of the organisations of consumers which are established in the urban areas need to be encouraged and assisted to penetrate into the rural areas, establish contacts with *gram panchayats*, disseminate information in the shape of pamphlets and leaflets etc., for promoting awareness in the villages.

(c) Special programmes for generating awareness and for dissemination need to be prepared for utilization through the electronic media i.e., radio and T.V. which have a high reach in the rural areas and small towns. Steps should also be taken to see that these programmes catch the imagination of the audience and carry the message of consumerism convincingly.

(d) Materials in the shape of leaflets and pamphlets explaining in simple local languages, the concept of consumer rights and measures available for their protection and redressal, need to be prepared and widely disseminated at regular intervals.

(e) Information about the types of cases taken to consumer courts and decisions thereon have also to be conveyed to the public for creating awareness and concretisation of the benefits that can be derived in seeking redressal.

(f) It is also necessary that ways and means should be explored for incorporating certain basic essentials of consumer protection in the curricula of studies in schools, colleges and universities. A beginning has already been done and it has to be carried forward with sincerity.

(g) Symposiums and seminars may be organised by the Government and educational institutions with the participation of voluntary consumer associations in every district at frequent intervals.

(h) Training programmes should be organised through which the important provisions of the Consumer Protection Act and the essentials of consumer movement are passed on to the activists, operatives and volunteers of the organisations of consumers in various parts of the country. These programmes may be of short duration and the primary objective of these should be to equip these functionaries and operatives of the consumer movement to assist in carrying the message of consumer protection to the people and to provide assistance to the consumers to secure redressal of their grievances.

(i) It is suggested that expenditure involved in spreading awareness and for equipping people to seek and secure redressal of their grievances may be met out of the consumer welfare fund which has been created by the Government of India from out of the accounts of excise refund.

(j) It is further suggested that a reasonable percentage of surcharge or income tax collected from national and multinational companies and manufacturers of goods and providers of services be contributed to augment the resources of a consumer welfare fund already created.

10.3.2 Strengthening the Legislation: In order to make consumer justice easy, cheaper and expeditiously available to the consumers as envisaged by the Act, the following measures are suggested.

Establishment of lower tribunals for broadening the

existing three tier CDRAs, as they are found to be inadequate to cope up with the needs of the consumers, particularly the rural consumers. Therefore, matters of value worth less than ₹ 5,000 may be entrusted to the panchayat tribunals and those of value up to ₹ 1,00,000 to the *mandal* or *taluk* tribunals with right of appeal to the district forum. The panchayat consumer forum may be presided over by the president of the panchayat and the *mandal* or *taluk* consumer forum may be presided over by the samithi president with the panchayat president concerned as members.

This helps the consumers in rural areas as it avoids the necessity of their going all the way to the district forum to settle their dispute involving much expense and time. This will also assure that justice is taken to the door step of the consumers more cheaply and expeditiously in conformity with the objects of the Consumer Protection Act.

It is suggested that the remuneration of the president and the honorarium payable to members should be commensurate with the work they do. The present rates fixed by the Rules are grossly inadequate and therefore be revised appropriately.

It is suggested that adequate and essential infrastructure should be provided to enable the district forums, State commissions and National Commission to function effectively as the Government both Central and States are found to be more or less indifferent in this regard.

It is also suggested to ensure that non judicial members who are selected to work on the benches of those tribunals are above political bias and consideration.

It is further suggested that panels of specialists like doctors, engineers, architects, industrialists and other experts should be prepared for each tribunal with the approval of the State Government and whenever a dispute involving a technical matter arises, the president be authorised to cooperate the concerned individual as an additional expert non-judicial member for settlement of that dispute.

The present practice of appointing retired district judges as president of the district forums should be discouraged.

It is suggested that the presence of lawyers should be permitted only where the case justifies engagement of a lawyer. In other cases, a lawyer should be allowed only where the court specifically permits or considers it necessary as there is a general clamour that the lawyers make it difficult for the tribunals to dispose of the cases expeditiously.

In cases where the parties engage lawyers, the tribunal must be allowed to collect ad valorem or fixed court fee from the unsuccessful party.

The researcher suggests the establishment of the office of the consumer ombudsman as a check over the Governmental omissions and commissions/indifference in the implementation of the provisions of the Act and to plug the deficiencies in the nature of administration of consumer justice by the CDRAs.

In fact there are a number of vacancies in the CDRAs due to the indifference of the government, both at Central and State level. The statutory time limit for disposal of a consumer complaint by the CDRA is 90 days where no laboratory report is required and within 150 days if it involves one, which at present is observed more in its breach than compliance by the CDRAs at all levels.

It is suggested that the number of adjournments in the disposal of the consumer complaints at all levels should be statutorily limited to discourage the prevailing practice of granting adjournments indiscriminately.

It is suggested that in all cases of frivolous or vexatious litigation before the CDRAS at all levels, heavy compensation may be ordered in the form of costs to be paid by the party indulging in such practices to the opposite party of which a part may be retained by the CDRA.

It is suggested that presidents of district forums should be sitting or retired district judges only and not those who are qualified to be appointed as district judges.

It is suggested to prescribe a procedure on the lines of admission bench in the High Court, wherein any complaint received by the CDRA initially is scrutinized by authorized and competent personnel to determine whether the case falls within the purview of the Consumer Protection Act and whether it should be pursued as opposed to the present practice of sending straightaway a copy of the complaint to the other party in every case.

Once a study of this dimension is undertaken, some broad conclusion automatically emerges which more or less throws light on some new aspects. The researcher suggests the following measures for overall supervision of the functioning of the administration of consumer justice in the interest of affording devoted consumer protection under the legal domain of the Act.

It is suggested that a separate Ministry—Ministry of Consumer Affairs and Justice—be constituted both at the Central and State level.

It is suggested that a consumer code, comprising of the existing segments of civil and criminal laws including the various post-Independence social welfare enactments concerning consumer protection be prepared along with various notification etc., at both the State and Central Government levels. It is suggested that consumer redressal agencies be given exclusive jurisdiction in all matters of consumer disputes to avoid confusion created by concurrent jurisdiction with other bodies. The concept of consumer may be widened excluding the requirement of consideration, as gratuitous consumers deserve as much protection as other consumers for consideration. This will solve the difficulties experienced by consumers at the hands of Government and charitable hospitals.

It is suggested that the practice of conducting consumer *adalats* by various public sector undertakings and banks be extended to other multinational and big national companies and manufacturers and that such *adalats* are held by them at least once in a quarter.

The consumer does not want compensation but expects full satisfaction from products and services of good quality which is paid for from his hard earned money. The object of a consumer protection law is to make the manufacturers of products and provider of services realise that they exist for the consumers and their satisfaction. The ideal consumer protection laws should aim at enabling the dethroned consumer to regain his sovereignty and supremacy in the market place. Attempts are afoot in this direction and if steps are taken on the lines of the above suggestions, before long, the consumer will regain his sovereignty.

10.4 Challenges Ahead

It is now over two decade and half since the Consumer Protection Act, 1986 was passed after years of lobbying by various consumer organisations. Viewed from a critical angle, the functioning of the redressal machinery is far from satisfactory. As a result, the number of cases pending in the various forums is piling up and increasing year after year.

Unless consumer groups take determined action to see that the institutions set up for their protection work effectively, the redressal agencies will go the way of civil courts, where litigants have to wait for years and spend fortunes for the settlement of their disputes. Making Consumer Protection Act effective, is therefore, the first challenge facing the consumer movement in India.

Although there are now about 1,000 consumer organisations in existence, yet all the cities and towns have not been covered. Rural areas where the greater part of our nine hundred million consumers live, are still virtually untouched by the consumer movement. Though the aim is to have a consumer complaints redressal forum in every district, it is not easy for poor rural consumers to go to the forum with complaints, nor do many consumers have an awareness of ways to assert their consumer rights. The solution lies in training rural workers who are already active in the villages. Mass media should be used to penetrate rural houses. Creating consumer awareness in the vast reaches of rural India with its variety of customs, traditions and languages and little formal education is the second challenge for the consumer movement.

Another matter of concern for the consumer is the likely fall out of the liberalisation policy adopted by the government. Undoubtedly, liberalisation has brought to us many benefits, notably, up to date technology, greater competition and better products, enhanced employment and investment opportunities. But some possible adverse effects must also be taken into account. The import to India of drugs, pesticides and cosmetics which are sometimes banned in the countries from which they originate is likely to be much easier with liberalized import laws. Consumer groups will have to be on their guard against such products and services. For example, obesity treatments, hair restoration treatments and arthritis cures which were not approved in the countries of origin have been brought in here through collaboration and launched with tremendous publicity. Consumer organisations need to take action against them for their misleading and highly exaggerated claims. Laws against cigarette and liquor advertising are being openly flouted through advertising on hoardings and through cable television. Consumer movement needs to be extremely alert regarding dubious or hazardous products entering the country in the wake of liberalization.

Some other emerging areas of consumer protection are environment protection, investor protection and freedom of information. Relentless increase in environmental pollution of all kinds has totally impoverished the quality of our lives and is taking a heavy toll of our health. Consumer groups need to strongly support and work with environmentalists. Every consumer will have to join with others to reduce pollution in his/her own neighbourhood.

Lastly, the concern of consumer movement should also be to discourage racism, communalism, violence and conspicuous consumption. Violence is today the real hero in most TV serials and films. It enters our homes, assaults our senses and affects all of us, specially our children. In the words of Anwer Fazal,

Regional Director, United Nations Development Programme for the Asia Pacific Region, "consumer movement should be directed towards service to the people and the environment instead of just ensuring value for money for consumers". Consumer movement should cherish a new vision which embodies three new cultures, i.e. culture of balance and harmony (so well provided by nature), culture of trusteeship and stewardship (as we are only guardians of earth) and culture of accountability to the future.

Consumer protection in India has an ancient history. It was part of our culture and tradition. Generally, there were no shortages and exploitation. Culprits were punished heavily. However, this golden era got over with the invasion of foreigners and modernization.

The origin of consumerism can be traced to the emergence of co-operatives at the beginning of the present century with governments encouraging development of consumer co-operatives. In general, co-operatives have been successful in halting abuses of monopolies and improving conditions of the lower income groups. Consumer movement, in its present form in India, came into being only in the 1960s with the formation of Consumer Guidance Society of India in Bombay in 1996. With its success, the consumer movement spread over to fight for availability, purity and standard prices of commodities.

At present, there are about 1,000 organisations all over the country. One can say that the consumer movement in India has come of age. From simple awareness generation, it took over to direct action and then to testing and litigation. Its contribution to the passing of Consumer Protection Act, 1986, has been a historic one. Both businesses and bureaucrats have started taking consumers seriously. Consumer grievance cells have been launched by important organisations and corporations. Consumers are represented on a number of consumer welfare committees set up by various organisations. However, with liberalization and globalisation, serious challenges lie ahead for the consumer groups.

Bibliography

Bibliography

Books

Aaker, D., and George, S.D., "Consumerism: Search for the Consumer Interest", Free Press, New York, 1971.

Advani, R., "Consumer Protection Act and Its Implications", Consumer Education and Research Centre, Ahmedabad, 1990.

Agarwal, K.M., "Kautilya's Crime and Punishment", Almora Book Depot, 1990.

Agarwal, V.K., "Consumer Protection in India", Deep and Deep Publications, New Delhi, 2000.

Alur, S.S., "Myth of Consumer Protection" in P. Leelakrishnan (ed.) Consumer Protection and Legal Control, Lucknow, Eastern Book Company, 1981, p. 110.

Baby, M.A., "Parliamentary Debates on the Consumer Protection Bill", Rajya Sabha, 1986, p. 129.

Bakshi, P.M., "Consumer Protection Law", Ashoka Law House, New Delhi, 2004.

Best, A., "When Consumers Complain", New York, Columbia University Press, 1981.

Bhatt, R., "Buying Pattern of the Urban Poor and Distribution Systems", Consumer Education and Research Centre, Ahmedabad, 1976.

Bijlani, D., "Role of Mass Media in Consumer Education", Centre for Development Communication, Gujarat University, Ahmedabad, 1990.

Borrie, G., "Development of Consumer Law and Policy Bold Spirits and Timorous Souls", London, Stevens and Sons Ltd., 1984.

Boyd, F.L. and Stovall, R., "Handbook of Consumer Education", Allyn and Bacon Inc., London, 1978.

Buckhorn, R.F., "Nadar, The People's Lawyer", Prentice Hall Inc., New Jersey.

Buxi, U., "Bentham's Theory of Legislation", First Print, Tripathi Publication.

Campbell, P., "The Consumer Interest: A Study in Consumer Economics, Arno Press New York, 1976.

Cardozo, B.N., "The Nature of the Judicial Process", Yale University Press, London, 1974.

Chandratrae, K.R., "Handbook on Consumer Protection Law", Nidhi Publishers, New Delhi, 1993.

Choudhury, R.S., "Doctor and Consumer Protection", Maharashtra Law Agency, Nasik, 1991.

Cheshire, Fitfoot and Furmston, "Law of Contract", 11th Edition, Butterworth.

Choudhury, V.R., "Law of Consumer Protection", Premier Publishing Company, Allahabad, 2008.

Cranston, R. "Consumers and the Law", Weidenfeld and Nicloson, London, 1984.

Cranston, R., "Regulating Business: Law and Consumer Agencies", The Macmillan Press Ltd., London, 1979.

Das and Rao, "Law Practice and Procedure on Consumer Protection Act,1986", Sodhi Publications, Allahabad, 1990.

Datey, V.S., "Supplement to Business And Corporate Laws", Taxmann Allied Services (P) Ltd., New Delhi, 2010.

Davis, K. and Fedrick, W., "Business and Society", Mc-Graw Hill International Book Company, New Delhi, 1984.

Dighe, S., Parliamentary Debates (Lok Sabha) on the Consumer Protection Bill, 1986.

Dicey, A.V., "An Introduction to the Study of Constitution", MacMillan Universal Book Traders, 10th edition.

Feldman, L.P., "Consumer Protection: Problems and Prospects", West Publishing Company, U.S.A., 1980.

Fetterman, E. and Schiller, M.K., "Let the Buyer Be Aware", Consumer Rights and Responsibilities, Fairchild Publication Inc., New York, 1978.

Fitzgerald, P.J., "Salmond's Jurisprudence", Sweet and Mexwell, 12th Edition, 1996.

Friedmen, C., "Law in a Changing Society", Penguin Book Co., Ltd., 2nd Edition, 1972.

Fulop, "The Consumer Movement and the Consumer", The Advertising Association, London.

Galbraith, "The Affluent Society", Deutsch, London, 4th Edition, 1984.

Gambhir, C., "Consumer Protection Administration, Organization and Working", Deep and Deep Publications (P) Ltd., New Delhi, 2007.

Garg, O.P., "Consumer Protection Act, 1986," Vinod Publishing House, Delhi, 1990.

Giri, H.N., "Consumers, Crimes and the Law", Ashish Publishing House, New Delhi, 1987.

Goldring, J.L. and Maher, L.W., "Consumer Protection Law in Australia", Butter Worths Pvt. Ltd., 1983.

Gordon, L.J. and Lee, S.M., "Economics for Consumers", D. Van Nostrand, New York, 1972.

Guest, A.G., "Anson's Law of Contract", Clarendon Press Oxford, 26th edition, 1984.

Gupta, V.K., "Kautilya's Jurisprudence", B.D. Gupta and Co., Delhi, 1987.

Harvey, B.W., and Deborah, L.P., "Consumer Protection Laws and the Concept of the Perfect Market", Institute of Trading Standards Administration, USA, 1980.

Hawan, V.K.N., "Consumer Protection", Practice and Procedure, 1994, Vinod Publishing House, Delhi, 1994.

Hinich, M.J. and Staelin, R., "Consumer Protection Legislation and the U.S. Food Industry", Pergamon Press, New York, 1980.

Jayachandran, G., "Indian Consumers: Marketer's Anathema or Dilemma" in S. Neelamegham (ed.), Marketing Management and Indian Economy, 1970, p. 170.

Jayakumar, N.K., "Consumer Justice: Strategies and Institutions", in P. Leelakrishnan (ed.), Consumer Protection and Legal Control, Eastern Book Company, Lucknow, 1981, p. 110.

Jha, C., "History and Sources of Law in Ancient India", Ashish Publishing House, New Delhi, 1987.

Kamath, K.P.S., "Servants, Not Masters", Udupi Consumers Forum, Udupi, 1987.

Kapoor, N.D., Elements of Mercantile Law, Sultan Chand and Sons, New Delhi, 2005.

Kar, R.N., "Working of the District Consumer Forums: A Comparative Study of Delhi and Dhenkanal District Consumer Disputes Redressal Forums", unpublished M.Phil dissertation, Delhi University, 1995.

Kramer, L., "EEC Consumer Law", Centre De Droit De La Consommution, France, 1986.

Kumar, N., "Consumer Protection in India", Himalaya Publishing House, Mumbai, 2007.

Lokanath, P.S., "The Consumer at Sea", Neelamegham S., (ed.), Marketing Management and the Indian Economy, 1970, p. 180.

Laxminarayan, "Principles and Practice of Public Enterprise

Management", S. Chand and Co., 1st edition, New Delhi.

Lowe, R. and Woodroffe, G., "Consumer Law and Practice", Sweet and Maxwell Ltd., London, 1980.

Madhukar, S. and Sudhakar, V.S., "Information Labelling Review", Consumer Education and Research Centre, Ahmedabad, 1985.

Mahajan, V.D., "Jurisprudence and Legal Theory", Eastern Book Company, Lucknow, 1987.

Mahindra, H., "Law and Consumer", Council for Fair Business Practices, Bombay, 1980.

Majumdar, P.K., "Law of Consumer Protection in India", Orient Publishing Co., New Delhi.

Majumdar, P.K., "Law of Consumer Protection in India", 3rd Edition, Orient Publishing Commercial, New Delhi, 2000.

Malathesh, S., "Consumerism: An Opinion Survey", Consumer Education and Research Centre, Ahmedabad, 1981.

Maynes, E.S., "Decision-Making for Consumer: An Introduction to Consumer Economics", McMillan Publishing Co., New York, 1976.

McAnally, M. and Delbridge, R., "Buy Rights", Pan Books Ltd., London, 1981.

McLaughlin, F.E. (ed), "The Future of Consumerism", Proceeding of a Conference, Maryland Centre for Business and Public Policy, Maryland, U.S.A., 1981.

Mehta, P.S., "How to Survive as a Consumer", Consumer Unity and Trust Society, Jaipur, 1998.

Misra, M.N., "Sales Promotion and Advertising Management", 1st edition, Himalaya Publishing House, New Delhi, 1994.

Mohanty, B., "Consumer Protection: A Challenging Task", in P. Leelakrishnan (ed.), Consumer Protection and Legal Control, Eastern Book Company, Lucknow, 1981, p. 24.

Murthy, P.V.V.S., "Consumer Justice", A Manual for Consumer Forum Members, Indian Institute of Public Administration, New Delhi, 2006.

Naik, R.K., "Consumer Protection Law in India", N.M. Tripathi (P) Ltd., Bombay, 1st edition, 1991.

Nayak, R.K., "Consumer Protection in India: An Eco Legal Treatise on Consumer Justice", The Indian Law Institute, 1991.

Oughton, D.W., "Consumer Law: Text Cases and Materials", Blackstone Press Ltd., London, 1991.

P., Leela Krishnan (ed.), "Consumer Protection and Legal Control",

Eastern Book Company, Lucknow, 1st edition.
Paduval, P.R., "Consumerism: Social Significance and Effectiveness", P. Leelakrishnan (ed.), Consumer Protection and Legal Control, Eastern Book Company, Lucknow, 1981, p. 41.
Painter, A.A., "Guide to Consumer Protection Law", Barry Rose Ltd., London, 1978.
Pattnaik, N.C., "Consumer Protection In India: A Socio-Legal Study of Consumers' Attitude Towards Consumer Protection Act, 1986, With Special Reference to Orissa", Unpublished Ph.D. Thesis, Berhampur University, 1996.
Pylee, M.V.,. "Consumer Protection in Developing Society", P. Leelakrishnan (ed.), Consumer Protection and Legal Control, Eastern Book Company, Lucknow, 1981, p. 10.
Rao, R., "Consumer is King: Know Your Rights and Remedies", Universal Publishing Co. Pvt. Ltd., Delhi, 2009.
Rathor, S.C.P., "Consumer Protection: A Critical Study of Legislation and its Enforcement with Special Reference to Orissa", Unpublished Ph.D. thesis, Berhampur University, 2001.
Reich, N. and Micklitz, H.W., "Consumer Legislation in the EEC Countries: A Comparative Analysis", Van Nostrand Rein Hold, New York, 1980.
Riswadkar, S., "Unfair Fair Price Shops", Consumer Education and Research Centre, Ahmedabad, 1983.
Sahoo, S.R., "A Study on Consumer's Awareness with Special Reference to Consumer protection Act", unpublished M.Phil. dissertation, Berhampur University, 1993.
Saraf, D.N., "Law of Consumer Protection in India", Bombay, N.M. Tripathy, Bombay, 1995.
Sarkar, A., "Problem of Consumers in Modern India", Discovery Publishing House, Delhi, 1989.
Sarma, K.V.S., "A Critical Appraisal on Consumer Protection: A Socio Legal Study", Unpublished Ph.D. Thesis, Berhampur University, 1999.
Seshadri, V., "Consumerism with Reference to Selected Home Appliances", Mittal Publications, New Delhi, 2006.
Shah, M., "Consumer and Clothing", Consumer Education and Research Centre, Ahmedabad, 1979.
Shah, P., "A Guide to Sources of Consumer Information", CERC, Ahmedabad, 1991.
Shapiro, A.A., "Economic Analysis of Consumer Redress

Mechanism", Consumer and Corporate Affairs, Canada, 1980.

Sharma, D., "Consumer Grievance Redressal under the Consumer Protection Act", New Century Publications, Delhi, 2002.

Sharma, K.M., "Key to Consumer Laws", Vinod Publishing and Co., New Delhi, 1994.

Singh, A., "Law of Consumer Protection: Principles and Practice", Eastern Book Company, Lucknow, 2000.

Singh, G., "Law of Consumer Protection in India: Justice within Reach", Deep and Deep Publication, New Delhi, 1996.

Singh, J., "Medical Profession and Consumer Protection Act", Bharat Law Publication, Jajpur.

Smith, P. and Swann, D., "Protecting the Consumer: An Economic and Legal Analysis", Martin Robertson and Company Limited, Oxford, 1984.

Tribilook, "Consumer Protection and the Affluent Society", McGraw Hill, 1971.

Thurstone, L.L. and Chate, R.J., "The Measurement of Attitude", Chicago University Press, Chicago 1932.

Vatas, R.M., "Consumer and the Law", Universal Book Traders, New Delhi, 1994.

Wraith, R., "Consumer Cause: A Short Account of its Organization Development, Power and Importance", Royal Institute of Public Administration, London, 1976.

Journals, Periodicals and Others

Aaker, D., and George S.D., "A Guide to Consumerism", *Journal of Marketing*, 12th July 1970.

Agarwal, S.K., "Court and Accountability of Universities: Some Recent Developments", *Consumer Confrontation*, Vol. 12, No. 2, 1992, p. 35.

Asante, S.K.B., "United Nations: International Regulation of Transnational Corporation", *Journal of World Trade Law*, Vol. 13, No.1, 1979, p. 55.

Basu, P., "Damages and Compensation in COPRA", *Consumer Protection Reporter*, Vol. 1, Part 3, 1995, pp. 477-478.

Bhanot, A., "Consumer Advocacy: A Growing Influence", *Span*, 1998, pp. 33-37.

Bharatiya, V.P., "Consumer Protection: So Much Done, Much More to be Done", *The Indian Journal of Legal Studies*, Vol. IX, 1989, p. 177.

Bijawat, C., "Medical Negligence, Medical Practice: American Experience", 1995, 37, *JILI*, Notes and Comments, p. 390.

Bustric, R.H., and Rothi, J.T., "Consumerism: An Interpretation", *Journal of Marketing,* 1970, Vol. 34, October, pp. 61-65.

Cardwell, K., "The Consumer Protection Act 1987: Enforcement of Provisions Governing the Safety of Consumer Goods", *The Modern Law Review*, Vol. 50, 1987, p. 622.

Cassels, J.M., "The Clarification of Consumer Thinking", Proceeding of Business-Consumer Relations Conference, New York, 1940.

Chandrachud, Y.V., "Law and the Consumer: Role of Judiciary", *Consumer Confrontation*, Vol. 6, No. 1, 1986, p. 13.

Clark, A., "The Consumer Protection Act", *The Modern Law Review*, Vol. 50, 1987.

Cohen, D., "Remedies for Consumer Protection: Prevention, Restitution or Punishment", *Journal of Marketing*, Vol. 39, No. 4, 1975, pp. 24-31.

Compendium of Important Orders of State CDR Commission and District Consumer Forums, State Institute of Consumer Awareness (SICA), Bhubaneswar, 2008.

Dameron, K., "The Consumer Movement", *Harvard Business Review*, Vol. 18, No. 8, 1989, pp. 271-289.

Das, N. "Consumer Protection Act and the Common Man", *All India Reporter*, 1991, p. 158.

Dimond, S.L, Word, S. and Feber, R., "Consumer Problems and Consumerism: An Analysis of Calls to a Consumer Hotline", *Journal of Marketing*, June 1976.

Dutta, N.K., "Origin and Development of Criminal Justice in India", Federal Legislation and Programs Relating to Consumer Protection, *Consumer Research Report*, No. 6. Department of Consumer and Corporate Affairs, Canada, March 1977.

Eradi, V.B., Welcome Address at the National Convention of Presidents and Members of State Consumer Disputes Redressal Commission held at New Delhi on 24th January, 1994 and reported in 1994, Consumer Protection Journal, Vol. 1, p. 29.

Essien, V.L.K., "Consumer Protection in Nigeria: The Case for Reform", New York University Journal of International Law and Politics, Vol. 16, No. 3, Spring, 1984, p. 515.

F. Kessler, "Contract of Adhesion- Some Thoughts about Freedom of Contract", 1945, 43, Col. L.R. 629.

Fulop, C., "The Costs and Benefits of a Duty to Trade Fairly", *Economic Affairs*, U.K., Vol. 8, 1987, p. 33.

Fulop, C., "Consumers Right to Information", *The Council for Fair Business Practices Bulletin*, Vol. 15, No. 3, 1981, p. 1.

Gaedeke, R.M., "Filing and Disposition of Consumer Complaints: Some Empirical Evidence", *Journal of Consumer Affairs*, Vol. 6, No. 1, 1972, pp. 45-56.

Galanter, "Justice in Many Rooms", Working Paper (1979) Disputes Processing Research Programme, University of Wisconsin Law School, Quoted in *University of Torento Law Journal*, Vol. 31, 1981, p. 119.

Girimaji, P., "Jurisdiction of Consumer Courts: NC Order Clears Doubts", *The Tribune*, 1993, p. 10.

Gupta, R. and Gunjan, G., "Law Relating to Consumer Protection in India: Concept and precept: Jurisprudential Foundation", *Consumer Protection Judgments*, Vol. 1, Part 2, 1995, pp. 31-43.

Gupta, R., "Redressal Agencies under the Consumer Protection Act 1986: Their Character, Scope and Dominance over Domestic Tribunals: Some Issues", *Consumer Protection Judgements*, Vol. 2 Part I, 1995.

Gupta, R., "Redressal Agencies under the Consumer Protection Act, 1986: Their Character, Scope of Power and Dominance over Domestic Tribunals", *Consumer Protection Journal*, JS, 1995, p. 10.

Gurjeet, S., "Consumer Disputes Redressal Mechanism under the Consumer Protection Act, 1986: Critical Analysis and Observations on the District Forums", 1996, II, CPJ 8.

Gurjeet, S., "Enforcement of Orders of Consumer Disputes Redressal Agencies and Imposition of Penalties under the Consumer Protection Act, 1986", 1994, I CPJ 17.

Gurjeet, S., "Increasing Ambit and Amplitude of the Consumer Protection Act, 1986: A Case Study of its Applicability to Educational Services", 1995, I CPJ 46.

Gurjeet, S., "Significance of International Co-ordination in the Arena of Consumer Protection: A Case Study of United Nations Guidelines and the International Organization of Consumer Union", 1995, I, C.P.J. 16.

Gurjeet, S., "The Concept of a 'Consumer' and the Rationale of Consumer Protection in the Contemporary World", 1994, II, C.P.J. 21.

Gurjeet, S., "The Problems of Consumer Protection in India: A Historical Perspective", 1987, II, CPJ 1.

Gurjeet, S., "The Concept of Commercial Purpose under the Consumer Protection Act, 1986", 1994, III, CPJ 1.

Gupta, R., "Writ Jurisdiction of the High Court under Consumer Protection Act, 1986: Dr. K. Subramanyam's Case-An Eclipse", 1994, III, CPJ 31.

Gupta, R., "Tax payer under the Consumer Protection Act, 1986, Knock the Right Door Please", 1994, III, CPJ 1.

Harland, D., "Some International Dimensions of Law and Policy", 1987, 29, JILI, 451.

Harland, D., "The United Nation's Guidelines for Consumer Protection", 1987, *Journal of Consumer Policy*, p. 246.

Harald, D.J. "Some International Dimensions of Consumer Law and Policy", 1987, 29 I.B.R, 451, October-December, No. 4.

Harland, D.J., "Some International Dimensions of Consumer Law and Policy", *Journal of Indian Law Institute*, Vol. 29, 1987, p. 460.

Harland, D.J., "Unfair and Deceptive Trade Practices", Proceedings of the IOCU Seminar, Hong Kong, January, 1980, p. 47.

Himachalam, D., "Consumerism in India", *Indian Journal of Marketing*, February 1990.

Inamdar, N.R., "Role of Voluntarism in Development", *Indian Journal of Public Administration*, Vol. 33, 1984, p. 420.

Jaswal, P.S. and Jaswal, N., "Protection of the Consumer and the Constitution: An Aspect of Socio-Economic Justice", Paper Presented at the National Seminar on "Consumer Protection and Law", Chandigarh, 24-25th March, 1990, p. 11.

Jewa, K., "Role of Members of Redressal Agencies for Effective Implementation of Consumer Protection Act, 1986", *Consumer Protection Judgments*, Vol. 1, 1995, p. 10.

Jolowicz, J.A., "The Protection of the Consumer and Purchaser of Goods Under English Law", *Modern Law Review*, Vol. 32, No. 1, 1969, p. 1.

Joseph and Abraham, "Government Doctors and Consumer Protection Act, 1986", 1996, III, CPJ, p. 9.

Jena, K.N., "Role of Members of Consumer Dispute Redressal Agencies for Effective Implementation of Consumer Protection Act, 1986", 1995, CPJ, p. 10.

Jena, K.N., "Consumer Protection Act, 1986, Section 14: A Law to

Ensure Social Accountability", 1996, 1, C.P.J., p. 1.

Jog, L.N., "Changing Equations: Consumer Business and Government", *FBP Sliver Jubilee Bulletin*, 1992.

Kalpana, "Making Consumerism a Movement", *Yojana*, New Delhi, Vol. 36, No. 10, 1992, p. 10.

Khan, A.A., "The Flaws in the Consumer Protection Act, 1986", *All India Reporter*, 1986, p. 1.

Khanna, R., "Law for the Welfare of Consumers in India", *Supreme Court Journal*, Vol.1, 1986, p. 18.

Khurana, L., "Consumer Protection: The Growing Concern", *Yojana*, Vol. 39, No. 5, 1995, p. 26.

Kondaiah, C., "Marking Justice Speedy, Effective and Substantial", *All India Reporter*, 1976, p. 98.

Knapp, J. and Williamson, I.K., "New National Coalition for Consumer Education", *Advancing the Consumer Interest*, Vol. 1, No. 1, 1988, p. 1.

Kotler, P., "What Consumerism Means for Marketers", *Harvard Business Review*, May-June 1972, pp. 48-57.

Krishnan, R., "No Remedy against Post Offices and Couriers under the Consumer Law", 1993, Comp. L.J., p. 15.

Kumar, K.S., "Need for the Awareness of Consumer Protection", *Yojana*, Vol. 39, No. 5, New Delhi, 1995, p. 24.

Kumar, R., "Consumer Protection and MRTP Cases: Highlights and Analysis", *Consumer Protection and Trade Practices Journal*, Vol. 1, No. 11, 1993, pp. 218-221.

Kumar, S., "Consumer Movement: Its Need in our Era", *Consumer Confrontation*, Vol. 9, No. 3, 1980, p. 14.

Malve, G., "Consumer Education under Consumer Protection Act 1986", *Supreme Court Journal*, Vol. 1, 1993, p. 1.

Mandana, J., "Indian Market Place: Guidelines to Consumer Education", Brindaban Publishing House, Bangalore, 1977.

Mann, J. and Thornton, P., "Consumerism in Perspective", *The European Journal of Marketing*, Vol. 12, No. 4, 1978, p. 256.

Mathews, K., "Power that Paralysis: A Survey of Electricity Consumers in the Rural Areas of Gujarat", Consumer Education and Research Centre, Ahmedabad, 1981.

Mathew, K.K., "Poverty, Power and the Constitution", *The Academic Law Review*, Vol. 1, 1971, p. 1.

Mathew, N.M., "Consumer Movement in India at Crossroads", *Health for the Millions*, October 1995, p. 78.

Mathur, A.B.L., "Service Marketing by the Public sector and the Quality of Life", *The Indian Journal of Legal Studies*, Vol. X, 1990, p. 29.

N. Krishna Murthy, J., "The Consumer Protection Act, Features and Legal Analysis", *Chartered Secretary*, 1990, Vol. 20, October, pp. 834-837.

Nabi, M.K. and Raut, K.C., "Whither Consumerism", *The Southern Economist*, April 1 and 15, 1993, pp. 13-15.

Nayak, R.K., "International Consumer Movement Through Law: Some Reflective Measures", *Indian Journal of Legal Studies*, Vol. IX, 1989, p. 124.

Panigrahi, B., "Consumer Protection and the Law", *All India Reporter*, 1992, p. 33.

Paul, S., "Judicial Scrutiny of Medical Negligence Cases by Consumer Forum", *All India Reporter*, 1995, p. 28.

Prasad, A.R., "The Consumer Protection Act, 1986: A Critical Appraisal", *All India Reporter*, 1989, p. 12.

Prasad, R.N., "Consumer Protection Act, 1986: Some Suggestions for Improvement", *All India Reporter*, 1991, p. 163.

Ramesh, M.K., "Consumers Interest in Legal Profession: Problems and Prospectives", *Cochin University Law Review*, Vol. 13, No. 4, 1989, p. 405.

Rao, B.V., "Consumerism in India: A Prospect and Future", *All India Reporter*, 1994, p. 97.

Rao, K.S., "The Role of the Court in Protecting Consumers vis-à-vis Public Enterprises", *The Indian Journal of Legal Studies*, Vol. X, 1990, p. 43.

Rao, N.S.B., "Consumer Education in Villages", *Indian Journal of Marketing*, Vol. 20, No. 9, 1990, p. 26.

Reddy, A.R., "Consumer Protection and Consumer Movement in India: A Perspective", *Supreme Court Journal*, Vol. 2, 1994, p. 34.

Reich, R.B., "Towards a New Consumer Protection", *University of Pennsylvania Law Review*, Vol. 128, No. 1, 1979, p. 1.

Sahasrabudddhe, R.V., "A Successful Redressal", *Consumer Confrontation*, Vol. 12, No. 2, 1992, p. 33.

Saraf, D.N., "Some Facets of Consumer Justice through Consumer Disputes Redressal Agencies", *Journal of Indian Law Institute*, Vol. 34, No. 1, 1992, p. 28.

Saraf, D.N., "Public Utility Services with Special Reference to Air

Service and the Consumer", *Journal of Indian Law Institute*, Vol. 34, No. 2, 1989, p. 29.

Sarkar, A., "Consumer Problems and Consumer Protection in India", *Indian Co-operative Review*, Vol.10, 1970, p. 42.

Saxena, J.C., "The Consumer Protection Act, 1986: A View Point", *Journal of Indian Law Institute*, Vol. 30, No. 3, 1988, p. 321.

Scott, H. "Consumer Protection and Payment System: Regulatory Policy for the Technological Era", *Harvard Law Review*, Vol. 98, 1985, p. 1870.

Shah, M., "Consumer Protection in the 1990s", *Consumer Confrontation*, Vol. 10, No. 1, 1990, pp. 5-7.

Shapiro, C., "Consumer Protection Policy in the United States", Discussion Papers in Economics, Woodraw Wilson School, Princeton University, Princeton, New Jersey, 1983.

Sharma, D.D., "Some Reflections on Consumer Protection and the Role of Law", *The Indian Journal of Legal Studies*, Vol. IX, 1989, p. 49.

Singh, G., "Business Self-Regulation and Consumer Protection in India: A Critique", *Journal of Consumer Policy*, Vol. 16, No. 1, 1993, p. 1.

Singh, G., "Consumer Awareness and Role of Voluntary Organizations", *Marketology*, Vol. 17, No. 2, 1985, p. 31.

Singh, G., "Consumer Disputes Redressal Mechanism under the Consume Protection Act 1986: Critical Analysis and Observations on the District Forum", *Consumer Protection and Trade Practices Journal*, Vol. 3, No. 7, 1995, p. 8.

Singh, G., "Enforcement of Orders of the Consumer Dispute Redressal Agencies and Imposing of penalties Under the Consumer Protection Act, 1986", *Consumer Protection Journal*, 1994, p. 17.

Singh, G., "Group Action and the Law: A Case Study of Social Action, Litigation and Consumer Protection in India", *Journal of Consumer Policy*, Vol. 18, No. 1, 1995, pp. 25-54.

Singh, G., "Need for Consumer Education in India: A View Point", *Consumer Protection Journal*, 1994, p. 9.

Singh, G., "The Problem of Consumer Protection in India: A Historical Approach", *Consumer Protection Reporter*, Vol. 3, No. 11-12, 1994, pp. 204-219.

Singh, K. and Sangwan, I.V., "A Comparative Study to Assess the Problems of Rural and Urban Consumers", *Consumer*

Confrontation, Vol. 14, No. 1, Ahmedabad, 1994, p. 44.

Singh, K., Yadav and et al., "Consumer Awareness: A Survey", *Consumer Confrontation*, Vol. 12 No. 2, Ahmedabad, 1992, p. 13.

Singh, K., Lata, Y., Veera, S., and Suresh, G., "Consumer Awareness", *Consumer Confrontation*, 1992, pp. 16-17.

Singh, R., "How Do Consumers Perceive Consumerism: An Exploratory Study", *Management and Labour Studies*, Vol. 15, No. 3, 1990, p. 146.

Singh, R.M., "Consumer Attitude towards Consumerism: An Exploratory Study", *Consumer Confrontation*, Vol. 10, No. 1, 1990, pp. 16-17.

Singh, S.J., Address in the Seminar on Consumer Protection at New Delhi on 29th September, 1989, Reported in *Consumer Confrontation*, Vol. 9, No. 6, Ahmedabad, 1989, p. 3.

Singh, S.N., "Consumer Protection Legislation: A Critique", *Journal of Indian Law Institute*, Vol. 29, No. 3, 1987, pp. 380-386.

Singh, S.N., "Consumer Protection: Some Suggestions", *Corporate Law Advisor*, 1992, pp. 145-149.

Sinha, R.K., "Need for Organizing the Unorganized: A Call for Consumer Movement in India", *The Indian Journal of Legal Studies*, Vol. X, 1990, p. 99.

Srivastav, S., "Consumer Protection and Medical Profession", *Central India Law Quarterly*, Vol. VII, Part IV, 1994, p. 426.

Swamy, S.N., "Consumer Protection: No Lukewarm Attitude", *Consumer Confrontation*, Vol. 9, No. 2, Ahmedabad, 1989, p. 13.

Talib, J., "COPRA and Health Services under Government-run Hospitals", *Supreme Court Journal*, Vol. 2, 1994, p. 74.

Tench, D., "Legal Protection for Consumers", Proceedings of the IOCU Seminar, Hong Kong, January 1980, p. 22.

Trebilcock, M.J., "Consumer Protection in the Affluent Society", *McGill Law Journal*, Vol. 16, No. 2, 1970, p. 263.

Venkataramanan, T.S.R., "Where the CPA Steps in", *The Hindu*, Visakhapatnam, 11th August, 1992, p. 17.

Verma, S.K., "Consumer Protection: Challenges and Perspective", *The Indian Journal of Legal Studies*, Vol. 9, 1989, p. 44.

Vijaykkar, A.S., "Protecting the Consumer by a Landmark Legislation", *Uphokta Jagran*, 1994, pp. 6-10.

Vyas, R.C., "Consumerism and the Public Sector Industries", The

Indian Journal of Legal Studies, Vol. 10, 1990, p. 1.

Webster, F.Z., "Does Business Misunderstand Consumers", *Harvard Business Review*, September-October, 1973, pp. 88-97.

Zethamal, V.A., "Consumer Perception of Price, Quality and Value Evidence", *Journal of Marketing*, No. 2, July 1988, p. 2.

List of Reports

105th Report of the Indian Law Commission

8th Report of the Indian Law Commission

General Assembly Resolution, 32/248, 1985

Report of Molony Committee on Consumer Protection

Report of the High Powered Expert Committee (Sachar Committee) on Companies and MRTP Acts (1978), Government of India, Ministry of Law Justice and Company Affairs, New Delhi

Report of the Industrial Licensing Policy (1969), Government of India, New Delhi

Report of the Monopoly Enquiry Commission (1965), Government of India, New Delhi

Report of the Royal Commission on Civil Liability and Compensation for Personal Injury, 1978

Report of the Secretary-General on Consumer Protection: Resolution of United Nations General Assembly, 7-8 No.E/1983/71, 27th May, 1983, United Nations Economic and Social Council

Report of WHO Expert Committee on the Selection of Essential Drugs Technical Report Series No.615, 1977

Index

Index